NOTES AND QUERIES ON ANTHROPOLOGY

NOTES AND QUERIES ON ANTHROPOLOGY

By

JOHN GEORGE GARSON,
CHARLES HERCULES READ

GYAN

ISBN : 978-81-212-1648-7(HB)

First Published, 1874

Published, 2018

Published by

Gyan Publishing House
5, Ansari Road
Daryaganj, New Delhi-110002
Phone: 011-47034999, 9811692060
www.gyanbooks.com
E-mail: books@gyanbooks.com

Printed at: G. Print Process, Delhi.

PREFACE TO THE SECOND EDITION.

SINCE the publication of the first edition of this Manual, in 1874, Anthropological Science has made such great advances that for some time past a second edition brought up to the requirements of the present time has been urgently required. The British Association for the Advancement of Science appointed a Committee to consider and report as to the best means of doing this. The Committee recommended that the work should be transferred to the Anthropological Institute of Great Britain and Ireland. This recommendation was approved of by the Association, and to assist in defraying the cost of publication it has made grants amounting to £70. A further sum of £10 was presented by the late Dr. Muirhead, of Cambuslang, Glasgow, towards this object. The Council of the Anthropological Institute having undertaken the publication of the work, appointed the two editors and a Committee of its members to prepare the new edition under its supervision.

It has been found necessary to re-cast entirely the first part—Anthropography—owing to the great development of this branch of the science. In doing so the editor has had the assistance of Dr. Beddoe, who was author of almost the entire first part of the former edition. Mr. George Atkinson has rendered valuable assistance in the production of the coloured plate, which it is hoped will be more permanent than that in the first edition. The sections on Medical Anthropology in the former edition have been revised and rewritten, and several new sections added; for assistance in this department, thanks are due to Dr. Robert Felkin.

The second part—Ethnography—has, from its nature, not required such drastic treatment, but the whole has been revised and additional chapters have been written. The arrangement of the sections also has been altered, with a view of bringing into greater prominence the queries which present the least difficulty to those whose special knowledge may be slight.

The thanks of the editors are due to those friends who have contributed the new sections, to others who have kindly given help in revising the old, and not least to the writers of the original work, who have borne with calmness the process of editing.

PREFACE TO THE FIRST EDITION.

Edited by

Colonel Lane-Fox, now Lieut.-General Pitt-Rivers, D.C.L., F.R.S.

(ABRIDGED).

THESE Notes and Queries are published by the British Association for the Advancement of Science.

*　　*　　*　　*

The object of the work is to promote accurate anthropological observation on the part of travellers, and to enable those who are not anthropologists themselves to supply the information which is wanted for the scientific study of anthropology at home.

History has confined itself chiefly to the achievements of special races; but the anthropologist regards all races as equally worthy of a place in the records of human development. The more remote and unknown the race or tribe, the more valuable the evidence afforded of the study of its institutions, from the probability of their being less mixed with those of European origin.

Travellers have usually recorded only those customs of modern savages which they have chanced to observe; and, as a rule, they have observed chiefly those which their experience of civilized institutions has led them to look for. Nor are there wanting instances in which the information thus obtained has been lamentably distorted in order to render it in harmony with preconceived ideas; owing to this and other causes, the imperfections of the anthropological record surpass those of other sciences, and false theories are often built upon imperfect bases of induction.

* * * *

The rapid extermination of savages at the present time, and the rapidity with which they are being reduced to the standard of European manners, renders it of urgent importance to correct these sources of error as soon as possible.

It is hoped that the questions contained in the following sections, each of which is the result of special study of the subject treated, may be a means of enabling the traveller to collect information without prejudice arising from his individual bias. To this end it is particularly requested that he will endeavour to answer the questions as fully as possible, not confining himself to a detailed account of those things which exist, but also, by special inquiries directed to the subject, endeavouring to determine the non-existence of others to which attention is drawn.

* * * *

TABLE OF CONTENTS.

Part I.

Medical Sections.

Part II.

NOTES AND QUERIES

ON

ANTHROPOLOGY,

OR

A GUIDE TO ANTHROPOLOGICAL RESEARCH FOR THE USE OF TRAVELLERS AND OTHERS.

ANTHROPOLOGY may be defined as the natural history of man. It is divided into two main divisions, namely, ANTHROPOGRAPHY and ETHNOGRAPHY. The former treats of man and the varieties of the human family from a purely animal point of view, that is, from a structural and functional aspect; while the latter deals with him as a social and intellectual being, and includes inquiries as to his manners, customs, institutions, history, traditions, language, religion, intellectual aptitudes, industries, arts, &c.

The first part of this work is devoted to Anthropography and the second part to Ethnography.

The Editors will be happy to receive on behalf of Contributors any specimens, or papers, or records of observations, on any subject included in the scope of this work, addressed to either of them, Anthropological Institute, 3, Hanover Square, London, W., and to make arrangements for the description or publication of the same in the Journal of the Institute or elsewhere, in the name of the sender, as may seem best in his interests.

PART I.

ANTHROPOGRAPHY.

EDITED BY

JOHN GEORGE GARSON, M.D.,

Memb. Council and Past Vice-President Anthrop. Institute, Great Britain and Ireland; Hon. Corresp. Memb. Soc. d'Anthrop., Paris; Corresp. Memb. Berlin. Gesell. f. Anthrop. Ethnog. u. Urgesch.; Lecturer on Comparative Anatomy at Charing Cross Hospital, London.

B 2

ANTHROPOGRAPHY.

No. I.—INTRODUCTION.

Anthropography includes observations of an anatomical, physiological, and pathological character. Many researches in this branch of Anthropology may be easily undertaken by the general traveller who will find it a most interesting and fascinating field of study; others are of a more technical character and can only be undertaken by medical men and Naturalists who have had previous training in the subjects which it embraces. The general traveller may also do much to advance the study of the more technical part by collecting specimens of skeletons, hair, and even parts of the body, such as the hands, feet, brain, or the entire head, and sending them to our laboratories or museums to have their characters worked out by skilled anatomists.

The anatomical part of the subject consists of observations on the external characters of the body, and on the comparative morphology and ontogeny of its skeletal, muscular, nervous, and other systems. The external characters of the body are best observed in the living subject. Materials for research are therefore abundant, and may generally with a little tact be readily obtained. The information which they yield when systematically studied is most important, and urgently required for the advancement of Anthropological science. For these reasons, and because a technical knowledge of anatomy is not essential for their study, the general traveller is especially recommended to devote his attention to them.

Under "Anatomical Observations" he will find what he is to note regarding them. Researches on the comparative morphology of man are made on the skeleton and dead body. They are usually undertaken by anatomists and medical men in an anatomical laboratory or a hospital where anatomical works can be consulted and are outside the scope of this work. As however the traveller may have opportunities of examining the skeleton, though unable to secure it for the laboratory, and may possess some anatomical knowledge, a few directions are given to enable him to investigate its most important characters.

The physiological part includes observations on the senses, the physical powers, circulation, respiration, psychological development, &c. In this department the general traveller may make several important observations, while the more scientifically trained traveller will find it a still larger field for research. The same observation applies to the pathological part of the subject, which deals with abnormalities or deviations from the usual type.

These several branches of ANTHROPOGRAPHY are treated of in this work from the point of view of the general traveller, so as to guide him how and what to observe. At the same time many of the outlines of investigations given will be useful to the more scientifically expert traveller, and possibly suggest others to his mind.

For the purpose of stimulating medical men practising or stationed in various parts of the world to devote attention to Anthropography, as well as to the advancement of our knowledge of disease, some sections of a more purely medical character have been added to this part of the work. Some of these sections might more accurately have been placed in a different order, or even in the second part of the work—Ethnography—but it has been thought better to keep all the medical sections together near those of an anatomical and physiological nature, even at the expense of consistency in classification.

J. G. G.

A.—ANATOMICAL OBSERVATIONS.

1. EXTERNAL CHARACTERS.

No. II.—GENERAL INSTRUCTIONS.

The object of observations on the external formation of the body is to determine the differences which exist between human beings according to age, sex, race, and the locality in which they reside. These differences are ascertained by systematically examining and recording the characters and measurements of the several parts of the body separately and collectively in a number of individuals. The observations should be made on the greatest possible number of persons. Records of only a few individuals are of little use, because in every series of persons, whether of pure or mixed origin, there is always a wide range of individual variation present, and in even the most carefully made measurements of the living body a certain amount of personal error occurs. It is only by making observations on a large number of persons that these sources of error can be reduced to such a point as not seriously to influence the results; thus ten measurements of 100 persons are better than fifty measurements of twenty persons.

The traveller should devote himself chiefly to observations on adult males, as it is in them that questions of race, type, mixture and individual variations are best determined; they, moreover, submit themselves more readily to examination. Observations on women and children are also important, the former to show sexual differences and the latter in relation to the development history of the body, and the influence locality may have upon it. Except for special researches in connection with questions of Development and Decay, the adults examined should be between the ages of twenty and fifty years, or, still better, between twenty-five and forty-five years. They should not be picked out for their size or beauty, but taken indiscriminately with the view of getting a truly representative series of observations.

The Schedule of Observations, consisting of a series of descriptive characters and measurements, which has been drawn up with the object of enabling the traveller to examine the external characters of the human body in a systematic manner is chiefly based upon Dr. Topinard's "*Instructions*;" but includes also, as far as possible, the views of other Anthropologists.

J. G. G.

No. II.—INSTRUMENTS.

The instruments required for the measurements scheduled in the subsequent pages are few in number and very portable; indeed, if occasion requires, most of them can be improvised on the spot, though measurements with such are not so accurate as when proper instruments are used, hence the traveller is recommended to equip himself before starting on his journey.

The Traveller's Anthropometer, manufactured by Aston and Mander of 25, Old Compton Street, London, after my design, is perhaps the most compact and comprehensive instrument the traveller can procure. With it and a measuring tape all the measurements contained in the schedule may be made. It consists of a graduated rod, Pl. I, fig. 1, A, 2 metres long, jointed in three pieces with a sliding arm, D E, and one which may be fixed at the zero end of the rod, B C. The one extremity of each arm is curved so as to form callipers the exact pattern of Flower's Craniometer while the rest of the arm is straight, and terminates in a point. The rod being held vertically each arm, B and D, slides horizontally

PLATE 1.

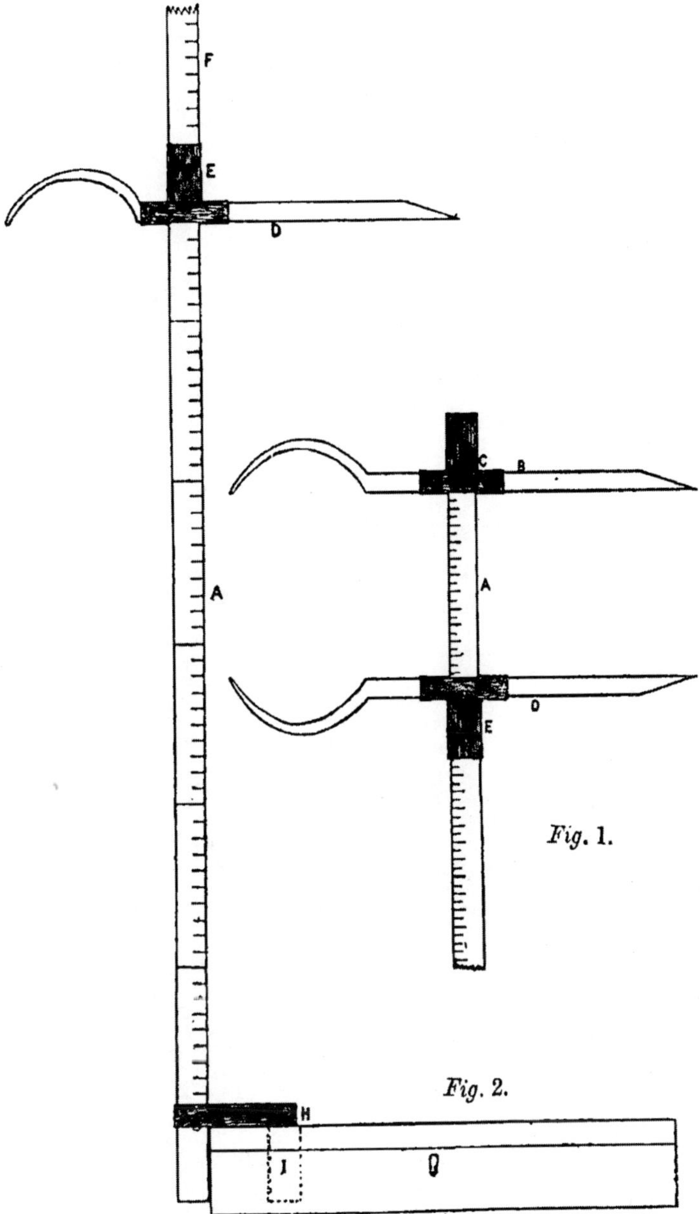

Fig. 1.

Fig. 2.

PLATE II.

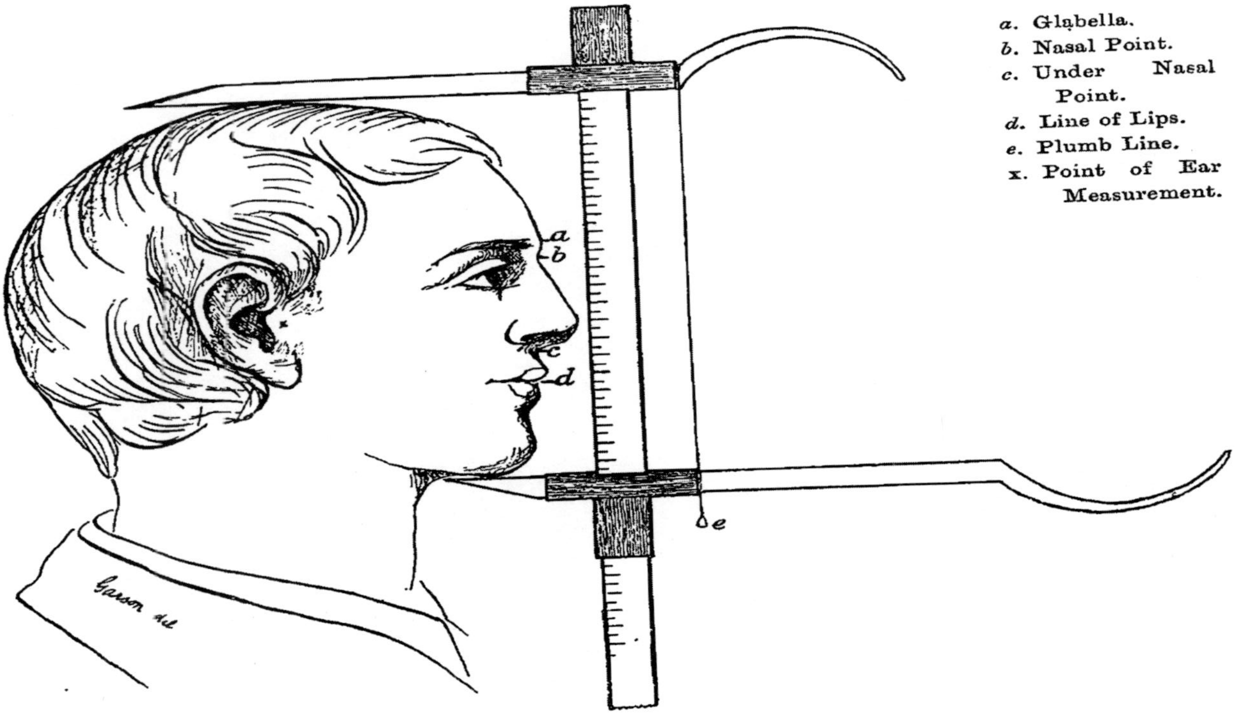

a. Glabella.
b. Nasal Point.
c. Under Nasal Point.
d. Line of Lips.
e. Plumb Line.
x. Point of Ear Measurement.

in its carrier, C and E, which fits on the rod, A, and can be lengthened or shortened in respect to its projection on either side of the rod. The sliding arm also slides vertically as well as horizontally while the fixed arm slides only horizontally; both arms and their carriers are easily removable from the rod, so that either one or both may be used as occasion requires. A foot-piece in the form of a shallow box, fig. 2, G, in which the arms and their carriers are packed, is supplied as part of the apparatus. To this the rod may be fixed in an upright position, by inserting it into the bore in the hole I, or by attaching a rest, H (also supplied with the instrument), to the zero end of the rod, it stands in a vertical position on the lid of the box.

To take the first four essential measurements, place the arms on the first segment of the rod with their extremities projecting equally on either side of it, Pl. I, fig. 1. The length and breadth of the head are measured between the curved ends of the arms, the dimensions of the nose between the straight and pointed ends. To measure the projections Nos. 5, 6, 7 and 8 slide the fixed arm horizontally till its curved end is prevented going further by the carrier, Pl. II, move the sliding arm horizontally in the opposite direction till the point of the straight end is only just seen beyond its carrier; adjust the head of the subject to the proper position for measurement and rest the fixed arm on the vertex, the pointed end directed towards the back of the head, while the rod rests against the point of the person's nose; slide the gliding carrier and arm, D E, vertically downwards to opposite the root of the nose, and finally slide this arm, D, horizontally forward till its pointed end touches the proper spot, *b*, Pl. II, at the root of the nose, when the measurement may be read off on the rod. The gliding arm is now moved horizontally from the face, drawn vertically downwards to opposite the mouth, and again projected horizontally towards the face, then by careful adjustment with the two movements of the arm the measurement from vertex to mouth, *d*, is obtained. The other projections are measured in a similar manner.

For the measurements of the face, cubit, hand and foot the arms are moved horizontally till they project equally on either side of the rod, as in measuring the length and breadth of the head, Pl. I, fig. 1. To measure the height of different parts of the body remove the fixed arm and carrier, B C, and attach the "rest," fig. 2, H, in its place, slip the other two segments into their sockets till the rod is the full length, slide the gliding arm vertically along the rod to about the middle of the centre segment, and also slide it horizontally till the pointed end projects as far as possible beyond the rod. The box foot-piece being placed on a stool or seat about 20 cm. high, and the subject having seated himself upon it, the rod is placed on the foot-piece behind the subject and the sliding arm is drawn down till it touches the vertex of his head. This measurement being made, the footpiece is placed on the ground and the subject kneels upon it, his body being held upright, the rod is this time rested on the foot-piece in front of the subject, and the sliding arm, which has been previously elevated, is moved vertically downwards till it rests upon the vertex as before. The arm may then be elevated and the subject made to stand on the foot-piece; the rod being placed behind him on the foot-piece, his height when standing is ascertained. After the subject has been measured the schedule is folded in two and the contour of the hand is taken on the one side, that of the foot on the other.

A graduated tape is necessary in addition to the Traveller's Anthropometer for some of the Additional Measurements in the schedule. It may be of linen, waxed or varnished, but as even such a tape is liable to stretch, the traveller should provide himself with a two-metre steel tape; those made by Chesterman are very good.

In absence of a Traveller's Anthropometer a pair of callipers may be used for measuring the head, length and breadth, and the dimensions of the nose, hand and foot, and height of malleolus, also the diameter of the face and ear. A wooden square with the longer limb graduated, and a small triangular indicator which can be held against the graduated limb will serve to measure the projections of the head, while the height of the body in different attitudes may be obtained by making the subject stand, kneel, or sit against a vertical wall on which a metre rule has been suspended one metre above the floor, or from the level of the stool, according to the measurement, and placing one limb of the square on the vertex of the head and the other against the rule.

Topinard's "Anthropometric Box," made by Collins of Paris, contains all the instruments required by the traveller, and is to be recommended.

Two or three strips of lead, 50 centimetres long by 1 cm. broad, and 2 millimetres thick, are useful for taking contours of the head or other part of the body to be afterwards traced on paper or on the schedule.

A photographic apparatus is useful in cases where the traveller is able to use it. Only two views are of any use in anthropography, namely, the full face and the profile. *See* Section PHOTOGRAPHY, p. 235.

J. G. G.

No. IV.—SCHEDULE.

Of Observations on External Characters.

PRELIMINARY PARTICULARS.

No.......................... Date.................................

Sex.......................... Age.................................

Tribe.......................... Locality.................................

Language or dialect..................................

General condition..

(1) Stout. (2) Medium. (3) Thin.

Descriptive Characters.

(A.) Colour of skin on parts not exposed to the air? ....

Black { Absolute (1.)
Sooty (2.)

Brown { Reddish (3.)
Yellowish (4.)

Red (5.)

Yellow (6.)

White { Yellowish (7.)
Brownish (8.)
Pale (9.)
Rosy (10.)

(For colour of skin *see* Plate II, Figs. 1—10.)

(B.) Colour of eyes? ....

Dark of all shades (1).

Medium { All medium shades, except green (2).
Green (3).

Light { All light shades, except blue (4).
Blue (5).

(For medium colours of eyes *see* Plate II, Figs. A, B, C, and D.)

(C.) Fold of skin at inner angle of eye? ....

(0) Absent. (1) Vestige remaining. (2) Covering $\frac{1}{3}$ to $\frac{1}{2}$ the caruncle. (3) Covering the caruncle.

(D.) Colour of hair? ....

(1) Black. (2) Dark brown. (3) Medium (4) Blond or fair of all shades. (5) Red.

(For medium shades of hair *see* Pl. II. Figs. A, B, and C.); if possible a lock of hair should be attached to the Schedule.)

(E.) Character of hair? ....

(1) Straight. (2) Undulating or wavy.
(3) Curly. (4) Woolly.

(F.) Amount of hair { On the face? .... / On the body?.... ....

(0) Absent. (1) Scarce. (2) Medium.
(3) Abundant.

(G.) Shape of face? ....

(1) Long and narrow. (2) Medium. (3) Short and broad. (4) Pyramidal, *i.e.*, narrowing upwards. (5) Wedge-shaped, *i.e.*, pointed towards chin.

(H.) Profile of nose? ....

(1) Straight, Pl. IV, Fig. 1. (2) Aquiline, Fig. 2. (3) Concave or turned up, Fig. 3. (4) High bridged, Fig. 4. (5) Sinuous or wavy, Fig. 5. (6) Chinese type, Fig. 6. (7) Negroid type, Fig. 7. (8) Australoid type, Fig. 8.

(I.) Prognathism or prominence of the region of the mouth? ....

(0) Absent. (1) Slight. (2) Moderately marked. (3) Considerable.

(J.) Lips.... ....

(1) Thin. (2) Medium. (3) Thick. (4) Everted.

(K.) Prominence of face transversely? ....

Proprosopic (face prominent, cheek bones not perceptible). { Considerable (1) / Moderate (2)
Mesoprosopic (3).
Platyoprosopic (face flat, cheek bones conspicuous). { Well marked (4) / Excessive (5)

Essential Measurements.

1. Head { Maximum length	....
2. Head { ,, breadth	....
3. Nose { Length from nasal spine to root ...	....
4. Nose { Breadth	....
5. Projections of Head. { From vertex to root of nose	....
6. Projections of Head. { ,, ,, to mouth	....
7. Projections of Head. { ,, ,, to chin	....
8. Projections of Head. { ,, ,, to tragus of ear ...	....
9. Bizygomatic breadth of face	....
10. Length of upper limb	....
11. Length of cubit	....
12. Length of the hand along its back	....
13. Length of foot	....
14. Sitting height	....
15. Kneeling height	....
16. Standing height (without shoes)	....
17. Height to chin	....
18. Height to sternal notch	.. ..
19. Height from internal malleolus to the ground	....
20. Span of arms	....

Additional Measurements.

21. Maximum breadth of shoulders	....
22. Maximum breadth of hips	....
23. Diameter of Face. { External biorbital breadth	....
24. Diameter of Face. { External biocular breadth	....
25. Diameter of Face. { Internal biocular breadth	....
26. Diameter of Face. { Bigonial breadth	....
27. Ear { Length (maximum)	....
28. Ear { Breadth (insertion of tragus to outer rim)	....
29. Height of umbilicus from the ground	....
30. Biorbito-nasal arc	....
31. Circumference of chest	....
32. Minimum supra-malleolar circumference of leg	....

33. Maximum supra-malleolar circumference of leg	....
34. Tracing of hand 35. „ of foot — Mark the sub-styloid and sub-malleolar points and the extremities of the metacarpo and meta-tarso-phalangeal joints	

Special Measurements.

(*a.*) Length of body from seventh cervical spine to lower end of coccyx	....
(*b.*) Bi-acromial breadth	....
(*c.*) Bi-iliac crest breadth	....
(*d.*) Length of arm. Acromion to humero-radial line	....
(*e.*) Length of forearm. Humero-radial line to tip of styloid process	....
(*f.*) Length of thigh. Anterior superior iliac spine to external femoro-tibial line	....
(*g.*) Length of leg. Femoro-tibial line to end of *external* malleolus	....
(*h.*) Height of external malleolus from the ground	....

Special Observations.

....

J. G. G.

No. V.—EXPLANATION OF SCHEDULE.

The "Preliminary Particulars" require little explanation. The *age* may offer some difficulty on account of the person not being able to express it; in such cases the observer must indicate it to the best of his judgment, inserting the word "about" before the number he enters for it.

The *condition of body* is to be noted, as it may explain some peculiarity in the measurements which might be thought to be due to error. To save time and trouble in writing, numbers within brackets are attached to each of the three conditions, so that if the person is thin it will be sufficient to write "3" in the blank column. This plan is also to be followed in recording the descriptive characters which follow.

The "Descriptive Characters" are next to be recorded, and while this is being done the observer may engage the subject in conversation, so as to gain his confidence and overcome any fear or repugnance he may have to be measured. When the colour or form in the subject does not correspond to any in the Schedule, but is intermediate between two colours or forms, the two numbers between which it lies should be entered in the blank column. If any difficulty is found in answering the questions in the Schedule, reference should be made to the section, DESCRIPTIVE CHARACTERS, for further explanation.

The measurements are divided into three sets. Of these the first set, the "Essential Measurements," should always be ascertained, as they are most important for the differentiation of races, and enable the whole figure of the subject to be reproduced and compared with those of other races. The second set, "Additional Measurements," should be taken also whenever it is possible. The third set, termed "Special Measurements," require of the observer a knowledge of the anatomy of the body, and are more particularly intended to be measured by medical men.

The points between which these various measurements are taken are explained in Section VII, page 22, with which the traveller should make himself familiar.

Printed Schedules, each containing a set of observations for a single person, may be obtained from Messrs. Harrison and Sons, of St. Martin's Lane, London, W.C., at a cost of 9*d*. per dozen. They also supply Schedules for measurements of the skeleton at the same rate.

After a little practice the traveller will be able to ascertain the Preliminary Particulars, Descriptive Characters, and the Essential Measurements of a subject in about 15 minutes.

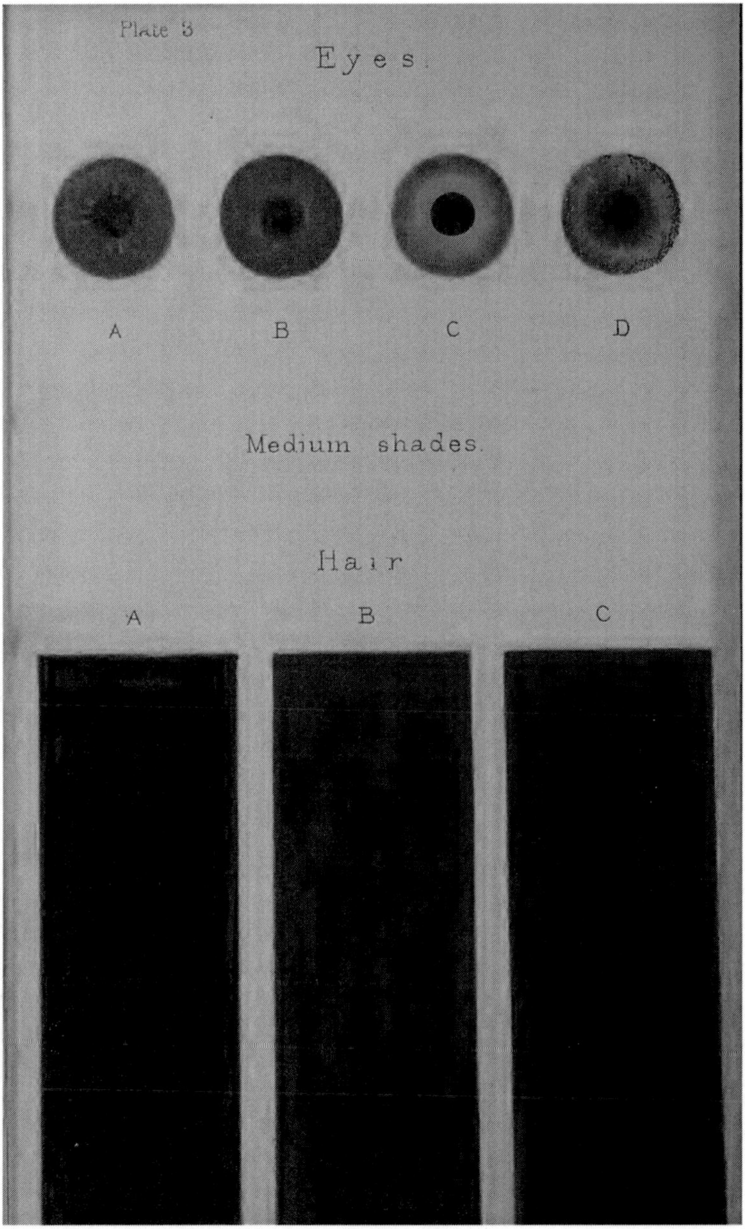
Plate 3
Eyes.
A
B
C
D
Medium shades.
Hair
A
B
C

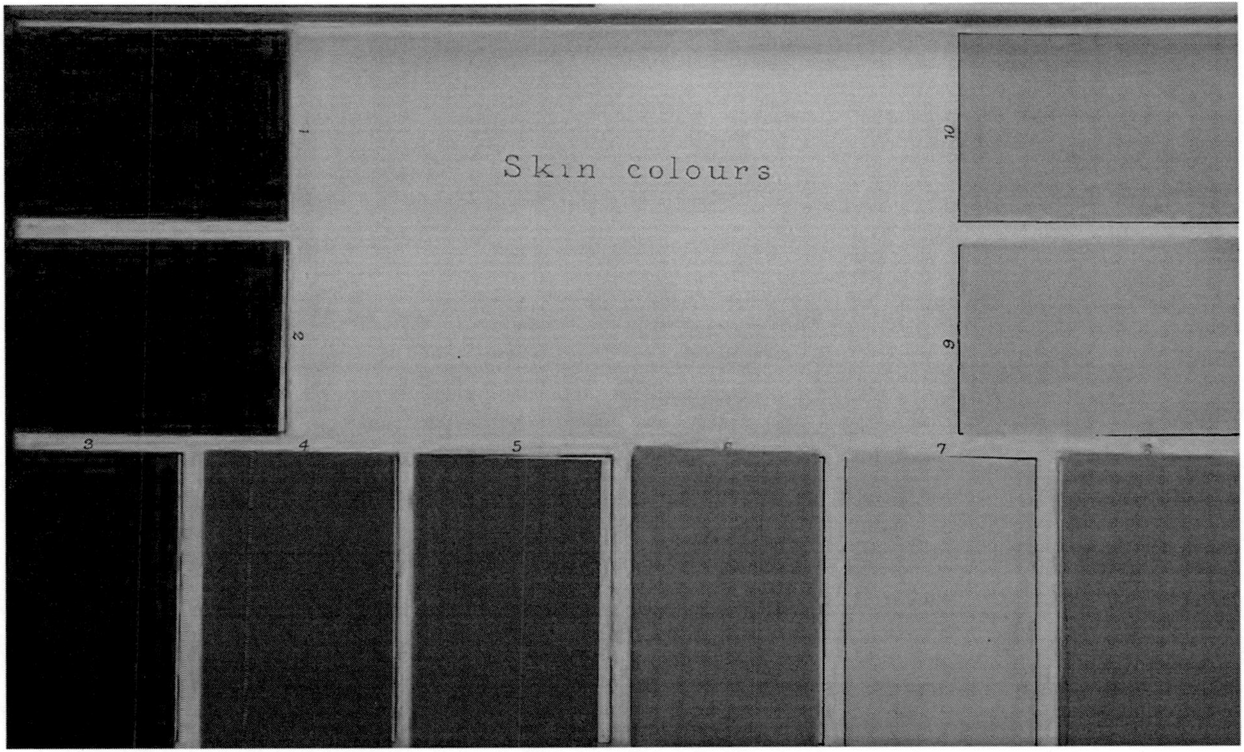
Skin colours
1
2
3
4
5
7
9
10

His work will be facilitated by the help of two assistants, one to write down the measurements and the other to assist him in taking them. The subject should be made to regard being measured as an amusement.

J. G. G.

No. VI.—DESCRIPTIVE CHARACTERS.

In the following Sections the various particulars regarding the Descriptive Characters asked in the Schedule are explained, and others supplementary to them which may with advantage be noted by the traveller are given.

Skin.

The colour of the skin may be easily enough indicated by the numbers of Broca's scale, which, though practically useless for hair, represent skin-tints very fairly.

A yet easier plan is that of Topinard, as follows:—

Is the skin—1. Black, coal-black? 2. Sooty-black? 3. Dark reddish-brown, chocolate? 4. Dark yellow-brown, dark olive? 5. Red, copper-coloured? 6. Yellow, olive? 7. Yellowish-white? 8. Brownish-white? 9. Pale white? 10. Florid or Rosy. (*See* Plate III., figs. 1–10.)

A very convenient part in clothed persons is usually the outer part of the upper arm. The part chosen should be stated in any case.

1. Is the skin smooth and velvety, or coarse and rough?
2. Is the oily excretion abundant?
3. Do the parts covered differ much in colour from those exposed to the sun?
4. Do different castes or sections of the population differ notably in colour?

5. What is the prevailing colour or complexion in parts *not* habitually exposed?

6. And what in those habitually exposed to weather and sunshine? Do freckles occur?

J. B.

EYE.

The colour of the iris is very important; next in importance are the form and position of the opening.

Colour:—The colour may be denoted in accordance with Broca's scale, which distinguishes four colours—orange or brown, ranging from very dark (1), through dark (2), medium (3), light (4), to lightest (5); green, similarly graduated from 6 to 10; blue, from darkest to lightest, 11 to 15; and grey or violet, from 16 to 20.

But Topinard's plan adopted in the Schedule is preferable, as being simpler and easier of application. He recognised four classes—

1. Dark.—Including those which are called black-brown, dark hazel, &c.
2. Medium or Neutral.—Such as cannot at once, in a good light, be distinguished as light or dark. Among these are the dark greys; most of the greens; those with a predominance of orange towards the centre, but of grey or light green elsewhere, &c. Examples of some varieties of neutral eyes are given (*see* Plate III., figs. A, B, C, and D).

Light. { 3.—Other than blue (light grey very light green, &c.).
4.—Blue.

What are the relative proportions of these four classes? The eyes should be examined from a moderate distance, so as to get a general impression of the colours. Those distinctly darker than the neutral examples given to be called *dark* those lighter to be called *light*

Form and position:—Are the eyes placed with their long axes nearly in one horizontal plane (as in most Europeans), or are their outer angles more or less visibly elevated (as in many or most Chinese)? Are they deeply-set, or *à fleur de tête*, prominent? Is the upper eyelid thick? Does it turn down at the inner angle, covering more or less the caruncle? Does the outer angle of the opening appear compressed and pointed, so as to suggest an almond shape?

J. B.

Hair.

1. Is the colour in adults—1. Black, coal-black? 2. Dark brown? 3. Medium, chestnut brown? 4. Fair blond, yellow, or flaxen? 5. Red, auburn?

Specimens are given of the colours, whether reddish-brown, yellowish, or dull (*cendré*), which are included under 3 (*see* Plate III., figs. A, B, and C). Shades much darker than these types are to be called dark-brown or black, those much lighter must be set down under 4 as fair, blond, &c.; red and auburn shades form a class of their own.

Only adults whose hair has not begun to turn grey should be selected for this purpose. The shades are best discriminated not in sunshine, but in the shade on a bright, clear day.

2. If the hair in adults is always or usually black, what colours prevail among children?

3. Is the natural colour of the hair interfered with in any way? Some races dye the hair.

4. Is there any colour which is preferred to others?

5. Obtain specimen locks of different ages, if possible, viz., (*a*) at birth, (*b*) between 1 and 2 years, (*c*) 2 and 4, (*d*) 4 and 8, (*e*) 8 and 16, (*f*) adult.

6. Is the hair straight, slightly or much waved, curly or frizzly, or what is called woolly? 7. If curly or frizzled, is this due to nature or art? 8. Is it in great quantity? 9. What length does it attain, whether measured by the apparent distance between points and roots of the locks, or

by stretching individual hairs? 10. Does it grow in separate tufts? or is it uniformly scattered over the hairy scalp? 11. Are the hairs coarse or fine in texture? round, flattened, or kidney-shaped in section?

12. Have the males any beard? If not, are they beardless by nature, or do they pluck out or otherwise destroy the beard?

13. On what parts of the body besides the head, armpits, and pubes does hair grow? at what age does it begin to grow on the different parts? and in what quantities? 14. What is the difference between male and female in this respect? 15. What difference is observed in the quality and colour of the hair on different parts of the body?

16. In what direction does the hair grow on different parts of the body, hands, arms, legs, &c.? 17. At what age do greyness and baldness appear? and in what parts first?

J. B.

Form of Face.

Where exact measurements of the facial features cannot be obtained, answers to the following questions may supply their place:—

1. Is the face, in a front view, square, oblong, round, elliptic, short-oval, long-oval, shield-shaped (like an escutcheon), or wedge-shaped?

2. In profile, is it convex or concave?

3. In profile also, are the chin, the nose, the mouth, the brow-ridges markedly prominent? and of the supra-orbital region, are the brow-ridges proper, or the glabella (central boss), the more prominent?

4. Is the nose (Plate IV.) straight, fig. 1; aquiline, fig. 2; hooked, fig. 3; concave, fig. 4; high-bridged (busqué), fig. 4: clubbed, or sinuous, fig. 5? Or has it the Chinese type (straight but flat), fig. 6; or the negroid (short, broad, nearly straight), fig. 7; or the Australoid or Papuan (broad, with the lower part forming a flattened and depressed hock) fig. 8?

5. Is the chin broad, narrow, angular, or round?

PLATE IV.

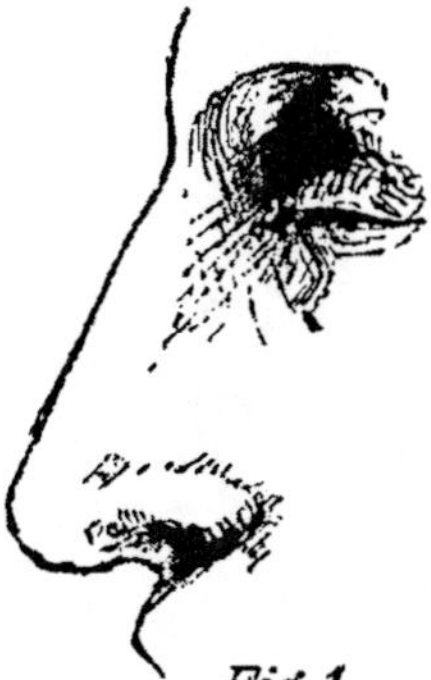

Fig 1.

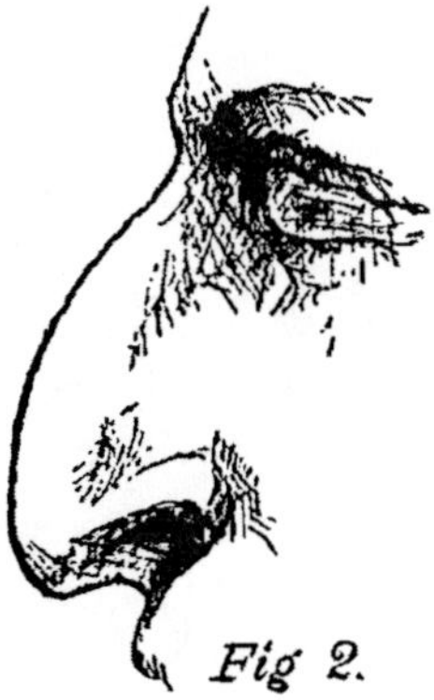

Fig 2.

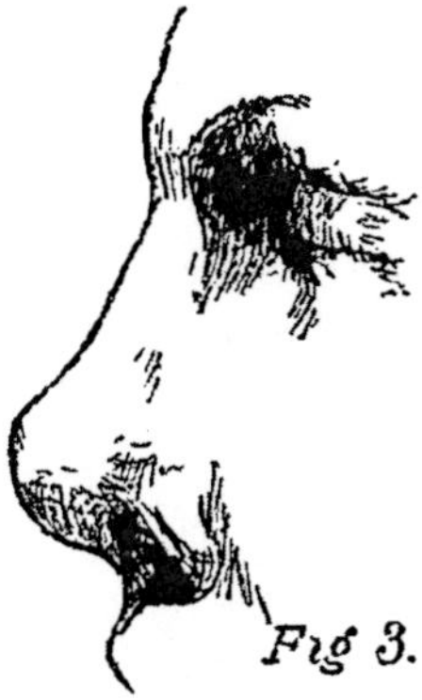

Fig 3.

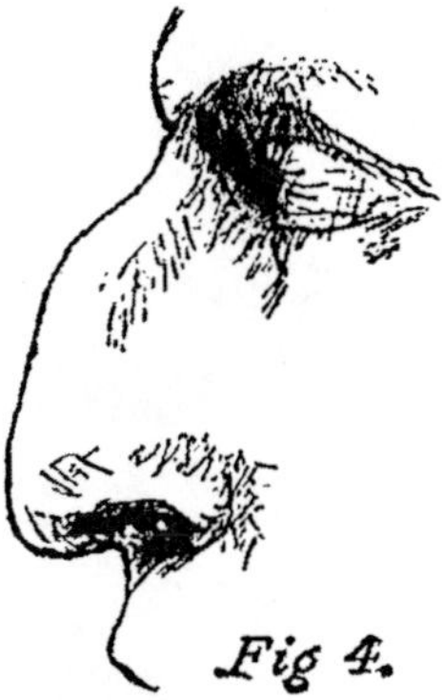

Fig 4.

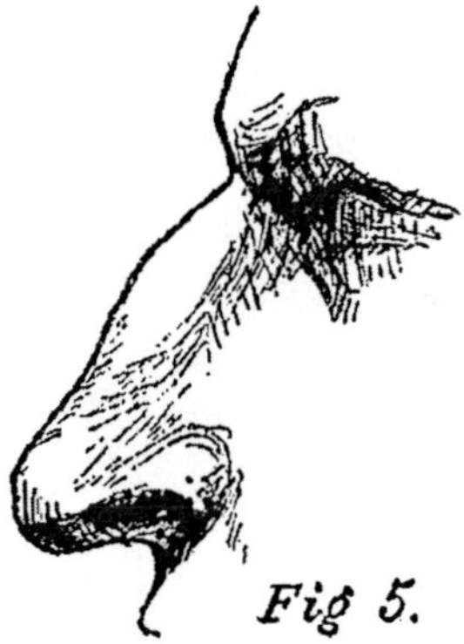

Fig 5.

Fig 6.

Fig 7.

Fig 8.

After Topinard.

6. Are the cheekbones broad, prominent forwards, or inconspicuous? or is the face in this region flat?

7. Are the lips thin, medium, or thick, or is the upper lip turned upwards and the lower lip turned downwards?

8. Are the ears large or small, flat or outstanding, simple or finely developed?

9. Are the lobes large or absent, attached or detached?

J. B.

Further Notes on the same Subject.

Proprosopic and Platyoprosopic are terms used to indicate whether the middle part of the face, between the level of the lower part of the nose and the supra-orbital level above, projects forward or is flat. In the former the breadth of the face at the level of the cheekbones appears diminished by these bones receding or being as it were pressed inwards, so that the face curves regularly forward from the ears to the nose, the latter is consequently prominent, and appears as a keel on the top of the arch. In the second the face is broad and flat in appearance, the cheekbones are prominent, and in extreme forms the side and front of the face are almost at right angles to one another, the bend of the angle being at the cheekbones, and the nose appears as if projecting from an almost flat surface. Extreme forms of the first type are frequently seen amongst English people, while the most marked type of the second is met with in the Eskimo and some of the Chinese. Two degrees of the proprosopic type and three of the orthoprosopic are given in the Schedule, while the intermediate condition of face is represented by the mesoprosopic form, of which the Celtic type of face may be taken as a fair example.

J. G. G.

No. VII.—DIRECTIONS FOR MEASURING THE BODY.

Essential Measurements.

1. *Length of Head.*—Measured from the most prominent point in the middle of the brow between the eyebrows, the *glabella*, Plate II*a*., to the most prominent point in the middle line of the occiput or back of head. It is the maximum length of the head in the middle line. In unsymmetrical heads the line of greatest length may be on one or other side of the middle line, such a length must *not* be taken.

2. *Transverse Breadth.*—The maximum breadth of the head wherever it may be (except low down behind the ears) measured transversely to the length. The points of the instrument must be exactly on the same level, otherwise the measurement will not be truly transverse, both in relation to the length and the horizontal plane.

These two measurements give the cephalic index which indicates the relation the breadth of the head bears to the length. It is obtained by multiplying the breadth by 100 and dividing the product by the length, the formula being

$$\frac{\text{Tr. B.} \times 100}{\text{Max length}} = \text{cephalic index.}$$

3. *Length of Nose.*—In making this measurement the instrument is held vertically, its lower point is placed lightly against the furthest back point of the under surface of the septum between the nostrils, Plate II*c*., where the upper lip begins, *not* on the tip of the nose, the upper point at the termination or root of the nose between the eyes, *b*; this is sometimes a little difficult to determine. There is a small transverse fold of the skin (sometimes two folds) at the root of the nose; it is on this fold, or when there are two folds, between the folds, that the upper point of the instrument

should rest, generally about two millimetres above the level of the transverse axes of the eyes.

4. *Breadth of Nose.*—Measured across the widest part without compressing the nostrils between the points of the instrument.

These two measurements give the nasal index, the formula of which is $\frac{\text{Breadth} \times 100}{\text{Length}}$ = nasal index.

The next four measurements show the distance their several levels project vertically below the plane of the top of the head. For directions as to how the instrument is to be used in determining them see INSTRUMENTS, p. 9. The position in which the head is held by the subject while these measurements, and also those of height, are being made is most important and requires the careful attention of the observer. The subject must sit with the body upright and the head straight, the line of vision directed horizontally forwards to a point at a little distance off, the same height as the eyes. Having adjusted the head in the proper position, the instrument is placed with one limb resting on the vertex while the body of the instrument is held vertically in front of the face; to secure this being done a small plumb-line should be temporarily fixed to the base of the curved part of its upper arm or on the end of the carrier, Plate II*e*. After each measurement is taken the observer should see that the subject is in the correct attitude before taking the next.

5. *Vertex to Root of Nose.*—The point on the root of the nose to which this measurement is taken is the same as that in measuring the length of the nose, Plate II*c*.

6. *Vertex to Mouth.*—The lower point is the line of the lips when closed, Plate II*d*.

7. *Vertex to Chin.*—The point on the chin is that corresponding to the under surface of the lower jaw, as shown in Plate II.

8. *Vertex to Tragus of Ear*, or supra-auricular projection, is measured by rotating the instrument to the side of the head, the horizontal arm still resting on the vertex. The

lower arm is projected against the middle of the tragus (the small projecting portion of the external ear which guards the opening of the meatus, in front), at the point where it starts from the side of the face, marked ×, Plate II.

By adding the length and breadth of the head, and the height from the tragus to the vertex together, and dividing the product by 3, the cephalic module of Schmidt is obtained, which enables us to compare approximately the volume of different heads.

9. *Bizygomatic breadth of Face* is the maximum breadth of the face between the bony arches in front of the ears.

This diameter compared with the length of the face from the root of the nose to the chin (obtained by subtracting the height from the root of the nose to the vertex, No. 5, from that between the vertex and chin, No. 7), forms a useful index, the formula of which is :

$$\frac{\text{Bizygomatic Breadth} \times 100}{\text{Height from chin to root of nose}} = \text{facial index.}$$

10. *Length of Upper Limb.*—This is measured with the arms straightened and hanging vertically at the sides of the body. The right arm should be selected for measurement unless both arms are measured. The point of the sliding arm of the instrument is applied to the depression which is found immediately below the bony prominence forming the tip of the shoulder, the acromion, between it and the head of the humerus or arm bone, the other arm of the instrument is drawn downwards till it reaches the extreme end of the middle finger. While making the measurement the instrument must be held parallel to the axis of the limb ; to do this its lower arm must be moved horizontally till it projects the requisite distance beyond the other, as in taking the projections of the head.

11. *Length of Cubit.*—The forearm is fully flexed upon the upper arm till the tip of the elbow is the most prominent point, the thumb being uppermost. The instrument is then placed along the outer edge of the forearm and the little finger side of the hand, the point of the elbow resting against the fixed arm of the instrument, while its other

arm (which has been previously drawn along the rod) is moved backwards again till it touches the end of the middle finger.

12. *Length of Hand.*—With the forefinger and thumb find the extremities or styloid processes of the bones of the forearm situated on the thumb and little finger sides of the subject's wrist, and tie a small cord over them, so as to show their line of junction. The length of the hand is measured from the centre of this line along the back to the tip of the middle finger.

These three measurements enable the length of the three segments of the upper limb to be determined, and compared.

13. *Length of Foot.*—Measured in the same manner as the shoemaker does for a boot.

In taking the three following heights, the measuring rod is used as described in the Section on INSTRUMENTS, p. 10.

14. *Sitting Height.*—The subject should be seated low. Care must be taken to see that the body is held perfectly erect, the head in the same position as when measuring its projections, and the legs should be close together. The measurement is taken between the vertex and the plane of the tuberosities of the ischia, or bony prominences of the buttock.

15. *Kneeling Height.*—The subject kneels down, holding his body erect and his head straight. The legs should be close together, and the point of the toes as nearly as possible on the same plane as the knee. Should the subject object to kneel properly, the height of the lower edge of the patella, or knee-cap, from the ground may be taken instead before measuring No. 19.

16. *Standing Height.*—This should always be measured without shoes, when possible. Should the subject object to take off his shoes, he may be measured with them on, and the thickness of the heel deducted.

17. *Height to Chin* is measured from the ground to the under surface of the lower jaw, the point at which the projection of the head to the chin ceased. While making this

measurement care must be taken that the head is held straight, as in measuring the projections.

18. *Height to Sternal Notch.*—The upper point of measurement is in the middle line of the body, on the upper edge of the sternum or breast bone, midway between the projecting ends of the collar bones.

19. *Malleolar Height.*—Measured from the tip of the internal malleolus (or downward projecting process of the large leg bone) to the ground, by sliding down the horizontal arm of the instrument to the level of the point of the malleolus.

The height of the head, from the vertex to the chin, having been previously ascertained, the difference between the heights to chin and to sternal notch give the length of the neck, while that between the sitting and the sternal heights gives the length of the trunk. The difference between the sitting and standing heights indicates the length of the inferior limb, from the level of the under surface of the tuberosities of the ischia to the sole of the foot; the sitting height subtracted from the kneeling height shows the length of the thigh from the lower end of the trunk to the knee; the difference between the kneeling and standing heights gives the length from the knee to the sole; the malleolar height deducted from this last indicates the length of the leg, while the malleolar height itself shows the height of the foot. In this way the amount contributed by each segment towards the stature of the body is indicated, and by reducing the measurement of each segment to hundredths of the whole stature the Canon of Proportion of the body is obtained.

20. *Span of Arms.*—The arms must be extended horizontally so that their axes are at right angles to the axis of the body, the palms directed forwards, the measuring rod is placed across the subject's back, *not* on front of the chest, and the maximum distance from the tip of the middle finger of one hand to that of the other with the arms extended is measured. This measurement is best made when the subject is standing with his back and arms resting against a wall.

Additional Measurements.

These measurements are next to be taken. If it is not possible to obtain all of them the traveller should measure as many as he can, as they are all important.

21. *Maximum Breadth of Shoulders*, measured between the external surfaces of the prominences of the shoulders about 5 cm. below the acromion, the subject standing in a natural position with his elbows to the sides.

22. *Maximum Breadth of Hips* across the prominences of the thighs, where the thigh bones are felt subcutaneously, while the subject is standing with the feet together and the weight of the body rests equally on both legs.

In making these two measurements the skin should be pressed firmly under the arms of the instrument. It may not be possible to obtain them on the nude, in which case they may be made with the clothes on. They form a good index, the breadth of the shoulders being taken as 100, thus:

$$\frac{\text{Hip breadth} \times 100}{\text{Shoulder breadth}} = \text{girdle index.}$$

23. *External Biorbital Breadth*, measured from the outer surfaces of the bony rim, bounding the orbit externally on the one side to the corresponding point on the rim of the other orbit. The level of the points of measurement is indicated by thickening of the bony rim, and is situated at or slightly above the external angle of the eye, and 2 or 3 millimetres below the external end of the eyebrow.

24. *External Biocular Breadth*, from the external angle of the one eye to the corresponding point of the other.

25. *Internal Biocular or Interocular Breadth*, between the internal angles of the two eyes.

26. *Bigonial Breadth*, is the breadth of the lower jaw at its angles which are easily felt below the skin.

The bizygomatic, external biorbital, and bigonial breadths of the face when compared with one another, or still better, with the projection of the head from vertex to chin, indicate the form of the face, whether it is long, short, oval or square in form, and thus assist the descriptive characters.

27. *Length of External Ear.*—The length of the auricle measured in its longest axis.

28. *Breadth of External Ear*, measured at right angles to the length from the point of junction of the tragus with the face, *see* 8, to the outer rim of the auricle.

29. *Height of Umbilicus or Navel* can usually be obtained only on nude savages, and should be ascertained after measuring the sternal height.

The next four measurements are made with the graduated tape.

30. *Biorbito-Nasal Arc*, measured over the root of the nose from the same points as 23. This arc, compared with the biorbital breadth, gives an index which has been found very useful in distinguishing races in India and elsewhere; its formula is $\frac{\text{Biorbito-nasal arc} \times 100}{\text{Biorbital breadth}} = \text{orbito-nasal index.}$ It indicates very well the degree of prominence or flatness of the face.

31. *Circumference of Chest.*—This measurement is more important in relation to the development of the chest, than as an indication of race character. In taking it, the subject must stand upright with shoulders back and arms hanging at the sides; the tape is placed immediately above the nipples, the lower edge touching them, and is brought horizontally round each side over the bladebones to the back of the subject where the observer stands, an assistant being in front to see that the tape is in the proper position and exactly horizontal. The measurement is read off while the chest is in repose. The circumference during forced inspiration and forced expiration may also be noted.

32. *Minimum supra-malleolar Circumference.*—This is the minimum circumference of the leg above the malleolus.

33. *Maximum supra-malleolar Circumference* shows the maximum girth of the calf of the leg.

In tracing the contours of the hand and foot care must be taken to keep the pencil quite perpendicular. The pencil should be split longitudinally, so that the outline it makes may be more exact.

34. *Contour of Hand.*—The hand is to be placed flat on a table, with the axes of the forearm and hand in line while the tracing is made. A mark should be made outwards from the contour line at the ends of the styloid processes of the bones of the forearm, and opposite the middle or highest points of the metacarpo-phalangeal enlargements, that is at the knuckles, of the forefinger and little finger, to indicate their position

35. *Contour of Foot.*—The foot is placed on a flat surface—the lid of the anthropometer box which will also serve as a table in tracing the hand—the leg being perpendicular to it. The pencil is held vertically, and the tracing begun opposite the lowest point of the internal malleolus, which should be indicated by an outward movement of the pencil, the tracing is brought round the front of the foot to the lowest point of the external malleolus, which should be similarly marked, and finally round the heel to the point where it was begun. The metatarso-phalangeal joint of the great and little toes should also be marked opposite the middle of the enlargements of these joints.

Further observations may be made by the traveller regarding any particular feature or peculiarity he may notice in the subject. Many of the peculiarities he will meet with are noticed in the Sections on Descriptive Characters, Abnormalities or Deformations.

Special Measurements.

(*a.*) *Length of the body from the seventh cervical spine to the lower end of coccyx.*—In making this measurement the subject stands with the body quite erect. The instrument is held vertically, and its arms adjusted till they touch the points of measurement on the body.

(*b.*) *Bi-acromial breadth* measure between the anterior and external angle of each acromion.

(*c.*) *Bi-iliac crest breadth.* The maximum transverse

breadth of the pelvis between the external margins of the iliac crests.

The next four measurements are supplementary to the lengths of the different segments of the limbs previously taken in the essential measurements, being direct measurements of the segments themselves. Their points of measurement are sufficiently defined in the Schedule. It is necessary to remember that they are vertical projections, consequently, while they are being ascertained, the instrument must be held vertically and its arms lengthened or shortened horizontally as may be required to make them touch the points of measurement, which should have been previously determined and marked on the skin.

J. G. G.

---

2. OSTEOLOGICAL CHARACTERS.

No, VIII.—GENERAL INSTRUCTIONS.

The skeleton (including the skull) should, if possible, be sent to an anatomical museum, such, for example, as the Natural History Museum or the Royal College of Surgeons' Museum in London, or the Museums of the Universities of Oxford, Cambridge, Edinburgh, or Dublin, where they can be examined by experts.* If the whole skeleton cannot be procured, the skull, the three pelvic bones, and the limb bones should be sent. The skeletons should be kept separate, and the locality, race, and, if known, the sex, rank, and probable age should be written upon each bone in addition to these particulars being written on labels attached to each, lest the latter be lost or injured by any chance in transit.

When the traveller is unable to procure specimens to

---

* See page 2.

send home but is able to examine them on the spot he should with his anthropometer and tape make the measurements of the skull, pelvis, and limb bones, and note the descriptive characters of the skull scheduled in the following scheme.

J. G. G.

No. IX.—SCHEDULE

of Observations on the Skeleton.

Preliminary Particulars.

No......................... Date....................................

Sex... .... Age........................ ....

Tribe........................ Locality ....

Language or dialect..................................

Measurements of the Skull.

1.	Maximum antero-posterior length	....
2.	" transverse breadth	....
3.	Minimum frontal breadth	....
4.	Height, basio-bregmatic	....
5.	Horizontal circumference	....
6.	Antero-posterior curve length	....
7.	Basio-nasial length	....
8.	Basio-alveolar (superior) length....	....
9.	Bizygomatic breadth	....
10.	Bigonial breadth	....
11.	Nasio-mental length	....
12.	Nasio-alveolar length	....
13.	Nasal height	....
14.	" breadth	....
15.	Orbital breadth	....
16.	" height	....

Measurements of the Pelvis.

17. Maximum iliac crest breadth		....
18. Pelvic height		....
19. Antero-posterior diameter of brim		....
20. Transverse diameter of brim		....

Measurements of Limb Bones.

21. Maximum length of humerus	....
22. " " radius	....
23. " " femur	....
24. " " tibia	....

Descriptive Characters.

The calvaria, or brain case—

a. Muscular ridges—(1) feeble, (2) moderate, (3) well marked	....
b. Chief sutures. Condition—(1) open, (2) moderately closed, (3) obliterated	....
Complexity—(1) simple, (2) moderate, (3) complicated	....
c. Wormean ossicles in sutures—(0) absent, (1) small, (2) medium, (3) large	....
d. Outlines or curves. Antero-posterior—(1) regular, (2) irregular; note whether elevated or depressed in the frontal, parietal, or occipital regions	....
Horizontal—(1) regular, (2) prominent or (3) flattened or depressed at any part, naming region ...	....
Transverse arch (1) pointed, (2) medium, (3) flat	....

Facial portion—

e. General form—(1) long and narrow, (2) medium, (3) short and broad, or square ....

f. Glabella and superciliary region—(1) flat, (2) moderately developed, (3) prominent ....

g. Orbits { Axes—(1) nearly horizontal, (2) set at an angle, *i.e.*, drooping externally ....
Form—(1) round, (2) broadened rectangular, (3) almost square ....

h. Inter-orbital region—(1) narrow, (2) medium, (3) broad ....

i. Nose { Lower Margins of openings—(1) sharp, (2) rounded, (3) sloping ....
Spine—(1) very small (2) small, (3) medium, (4) large ... ...
Profile outline—(1) straight, (2) convex, (3) concave ....

k. Profile of upper jaw—(1) straight, or nearly so, (2) prominent and convex above, (3) prominent and concave above ....

l. Teeth { Direction of incisors—(1) vertical, (2) projecting ....
Wear—(1) unworn, (2) somewhat worn, (3) much worn ....

m. Form of palate—(1) U-shaped, (2) elliptical (horse-shoe shaped), (3) parabolic (narrow in front) ....

n. Chin—(1) pointed and narrow, (2) medium, round, (3) square, flat ....

Special Observations.

....

J. G. G.

No. X.—DIRECTIONS FOR MEASURING THE SKELETON.

1. *Maximum Antero-posterior diameter of Skull.*—Measured from the glabella to the most prominent part of occiput in the middle line.

2. *Maximum Transverse breadth.*—Measured wherever it may be, except on the mastoid processes behind the auditory meatûs, transversely to the length. Care must be taken to hold the instrument perfectly horizontal, so that its points are on the same level.

3. *Minimum Frontal breadth.* — Measured across the narrowest part of the forehead on the lateral ridges of the frontal bone.

4. *Height.*—Measured from the basion (anterior edge of the foramen magnum) to the bregma (the point on the vertex where the frontal and interparietal sutures meet).

5. *Horizontal Circumference.*—Measured with the tape immediately above the superciliary ridges and over the most prominent part of the occiput.

6. *Antero-posterior curve.*—Measured from the nasion (the point at the root of the nose where the suture between the nasal bones ends at their junction with the frontal bone) over the glabella, bregma, occiput, and foramen magum to the basion.

7. *Basio-nasial length.*—Measured from the basion to the nasion in a direct line.

This measurement, added to the previous one, gives the antero-posterior circumference of the brain case.

8. *Basio-alveolar length.*—Also a direct radius from the basion to the alveolar point (the most prominent point of the alveolar border of the upper jaw, between and a little anterior to the roots of the two central incisor teeth).

9. *Bizygomatic breadth.*—The distance between the external surfaces of the zygomatic arches at each side of the face.

10. *Bigonial breadth.*—The distance between the external surfaces at the angles of the lower jaw.

11. *Nasio-mental length.*—The direct distance from the nasion to the under surface of the lower jaw in the middle line.

12. *Nasio-alveolar length,* from the nasion to the alveolar point.

13. *Nasal height,* from the nasion to the lowest level of the floor of the nasal openings in the middle line.

14. *Nasal breadth*, the transverse breadth across the nasal openings at the widest part.

15. *Orbital breadth*, measured from the spot where the posterior edge of the lachrymal groove meets the fronto-lachrymal suture, to the external border of the orbit in the line of its greatest axis.

16. *Orbital height*, measured at right angles to the axis of breadth between the upper and lower borders across the middle of the orbit.

---

17. *Maximum breadth of Pelvis*, measured between the outer edges of the iliac crests.

18. *Pelvic height*, or the maximum length of the innommate bone, from the highest point of the iliac crest to the lowest part of the tuber ischii.

19. *Antero-posterior diameter of the Brim*, measured from the middle of the anterior margin of the upper border of the sacrum to the nearest point opposite at the upper part of the symphysis pubis.

20. *Transverse diameter of Brim*, measured at right angles to the preceding across the broadest part of the brim, or margin of the pelvic cavity.

If the person has been buried for some time the two innommate bones and the sacrum which form the pelvis will probably be separate. To obtain the above measurements it will be necessary to fix the bones together by means of string, and when doing so a small piece of wood, about 5 or 6 millimetres thick, should be placed between the ends of the pubic bones in front, to represent the thickness of the soft tissues which have disappeared.

---

21. *Maximum length of Humerus.*—The bone is laid flat and measured by projection between the summit and the most dependent point of the lower articular surface, the body

of the instrument being parallel to the long axis of the bone.

22. *Maximum length of Radius*, from the upper border of the head of the bone to the extremity of the styloid process.

23. *Maximum length of Femur.*—The femur is placed on a table or flat surface, with its inner aspect downwards, so that the tuberosity of the internal condyle and the articular head of the bone rest against the table, the length is measured from the lowest point of the under surface of the internal condyle to the summit of the head of the bone in a direct line.

24. *Maximum length of Tibia.*—The central spine is not included, the measurement being taken from the highest part of the flat surface in front and at the sides of it, to the extremity of the internal malleolus.

NOTE.—The tape should only be used in measuring Nos. 5 and 6; all the other measurements are to be made with the anthropometer.

J. G. G.

B.—PHYSIOLOGICAL OBSERVATIONS.

No. XI.—INTRODUCTION.

Deductions regarding the comparative physiology of man to be trustworthy require to be based on even more numerous observations than anatomical characters. The study of this branch of anthropography offers excellent opportunities for medical men settled for some time in a country. It is only possible here to give an outline of the direction which such studies may take and to indicate some of the observations which may be most readily made by the traveller.

J. G. G.

No. XII.—TEMPERATURE OF THE BODY.

In making observations on the temperature of the body the observer should use a clinical thermometer which has been manufactured for two or three years and been afterwards tested with a standard instrument so as to ascertain the amount of error in its graduation. Such an instrument may be obtained with a certificate from Kew Observatory through any good instrument maker. If possible the traveller should have his thermometer re-tested at intervals to ascertain if any variation has occurred in it.

The temperature of the body is ascertained by placing the bulb of the thermometer under the tongue for from one to five minutes, according to the sensitiveness of the instrument used, the mouth meanwhile being closed round the stem and breathing carried on entirely through the nostrils. The temperature of the surrounding air must at the same time be ascertained with an ordinary thermometer and noted. Previously to the observation being made the subject should have been resting in the shade for a while and should not have partaken of food for about two hours. The observations should be repeated several times, and may be made under different conditions of body, the typical observation, however, is when the person is fasting and at rest. The temperature taken in the Axilla is not sufficiently accurate for Anthropographical purposes.

J. G. G.

No. XIII.—CIRCULATION AND RESPIRATION.

The frequency of the pulse-beat should be observed while the subject is at rest in a sitting posture, and should be noted at the same time of day and under the same conditions on each occasion the observation is repeated. The pulse should be counted during a whole minute at a time.

The respirations should be counted for at least a minute while the subject is resting, and without his being conscious of what is being done. Observations should be made as to whether the respiratory movements are similar or different in males and females, particularly as to the predominance of costal or abdominal breathing in one or other sex.

J. G. G

No. XIV.—MISCELLANEOUS.

1. Do the people bear cold well, or bear exposure to direct rays of the sun? Do they expose their heads to the sun uncovered? How do they bear privations of food, or drink, or sleep?

2. Is the voice deep, hoarse, or shrill?

3. Are there any peculiarities of the excretory functions, such as the habitual diarrhœa (as in Faeroe), constipation, or salivation, or alkalinity of urine, or abundance or absence of perceptible perspiration?

J. B

No. XV.—ODOUR.

Many curious things are known or reported on this subject. Thus the Peruvians have different names for the scent of a Negro, an Indian, and a white man. The North-American Indians have been reported, but on doubtful authority, to regard the smell of Jews as horribly offensive. The odour of Kaffirs is said not to be diminished by washing, but to be increased by muscular exertion.

1. Is there any notable peculiarity of odour attached to the persons of the tribe or people described? 2. Is it recognised as diagnostic by their neighbours, or by dogs or other animals? 3. Does it seem to depend on filthy habits and

neglect of ablution, or on any favourite cosmetic or unguent, or on peculiarities of diet? or to be natural and constitutional? 4. Does it belong equally to both sexes and to all complexions (where these latter vary)? 5. Does it vary at different ages?

J. B.

No. XVI.—PHYSICAL POWERS.

Strength, speed, endurance.

It is difficult to institute comparative tests of strength for Europeans or civilized men and savages or barbarians. "Knack" and custom or constant practice have so great an influence, that it is necessary to select as a test some action not habitually used by either party. The persons tested should be in the prime of life, and otherwise similarly circumstanced.

In countries where the women do most or much of the hard labour, their strength should be tested as well as that of the males: with a view to comparison, all trials should be timed, and the weights and distances carefully measured, and the previous condition or training of the individuals recorded.

M. Broca commends the traction-dynamometer of Mathieu. The force registered should be that put forth continuously during at least two seconds. The maximum got by a sudden jerk may, however, also be noted.

"Putting" or raising a heavy stone is a pretty good test.

Trials of speed should not be confined to short races. The American Indians in general, *e.g.*, are said to have more enduring speed than Europeans, though easily beaten by them in sudden bursts: with some other savages the case is reversed.

1. What is the weight of the burden which a native will carry? 2. How far will he carry it in one day? 3. For how many days in succession without suffering thereby? 4. What distance can a man walk in one day? 5. What distance can

he ride in one day? 6. What distance can he run in one day? 7. In what time can he run an English mile of 1760 yards, or 2112 paces of 30 inches, on a level road or grass? 8. In what time can he walk ten or twenty miles on a fairly level road or grass? 9. In all trials of speed or endurance the temperature and the manner in which the individual is shod and clothed should be recorded, as also a general description of the ground traversed. 10. What weight can a man raise one foot from the ground, the handle being properly adjusted? 11. How far can he shoot an arrow or hurl a spear? 12. How long can he abstain from food or drink, without inconvenience, when in exercise? 13. Ditto when not in exercise? 14. Have they any drugs, or practices of any kind whereby they conserve their energy during labour, or believe that they conserve it.

J. B.

Further Notes on the same Subject.

Valuable data on the above points, as well as those treated of in *The Senses*, p. 41, in the note to *Heredity*, p. 48, and in *Psychology*, p. 53, are easily obtained by recording the number of persons out of any rather large number of them (say of more than 50) who succeed in achieving two (or better, three) definite tests of different degrees of severity. Thus—

How many succeeded and how many failed to lift the specified weights A, B, C, respectively?

How many succeeded and how many failed to run the specified distance D in *k*, *l*, and *m*, seconds; or else, how many succeeded and how many failed in running the specified distances E, F, G, in *n* seconds?

How many dropped out, and how many marched on after eating no food for *r*, *s*, *t* hours respectively? and so on.

The magnitude of the tasks or tests selected should be such that, very roughly speaking, a quarter of the whole number of persons observed may be expected to fail in the first, one-half in the second, and three-quarters in the third. The method of drawing conclusions from these data is indicated in the paragraph on Statistics, p. 226. They afford a *complete* and approximately correct picture of the distribution of the qualities tested, and not merely general averages.

F. G.

No. XVII.—THE SENSES.

Sight and hearing are generally supposed to be more acute in persons belonging to tribes who have long dwelt in open countries and led a nomadic or insecure life. *Myopia* (short sight) is thought to be extremely rare among savages, who exercise the eye very little on minute objects, while their smell is more acute than fastidious. But exact data on these subjects are wanting.

(a.) *Sight.*

For testing clearness of vision, the test-dots employed for testing the sight of recruits in the British Army (*see* Pl. V), and the directions for using them by Prof. Longmore, may be useful:—

Each test-dot is $\frac{1}{5}$-inch square, and corresponds at a distance of 15 feet with a bull's-eye 2 feet square at 600 yards, which must be distinctly seen by every acceptable recruit.

With *perfectly* acute vision these test-dots ought to be clearly visible in full daylight at 19 yards.

Directions for using the Test-dots.

1. Measure off 15 feet with precision.
2. Hold the test-dot card or paper perfectly upright in front of the man, and *let it face the light so as to be fully illuminated.*

3. Expose some of the dots (not more than seven or eight at a time) by covering the remainder with a card or a piece of paper, and desire the man to name their number and relative positions.

4. Vary the groups frequently to provide against deception; by using a covering card with a square portion cut out of one corner, six different groups of dots may be exposed without exceeding the number of dots above-mentioned. The test-dots should be kept perfectly clean.

At what distance can a man count the test-dots in conformity with the instructions on that head?

Power of distant vision can only be tested by extemporised modes of comparisons with that of Europeans. It has been noticed that amongst North American Indians a small distant object on the prairies will be recognised by each individual at the same instant and give rise to a simultaneous exclamation from the whole party. The power of judging distance may be greatly improved by practice; but some men show far greater natural aptitude than others. In the case of native troops, when judging-distance practice is conducted according to the English method, the results of the practice should be recorded.

The following are the rules for judging-distance practice; the object judged from is usually a group of two or three men; the number of answers and points obtained should be recorded. The value of men's answers, by points, in the several classes is as follows :—

3rd class, or when judging distance between 100 and 300 yards	within 5 yards	3 points
	„ 10 „	2 „
	„ 15 „	1 point.
2nd class, or when judging distance between 300 and 600 yards	within 20 yards	2 points.
	„ 30 „	1 point.
1st class, or when judging distance between 600 and 900 yards	within 30 yards	2 points
	„ 40 „	1 point.

PLATE V

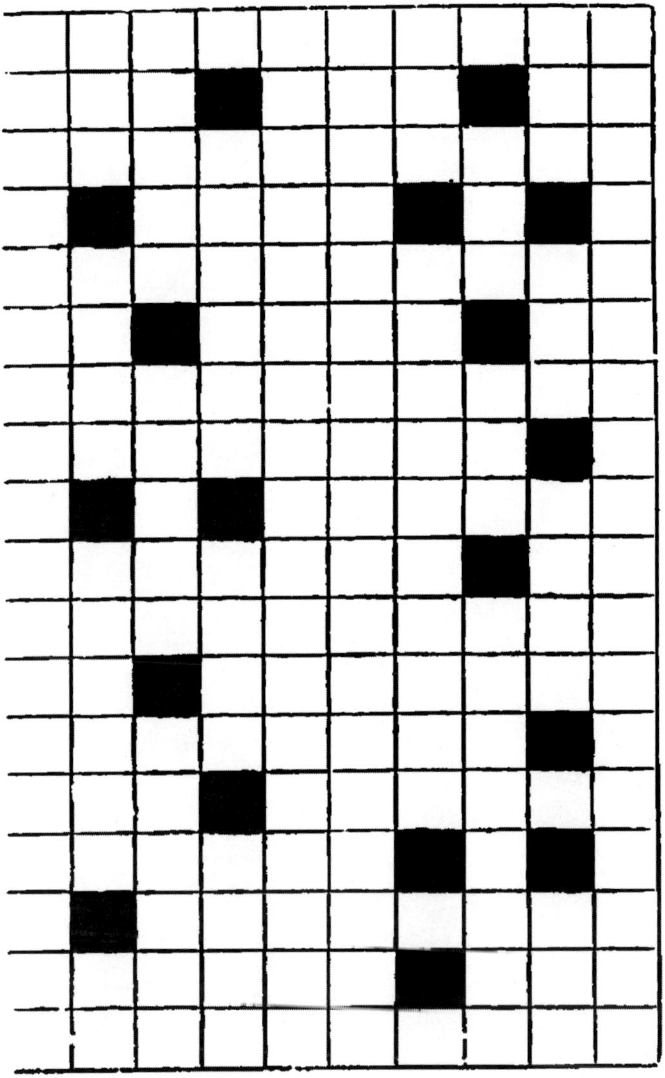

The following questions may also be answered (but due allowance must be made for the state of the atmosphere, colour of object and background; and too much reliance must not be placed on the answers as a means of comparison with similar observations made in distant countries):—1. At what distance can he distinguish the form of a human figure moving? 2. At what distance can he distinguish a man on horseback?

The existence of *Myopia*, where suspected, may be ascertained by the improvement gained by the use of biconcave (short-sighted) spectacles.

J. B.

Further Notes on Testing Sight.

Perhaps the simplest and the surest measure of keenness of eyesight is the greatest distance at which a square of known size that has two of its sides vertical as in Fig. 1, can be

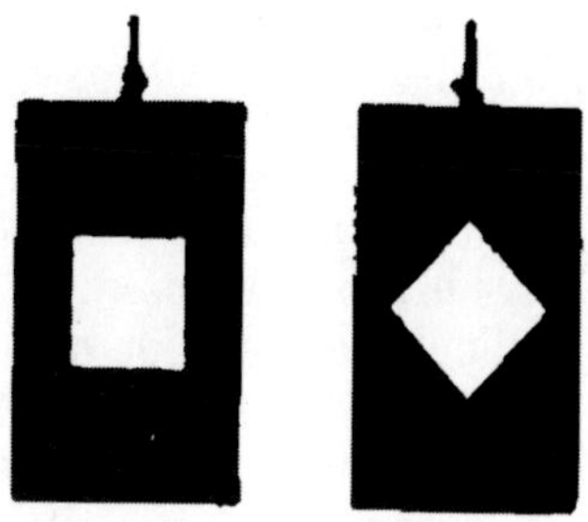

Fig. 1. Fig. 2.

distinguished from another of the same size that has one of its diagonals vertical as in Fig. 2. These two figures represent the opposite faces of the same card (or of painted zinc, which would be more durable), which is intended to be hung against a rather dark background. Procure three such pieces of card with squares on them of 1¼, 1, and ¾-inch in the side, respectively. An assistant displays and changes them, you stand by the person who is being tested, and using an opera glass, note the greatest distance at which he can distinguish with certainty the two positions of the 1-inch square. The object of the larger and of the smaller card is partly to discover that distance quickly, and partly to serve as a check against the man's apparent power of distinguishing the positions being due to lucky guesses. The cards must hang truly, and this will be the more easily ensured if weights are attached to holes in their lower ends.

The testing must be performed when the light is perfectly good, but not dazzling. Always test yourself when you are testing others, because if your own efficiency comes up to its normal standard, it is fair evidence that the conditions of light, &c., are normal also, otherwise very probably they are not.

F. G.

(b.) *Hearing.*

Hearing may be roughly tested by the ability to hear words spoken or the ticking of a watch.

Test by words in speaking.—The subject should hold his head straight and have his mouth closed. The observer places himself first behind then at either side of the subject, taking care that his face is not seen by the latter, who should repeat the words spoken. The hearing should be tested first with both ears open, the observer being behind. The subject then stops up one ear with his finger and listens to the observer, who now places himself opposite and rather behind the clear ear, which he proceeds to test. The same plan is followed for the other ear. The observer should begin by testing the subject with single words such as "tip," "fish," &c., containing soft vowels and little emphasized consonants, such words being the most difficult to hear. The test words should be spoken in a loud whisper and the distance from which they are heard with both ears, and then by each ear alternately, should be recorded. The observer should stand at a distance from the subject and gradually approach him till he hears the test words.

Test with a Watch.—Ascertain the normal distance the particular watch can be heard by examining several persons. The subject closes his eyes and puts his finger in one ear, the watch is brought towards the clear ear from a distance at which it is not heard to the point at which its ticking is just perceived. The distance between this point and the ear is then measured and recorded. This observation should be repeated two or three times. The second ear is then tested in a similar manner. Care should be taken to see that the subject keeps his eyes closed throughout the test.

J. G. G.

(c.) *Smell.*

For this no positive rules can be given.—Note whether any particular odours are disliked or enjoyed. Can they distinguish individuals in the dark by smell, as is said to be the case with some races? Can fires be smelt at great distances?

J. B.

(d.) *Touch.*

The subject having closed his eyes, apply the points of an ordinary mathematical compass to different parts of the body, varying the interspace between them so as to ascertain the minimum distance, for each part of the surface tried, at which the two points cease to be felt as one.

J. B.

No. XVIII.—ATTITUDES AND MOVEMENTS.

There is greater variety in the postures habitually assumed by different races of men than is generally known; thus the Tibetans are said to sleep, by preference, on an inclined plane with the face downwards. Nothing is more characteristic of the temperament than the carriage and motions of the body, and they should be closely observed. Should there be any peculiarity in the walk, it might be desirable to ascertain the average time and length of pace; this might be done by measuring off a piece of level ground over which the people are in the habit of walking, and counting the paces. It may be convenient to bear in mind that the regulation pace of the British infantry is 116 per minute, and the length 30 inches, making 96 yards 2 feet in a minute, and 3 miles 520 feet in an hour: this, however, is quicker and probably shorter than the pace of an average Englishman, and is never maintained on the line of march: probably the old regulation pace of 108 per minute is nearer the natural standard.

1. What is the habitual posture in sleep? 2. In standing at ease? 3. In micturition? 4. In the accouchement of women? 5. In riding? [Swimming? *see* p. 98.] 6. Is the body well balanced in walking? 7. In riding, walking, or running, do they turn the toes in or out? 8. Is the foot firmly planted in walking? or do they walk on the heels or toes? (*Note.* This will in some degree depend on the manner in which they are shod.) 9. What is the average length of pace and cadence of the step in men? 10. In women? 11. Is the body erect and the leg straightened? or do they stand and move with the knee slightly bent? 12. Is the gait energetic or slouching? 13. How do they carry the head? When the head is in the customary position, what would be the line taken by a horizontal plane drawn through the meatus auditorius (opening of the ear)? 14. Do they swing the arm in walking? 15. Are the attitudes stiff or easy? 16. Does the arm hang habitually with the palm of the they to the front, rear, or side? 17. In

moving any heavy object, do they habitually pull or push? is power generally exerted from or towards the body? and what muscles do they chiefly employ? (*Note.* It has been found in some parts of India that the natives cannot use a European saw until the teeth are reversed so as to cut with a pulling motion.) 18. What is their favourite method of carrying weighty objects or burdens? 19. Do they climb trees well? and have they any peculiar mode of doing this? 20. Have they much power of moving the ears, scalp, or features? 21. Can they shut one eye without closing the other? 22. Can they extend one finger without opening the hand? and do they habitually point with one finger or with the open hand? 23. Have they any tricks of sleight of hand? 24. Do they make much use of the feet in holding objects? and is the great toe in any degree opposable? 25. Are the joints generally stiff or pliable.

J. B.

Reproduction and Development.

(*See* Medical Section, pp. 55 and 58.)

No. XIX.—HEREDITY.

With regard to original or congenital physical and mental qualities, it is not the existence and importance of heredity that is questionable, but its extent, limits, and conditions. Acquired physical traits are usually, if not always, intransmissible, but the existence of exceptions to the rule has been asserted. As regards acquired mental qualities, little inquiry has hitherto been made.

Where any system of castes exists, or where the intercourse of the sexes is rigidly regulated, there is much room for observations of this kind.

Examine, for example :—1. How far stature, strength,

beauty, descend in the families of the chiefs. 2. How far intellectual ability or cunning in those of the priests and wizards. 3 Whether albinism, erythrism, or other abnormalities (*see* p. 60) are thus transmitted, and to what proportion of the children in a family, or if not to children, whether they are ever transmitted to grandchildren. 4. Whether instances occur in which a tribal mark or something like it appears naturally in a child. 5. Whether a natural aptitude for a particular art appears in the children of a caste who practise that art. 6. Whether there is any power of resistance to malarial poison transmitted from parent to child in certain tribes or clans.

J. B.

Further Notes on the same Subject.

The nature of man appears to be as plastic as that of any domestic animal, and equally to admit of differentiation. The inquiries of a traveller might often show the directions in which the tendency to a spontaneous establishment of new breeds is most common; but he must distinguish with all the care he can between *natural* and *acquired* gifts, by seeking appropriate cases and investigating them thoroughly. Children of savage races educated in the houses of missionaries, quite away from their own people, deserve close study, to see how far the natural character, apart from the traditions, &c., of their race, persists in showing itself. Also the children of foreign slaves who are bred up by barbarians. The large families of polygamatous parentage afford good studies for heredity. Among the hereditary characteristics of a race which admit of precise testing (*see* note by myself on Sight, p. 43) are:—Acuteness of sight. Delicacy of hearing. Aptitude to music. Neatness in handicrafts, and taste in design. Love of pursuits connected with the water: thus the South-Sea Islanders swim well early in childhood; is this really a natural or is it wholly an acquired faculty? Power of path-finding: the stories told of this gift are mostly gross exaggerations, but the subject deserves careful measurement; an ingenious traveller having a theodolite and skilled in its use could make many experiments, which would give trustworthy results. Power of sustaining hunger and thirst. Craving for particular kinds of narcotics and drinks. Recuperative power after accidents, and strength to withstand severe shocks and mutilations. Immunity from, or liability to, particular diseases. Psychological peculiarities, as:—the inherent gifts of ruling races; the early check of the development of the mind; excessive powers of imagination, as shown in hearing unreal voices, seeing fancied apparitions; also the convulsionary habits of wizards, and their hereditary nature. Half-castes deserve careful study. It is not easy to suggest beforehand what inquiries should be made. The traveller should be ever on the watch, and when an appropriate case presents itself to his notice, he should investigate it with great care. Those who confuse the effects of nature and of nurture, give information that is of very little use. The appearance of any natural peculiarity among the brothers or sisters of a large family, and the proportion of its members who show it in varying degrees, is an indirect datum for estimating heredity that is often more valuable than direct data.

F. G.

No. XX.—CROSSES.

The principal moot points on this subject have reference to either:—

(*a*) the fecundity of mongrels, or

(*b*) the physical or mental improvement or deterioration produced by crossing, or

(*c*) the points, if any, derived preferentially from either race or sex.

The following is M. Broca's method of indicating the racial position of mongrels or mestizos:—

Pure Races................	A	and	B	[(Mulatto).
First Cross................		AB		Mestizo of first blood
First Return Cross (Quadroon)		A^2B or B^2A		Do. of second blood.
Second Return Cross (Octoroon)		A^3B or B^3A		Do. of third blood.
Third Return Cross	A^4B	or	B^4A	Do. of fourth blood.
Return to pure race	A	or	B	....

The offspring of an octoroon and a mulatto, for example, would be designated thus, A^3B+AB ; and the same principle would be applied to cases where three races were crossed.

Another and a simpler, and perhaps preferable, method, consists in indicating the shares of the several races by fractions. Thus the result of a union between a quadroon and a zambo (half negro, half Indian) would be represented thus, $A\frac{3}{8}\ B\frac{3}{8}\ C\frac{1}{4}$, a quadroon being $A\frac{3}{4}\ B\frac{1}{4}$, a zambo $B\frac{1}{2}\ C\frac{1}{2}$.

1. Are connexions between the races under consideration likely to be frequent? 2. Is the mulatto or mongrel population numerous in proportion to the supposed number of unions? 3. Are individuals of the two races more or less fruitful in their unions among themselves than in crossed unions? (The Polynesians are said to be *less* so, the Australians much *more* so; but the latter, probably, usually destroy the mulatto infants.) 4. Are inverse crosses (male of inferior with female of superior race) equally fruitful with direct ones? Are the children of the first cross as strong, viable, and long-lived as those of pure blood in the same country? and do they yield as few examples of blindness, idiocy, &c.? 6. What is the relative degree of their fruitfulness among themselves and in their crosses with the pure blood? 7. Do they continue fruitful among themselves, without being reinforced with crosses of pure blood? The Liplappens (Dutch-Javan mestizos) are said in the third generation to yield only females, and these sterile; but the pure Dutch race is also said to become speedily sterile in Java. 8. Do

the products of the first cross resemble most the male or the female parent? and is there any difference between those of the direct and of the inverse cross? 9. How many return crosses restore apparent purity of blood? and what characteristic marks of the cross remain longest (hair, eyes, nails, &c.)? 10. What is the intellectual and moral position of mixed breeds between races, one of which is greatly superior to the other? (Social conditions may interfere with this problem; a despised and helot race can hardly maintain a high moral standard.) 11. Does a mixed breed develop any new and special aptitudes or talents? or is it superior in any respect to *both* its constituent stocks? 12. Can any direct cause be alleged for sterility where prevalent, *e.g.*, physical unsuitability, frequency of prostitution or of abortion, &c.? 13. Does the external form seem to be taken from one parent, and the constitutional habits from the other? 14. Do individual members of one family of mongrel blood differ greatly from one another by approximation to one or other parent?

J. B.

No. XXI.—PHYSIOGNOMY.

Observations on natives who have had little communication with Europeans would be of course the most valuable, though those made on any natives would be of much interest. General remarks on expression are of comparatively little value; and memory is so deceptive that it ought not to be trusted. A definite description of the countenance under any emotion or frame of mind, with a statement of the circumstances under which it occurred, would possess much value.

1. Is astonishment expressed by the eyes and mouth being opened wide, and by the eyebrows being raised? Are the open hands often raised high up, with the fingers widely separated, and the palms directed towards the person causing astonishment? Is the open mouth in some cases covered by the hand? or is the hand carried to some part of the head?

2. Does shame excite a blush when the colour of the skin allows it to be visible? and especially how low down the body does the blush extend? 3. When a man is indignant or defiant, does he frown, hold his body and head erect, square his shoulders and clench his fists? 4. When considering deeply on any subject, or trying to understand any puzzle, does he frown, or wrinkle the skin beneath the lower eyelids? 5. When in low spirits, are the corners of the mouth depressed, and the inner corner of the eyebrows raised by that muscle which the French call the "Grief muscle"? (The eyebrow in this state becomes slightly oblique, with a little swelling at the inner end; and the forehead is transversely wrinkled in the middle part, but not across the whole breadth, as when the eyebrows are raised in surprise.) 6. When in good spirits do the eyes sparkle, with the skin a little wrinkled round and under them, and with the mouth a little drawn back at the corners? 7. When a man sneers or snarls at another, is the corner of the upper lip over the canine or eye tooth raised on the side facing the man whom he addresses? 8. Can a dogged or obstinate expression be recognised, which is chiefly shown by the mouth being firmly closed, a lowering brow, and a slight frown? 9. Is contempt expressed by a slight protrusion of the lips and by turning up the nose, with a slight expiration, or by the closure of the eyes, or by other gestures? 10. Is disgust shown by the lower lip being turned down, the upper lip slightly raised, with a sudden expiration, something like incipient vomiting, or like something spat out of the mouth? 11. Is extreme fear expressed in the same general manner as with Europeans? 12. Is laughter ever carried to such an extreme as to bring tears into the eyes? 13. When a man wishes to show that he cannot prevent something being done, or cannot himself do something, does he shrug his shoulders, turn inwards his elbows, extend outwards his hands and open the palms, with the eyebrows raised and mouth somewhat opened? 14. Do the children when sulky pout or greatly protrude the lips into a tubular form? Do they at the same time frown or utter any noise? 15. Can guilty, or sly, or jealous expressions be recognised? though I

know not how these can be defined. 16. Is the head nodded vertically in affirmation, and shaken laterally in negation? or is the hand or finger so used?

C. D.

No. XXII.—PSYCHOLOGY.

Under this head may be included inquiries respecting the degrees of quickness of perception, the power of reasoning, learning, and generalizing, of fixing the attention, of memory, of perseverance, exhibited by the tribes or races observed. It would not be possible to lay down precise tests for the use of the investigator.

The power of forming abstract ideas seems to be extremely limited in the lowest races. The faculty of attention is apt to be easily wearied. The memory may be keen with regard to particular classes of objects or events, but in other respects almost a blank. The power of drawing a map of the neighbouring country varies immensely, and may be tested with advantage. (The Esquimaux seem to equal or surpass most Europeans on this point.) Ideas as to lapse of time are usually very vague, and may be tested.

Acquaintance with the languages of neighbouring tribes should be noted where met with, and its extent ascertained. Perseverance may be estimated by the skill displayed and success attained in hunting, carving, and other occupations. The degrees of curiosity manifested respecting objects new to the people, and of imagination and intelligence as to their probable or explained uses, should be taken note of.

Any observations on the sequence of ideas in the minds of savages who have not come in contact with Europeans would be extremely valuable.

Care should be taken to ascertain whether the slight progress made by savages in acquiring habits of civilized life arises from incapacity or from the influence of acquired habits, customs, and modes of thought which are antagonistic to progress. Particular notice should therefore be taken, on the one hand, of the effect of European customs when introduced amongst savages and exposed to contact with native surroundings; and, on the other hand, of the influence of culture upon natives of the same race who have been removed at an early age from native surroundings and brought up in European schools. It is to the latter that the following questions chiefly refer :—

1. Are they precocious or otherwise? 2. If the former, is intelligence maintained? or is there any definite age, or level of attainments, at which Europeans habitually excel them? 3. Is the memory generally good or only in particular branches? and if the latter, is it shown in matters in which the intellects of their parents have been cultivated in the savage state (*see* HEREDITY, p. 47)? 4. Do they show perseverance in their studies? 5. As compared with Europeans, are they proficient in :—(*a*) arithmetic, (*b*) languages, (*c*) drawing, (*d*) reading, (*e*) science, (*f*) religion, (*g*) trade, (*h*) mechanics? 6. Are they honest? 7. Truthful? 8. Affectionate? 9. Courageous? 10. Have they good powers of reasoning? 11. Generalizing? 12. After being educated do they evince a desire to return to the savage state? 13. In the construction of their tools, weapons, and other arts, do they appear to act automatically or with intelligence? 14. Do they show strong power of will? 15. Imagination? 16. Is the speech voluble? 17. In conversation, drawing, &c., do the same ideas constantly repeat themselves? 18. Are they subject to strong emotions? 19. Illusions? 20. Much affected by dreams? 21. Somnambulism? 22. Unconscious cerebration? 23. Trances? 24. Insanity? (*see* p. 82).

J. B.

C.—PATHOLOGICAL OBSERVATIONS.

(*See* Medical Sections, Nos. IV, V, and VI.)

MEDICAL SECTIONS.

No. I.—REPRODUCTION.

I. *Manners and Customs Affecting the Sexes Previous to Marriage.*

(*a*) Relating to males :—

Is there any evidence of special physical training for sexual purposes before or after puberty and preparatory to marriage (*e.g.*, circumcision, the "mika" operation, *i.e.*, artificial hypospadias, &c.)? Is there any minimum limit of age? Is any proof of virility required? Is promiscuous intercourse, with or without precautions against pregnancy, permitted before marriage? If so what steps are taken to enforce the rules, and what punishment follows their breach?

(*b*) Relating to females :—

Is there any special interference with the sexual organs in girls previous to puberty (*e.g.*, dilatation of organs, closure of vulva, &c.)? Is there any minimum limit of age? Is connection permitted before marriage, or what steps are taken to ensure chastity or prevent pregnancy?

II. *Menstruation.*

At what age does menstruation usually occur? Are there any special customs or superstitions connected with (1) ordinary; (2) precocious; (3) deferred menstruation? Is purification practised subsequent to each menstruation?

III. *Marriage.*

What is the average age of both sexes at marriage? Note any special customs relating to marriage ceremonies.

IV. *Pregnancy.*

What means are adopted for determining that a woman is pregnant? Is she debarred from cohabitation or otherwise secluded during pregnancy? Note any special diet or other customs during pregnancy relating either to husband or wife (*e.g.*, the "couvade," &c.)?

V. *Labour.*

What preparations are made in anticipation of labour (*e.g.*, as to food, dwelling, bed, assistance, seclusion, &c.)? What position is usually adopted? Note exceptions and reason for the same. What is the average duration of labour? Note any customs or superstitions regarding the caul, treatment of cord, disposal of placenta, &c. Are difficult labours common? To what are they chiefly due? How and by whom are complications treated? If a woman dies undelivered are any means taken to save the child?

VI. *The Puerperium.*

How long is a woman confined to bed? Is she subject to any special diet, system of purification, &c.?

VII. *Lactation.*

What is the average duration of suckling? Is any special diet enforced? Is she restrained from sexual intercourse during this period?

VIII. *The Child.*

How is the child treated immediately after birth? How are still-born children resuscitated? Is there any special treatment of the head? Are there any special customs with regard to twins or preternatural births? Are there any customs or ceremonies connected with the naming of the child akin to baptism?

IX. *General.*

What is the average number of a family? What is the relative proportion of the sexes? What is the greatest number in a family? How many have been produced by one mother, and of these how many grew up? Do twins or triplets, &c., occur frequently? Ascertain, if possible, the total number of boys and girls respectively born in one given area or tribe. (This is of importance in districts where polyandry exists.) Are there any restraints on population? Is sterility in women common? Is want of virile power complained of by men? Are drugs or other means used to produce abortion, or stimulate sexual desire and power? If so, what are they? If possible, obtain samples (*see* Therapeutics). Are births out of wedlock common? What is done with the children? Whether do the lower or upper classes produce the larger families? Does population seem to be increasing, or the reverse, judging by extent of occupied land, size of cemeteries, ruins of villages, &c., as well as by report? Can the ratio of births and deaths in a community of known population be obtained?

R. M. M.

No. II.—DEVELOPMENT, GROWTH AND DECAY.

1. Weight and height and condition of the hair and nails, and colour of the iris at birth.

2. Time at which the milk teeth appear.

3. Are the children who do not observe the rule put to death?

4. When do the fontanelles close?

5. What is the rate of growth in height during infancy and childhood?

6. Time of appearance of the teeth of the second dentition?

7. Is there any peculiarity in connection with the eruption of the wisdom teeth?

(Monthly observations should be made, if possible, on Nos. 2–7.)

8. Is caries of teeth common? are they worn down by hard or gritty food.

9. What is the usual age of puberty as indicated in females by commencement of menstruation and development of breasts, and in males by change of voice, and development of hair on face, or other parts of body?

10. Age of union of epiphyses and closure of sutures.

11. At what ages in the two sexes do the maxima of stature and of bulk or general physical development seem to be attained?

12. What are the average and the extreme length of life observed or reported?

13. About what age do women cease to menstruate? and 14 what are the extremes of child-bearing age?

15. Are old people allowed to reach the natural term of life, or are they killed or allowed to starve? 16. If the age in years cannot be ascertained inquire how many generations may exist simultaneously, *e.g.*, whether a man often sees his great grand-children. 17. Condition in old age of teeth and jaws; of hair, as to changes in colour or quantity; of eyes, as to transparency of lens and cornea (arcus senilis). 18. Acuteness of sight and hearing in old age. J. S.

No. III.—NATIVE DIETARY AND LAWS OF DIET.

By the food, the matter and energy daily lost from the body is replaced. The energy required depends on the amount of mechanical labour to be performed, and the amount of heat which must be produced to maintain the temperature of the body. More, therefore, is required in cold than in hot climates. The nature of the matter excreted appears to depend largely on the nature of the food taken; but it always contains a certain proportion of nitrogen which must be replaced by nitrogen in the food in the form of proteids, such as albumen, myosin, gluten, &c. The amount of proteids consumed varies greatly in different races, and among some people nearly all the required energy is derived from this source. Among others it is largely derived from fat and such carbohydrates as starches and sugars.

It is of the utmost importance to determine the relative amount of these ingredients in various native dietaries, and this may be done by estimating, however roughly, the amounts of the various articles of food usually consumed per diem. If any exceptional article is used it should, if possible, be dried and sent home for analysis.

1. As nearly as possible ascertain the nature and composition of the diet of different classes, noting at the same time the amount of mechanical work usually performed, the external temperature, and the nature of the clothing.

2. Average amount of various foods consumed by adult. 3. Do they adhere constantly to the same food or do they vary it—(*a*) According to the seasons? (*b*) At any special periods? (*c*) When opportunity offers? 4. Do great differences in this respect prevail among neighbouring tribes? and do these differences coincide with diversities of physical type? 5. Is there any alimentary principle, which, being absent or scarce in the dietary of the people, is eagerly sought and hungered for by them? 6. Does any apparent perversion of appetite

prevail, such as that for "eating dirt" in the West Indies? 7. Is common salt, or any other mineral substance, used or relished? 8. How many meals are commonly eaten in the day? and what appears to be the average quantity of food consumed by an adult?

9. What stimulants or exhilarants or narcotics are in use among the people? and to what extent? 10. Are any substances of this nature used which are not known in Europe? If so, note carefully their mode of use and supposed or observed effects on health, and on capacity for abstinence or labour.

11. Are there any prevalent diseases attributed or attributable to the dietary, *e.g.* scurvy from want of fresh vegetables or potash salts, ophthalmia from defect of nitrogen (as in a pure rice diet), gangrene &c., from use of diseased grain, paralysis from too much pulse, leprosy or skin-disease from too much fish or fish-oil, consumption from scantiness or poverty of food, especially poverty in fat? 12. Does the quality or quantity of food consumed vary much with the seasons? and do such variations affect the health and condition of the people?

J. B. and D. N. P.

No. IV.—ABNORMALITIES.

(*Natural* Deformities.)

1. Albinism.—Is this common? Are any causes assigned for it? Do Albinoes differ physically from other people? How are they regarded and treated? Do they intermarry? Are they allowed to marry other members of the community? Examine carefully any specimens which may be met with, noting the colour of the skin, hair, and eyes.

2. Hair.—Is Erythrism or red hair met with in the midst of a blackskinned population? If so, note the colour of the skin and eyes. Does excessive hairiness of face or body (Hypertrichosis) or total absence of hair ever occur?

3. Deformities of the face, &c., such as supernumerary auricles, hare lip, cleft palate, cleft tongue, cleft cheek (macrostoma), abnormally small mouth (microstoma), and any peculiarities of the teeth.

4. Deformities of the extremities, *e.g.*, supernumerary fingers or toes, webbed fingers, imperfect development, or absence of one of the bones of the forearm, hypertrophy of the limbs, club hand, club foot.

5. Deformities of the genitals, *e.g.*, abnormal length of the labia, imperforate hymen, undescended testicles, cleft penis epispadias or hypospadias, cleft scrotum with the testicles in what appear to be labia, absence of the anterior wall of the bladder, extroverted bladder.

6. Does excessive development of fat about the haunches, buttocks, *steatopyga*, or labia occur? Can any causes, artificial or otherwise, be assigned for the occurrence?

7. Note any deformities or malformations which may occur in the region of the umbilicus, and state how the cord is treated at birth.

8. Are any of the above deformities more common than usual, or any one of them frequently met with? Are there any of hereditary nature? How are they regarded and treated?

J.B. Revised by J. W. B. H.

No. V.—DEFORMATIONS.

(*Artificial* Deformities.)

The practice of artificially producing deformities in the human subject appears to have existed from the most remote times of which we have any record, and to have prevailed at one time or another in all parts of the world. In the investigation, therefore, of the ethnographical characters of a people, considerable interest attaches to observations respecting artificial "deformations," as the practice in question has been termed; for it is very possible that important information may thence be derived with regard to the relations between different tribes or races, even widely separated from each other.

The principal kinds of intentional deformation to be looked for may be arranged under the heads of :—

A. Cranial.
B. Facial, including the ears.
C. Dental.
D. Of the trunk and extremities.

As the practices of tattooing and circumcision, &c., are placed under other heads, they will not here be considered, although in one sense they may be regarded as kinds of artificial deformation.

A. *Cranial Deformation.*

Alteration in the natural form of the skull is, so far as is known, the most ancient and the most general of all kinds of artificial deformation, and consequently all observations relating to it will be of interest and importance.

There are two principal ways in which the change from its natural shape is produced in the human skull :—

The first consists in the application of pressure, usually both in front and behind, or in front or behind alone, by means of flat boards or pieces of bark applied in such a way as to exert continued pressure for a considerable time in early infancy, and commencing immediately after birth, when the shape of the head admits very readily of being moulded in almost any direction. It is to be observed, however, that under certain very common conditions a considerable modification of the form of the head, more especially in the hinder region, may arise, as it were unintentionally, from the child sleeping with the head resting on a hard substance or from the practice of swathing the infant continually upon a board for the convenience of carriage. Or, again, the form of the head may be affected even by the manner in which the child is otherwise habitually carried, either on the right or the left arm of the nurse, in consequence of which a considerable degree of unilateral deformity may be produced.

It will be necessary, therefore, to ascertain whether any observed deformity of the head or skull arises from an intentional or unintentional cause, and in all cases to note the mode in which infants are habitually carried or swathed.

The other principal mode in which the form of the skull is altered is by the methodical application of bandages encircling the head in various directions. The artificial forms produced in this way are usually more or less elongated or pyramidal, or, as some may be termed, cylindrical. In the case of this kind of deformation, however, as in the former, considerable abnormities of form may be produced, as it were, unintentionally, by the mode in which the head-attire, more especially is worn. A striking instance of this has been observed very extensively in France, but more or less of a tendency to the same kind of thing may be frequently observed amongst ourselves.

As the practice of cranial deformation, though probably innocuous, cannot in any case be supposed to possess any direct advantages, the *reason* for its extensive prevalence among all races of mankind is not very obvious, and is a very curious subject of inquiry.

One of the most probable reasons, and also the most ancient, is that assigned by Hippocrates, viz., that it arose from a desire to magnify any form of head, considered either as intrinsically beautiful or as distinctive of a superior race or rank.

In investigating this subject, the principal points, therefore, to be attended to are :—

1. The kind or form of the deformation.

2. Whether by a flattening process or by bands.

3. Whether, in the former case, the pressure is applied both in front and behind, or on either aspect singly, and how it is effected.

4. In the latter case, whether the elongation be upwards or backwards.

5. In both cases the length of time during which the pressure, &c., is continued.

6. Although the concurrent testimony of almost all recent observers would tend to show that deformation of the skull has no effect upon the moral, intellectual, or perceptive faculties, this is a point still worthy attention.

7. It should be ascertained whether in any given race the practice of deforming the head is general or whether it is confined to one or the other sex, or to any particular rank or station. And so far as may be possible the reasons assigned for the practice should be noted.

8. In view of the very probable assumption that the deformity is intended to magnify, as it were, the natural characteristic form of the skull, observations should be made as to the general form of the head, the natural indigenous form, whether it is *rounded* or *elongated*, *broad* or *narrow*, *high* or *low*.

To explain this more fully it may be remarked that, though all skulls are naturally symmetrical and have uniformly rounded curved contours, they differ very considerably in the proportions of their length or antero-posterior dimension and their breadth or transverse direction, and in a less degree as regards their vertical height (*see* Anatomical Observations).

B. *Deformations of the features of the face usually involve the* nose, cheeks, lips, *and* ears.

12. It is a custom among many savage tribes to flatten the nose, which is done either by continued pressure, or by such violence as to force in the bridge whilst the tissues are yet soft and cartilaginous. In some cases, however, attempts are made to improve the countenance by pinching the nose so as to give it greater prominence than it would otherwise have. A common practice also among some tribes is to perforate either the cartilaginous septum alone of the nose or the entire organ, inserting bars or rings of wood or metal and even of

stone. Incisions and other mutilations are practised so as to alter the shape of the nose.

13. The cheeks are sometimes perforated, the holes being occupied by articles of wood, bone, or metal.

14. In Africa, more especially, great pains are taken to produce hideous deformity of the lips, either upper or lower or both, by perforating them and wearing ornaments in the holes, sometimes of very great size.

15. In a similar manner the ears are perforated and made to support enormous weights, by which they become monstrously elongated and hypertrophied.

16. In many parts, more particularly of Africa, it is a common practice to produce large raised scars on the forehead, cheeks, nose, or chin, forming patterns peculiar to different tribes. The form and mode of making these scars should be noticed, and whether they are regarded as race, or family, or rank characters, &c.

C. *Dental Deformations.*

17. The custom of deforming the teeth is practised in several parts of the world; and as different modes of doing it prevail amongst different tribes, the characters afforded in this way will probably be found of considerable ethnographical importance.

The practice appears in general to be limited to the front or incisor teeth, and consists either in extracting, or, more usually perhaps, in breaking off one or more of them, or of filing them thin or to single sharp points or in serrate fashion.

The reasons for this practice, if any are assigned, should be ascertained, and, as in other cases, whether it is exercised upon one or both sexes, or is distinctive or not of rank, &c.

D. *Deformation of the Trunk and Limbs.*

The principal deformations to be noticed under this head are :—

18. As regards the trunk: (*a*) alteration in the form or hindrance to the development of the breasts, which is effected by the methodical application of bandages and compresses.

The most usual object, however, aimed at is to produce elongation of the mamma, which is thus rendered capable of being either thrown over the mother's shoulder or under the arm, so that the infant can suck whilst carried on the mother's back.

(*b*) Amongst some of the Kaffir tribes the preternatural elongation of the nipple is commenced in early life by manipulation and the binding of it round with a narrow fillet or tape.

19. The chief deformation practised upon the extremities is (*a*) that of the feet peculiar to the Chinese women, with regard to which we already possess a great amount of information.

(*b*) Amongst some African tribes it has been stated that amputation of part or the whole of one of the fingers is practised. Should this be observed, the fact is one well worthy of record, together with the reasons that may be assigned for it.

(*c*) The practice of castration may also perhaps be included under the head of deformation or mutilation, also infibulation. The mode in which the operation is performed, the age at which it takes place, and the reasons assigned for it should all be duly noticed.

(*d*) The practice of producing artificial Hypospadias for the purpose of limiting the population or the number in a family. Information is desired regarding the mode of operating and the instruments used, or other details in connection with this curious custom.

G. B., revised by J. G. G.

No. VI.—PATHOLOGY.

1. What endemic diseases are observed in the district?

2. How is the occurrence and course of such diseases affected by the following factors:—

(*a.*) Season of the year, (*b.*) temperature.
(*c.*) Dryness or humidity of the soil.
(*d.*) Geological conformation.
(*e.*) Physical conformation, *e.g.*, river basins, lakes mountains.
(*f.*) Forests, (*g.*) winds, (*h.*) cultivation.
(*k.*) Dietetic and other habits of the people.

3. What diseases are the native and immigrant population respectively affected by?

4. What epidemic diseases occur?

5. How is their occurrence influenced by the factors mentioned under question 2 and by such circumstances as movements of peoples (lines of commerce, pilgrimages, march of armies, migrations of tribes), by floods, tornadoes, famines, nature of food supply.

7. What are the effects of introduced disease in the native and immigrant population, respectively.

8. What appearances are found in post-mortem examination?

NOTE.—Pathological specimens should be preserved in absolute alcohol or methylated spirit (or failing these in strong whiskey, rum, or brandy). The pieces of tissue should be small, seldom more than half-an-inch thick. They should be wrapped in lint or linen, and placed in a relatively large quantity of spirit, in a bottle closed with a glass stopper. Descriptive labels should be placed inside the bottle, as well as gummed on the outside.

A. B.

No. VII.—MEDICINE.

The information which can be obtained in foreign countries with regard to medicine depends, in the first place, on the competence of the observer, that is to say, whether a qualified medical man or a traveller who has some knowledge of medicine, and again, whether the observer is resident in a foreign country or simply travelling through it. In this section the first general questions may be answered by any intelligent traveller. The latter questions are intended only for qualified medical men. It is of great importance that all returns should be made with the greatest accuracy, and that the place where the observations are made should be definitely stated, the latitude, longitude, and altitude being given. Observers should also remember that detailed observations are of a higher scientific value than general statements. With regard to statistics, they can for the most part be only obtained by persons resident for a considerable time in a given locality, but at the same time in travelling through a country many valuable statistics can be obtained if care is taken to give the number of the population, &c.

On first arriving in a foreign country it is necessary to investigate, as closely as possible, the action of the climate upon Europeans, and it will be found, as a rule, that the action of climate varies to some extent, at any rate, according to the nationality and birth place of the European. Northern and Southern Europeans for instance, being variously affected by a tropical climate. A person travelling through a country can do much to elucidate the geographical distribution of various diseases; on the other hand, a person stationed for a year or so abroad can obtain the most valuable information as to the etiology of disease, the prevalence of disease at various seasons, and the influence which race, food, and climate have upon the production of, or immunity from, disease. It is important to pay attention to the normal temperature of persons in various parts of the world, as up to the present this point has been greatly neglected, *see*

Temperature, p. 37. The influence of climate upon the blood and the circulation should also be carefully studied, and the relation between circulation and respiration.

1. What are the diseases suffered from by the natives? 2. Give the native as well as the ordinary English names. 3. What diseases are most prevalent? 4. To what are the diseases attributed by the natives? and mention any traditions or superstitions connected therewith. 5. Are charms employed or any superstitious ceremonies observed in sickness? If so, describe them accurately, as also any peculiar implements used in the practice of these charms. 6. Are sick persons waited on by their friends? 7. Is isolation practised? 8 Are any measures of a sanitary nature observed to preserve the health of communities or individuals? If so, describe them. 9. Is inoculation practised? 10. What is the treatment employed against various diseases? 11. Are native vegetables, *i.e*, simples or other remedies or both employed? If so, are there any rules of collecting, preparing, or administering such remedies? 12. What are the names of the simples, native or botanical or both, and what are the names of other remedies, if there are such? 13. Describe the mode of administration of remedies with regard to dose and frequency? 14. What is the limit of the administration of medicine or the sign by which it is decided to stop the medicine? 15. If natives carry bones on their persons of dead relatives or other objects of this kind, try to ascertain precisely what is their object in so doing, whether (*a*) out of respect for the dead, (*b*) as memorials and marks of affection, (*c*) as amulets to avert sickness or other evils, (*d*) as fetishes, (*e*) as charms, (*f*) or magical means of communicating with unseen talismans or powers, (*g*) or whether such objects so borne are ever used as remedies for sickness. 16. On a person's recovery, are there any ceremonies of purification or otherwise in vogue? 17. Do natives appear to suffer pain as acutely as Europeans? 18. Is massage practised in the treatment of disease or for other purposes? 19. Have the natives much vital power? Do they struggle against disease or do they readily succumb to it? 20. Compared with Europeans in the same country, do

they seem to suffer more from diseases of inflammatory or of asthenic type? 21. Do the natives endure cold well, or heat, especially the direct rays of the sun? 22. Do the natives suffer from pulmonary consumption? If so, is it particularly prevalent in certain localities or under particular conditions of life? 23. Are any of the following diseases common? State their frequency and anything peculiar observed in connection with them—epilepsy, neuralgia, rheumatism, gout, heart disease, asthma, bronchitis, pneumonia, pleurisy, scarlet fever, measles, typhus, typhoid, small pox, diarrhœa, dysentery, yellow fever, leprosy, yaws, beri-beri, &c.? And how are these diseases treated? 24. Do the people suffer from febrile diseases attributable to malaria or climate, such as ague or remittent fevers? Do different tribes differ in their susceptibilities to such fevers and how do Europeans or people of mixed breed compare with them in this respect? 25. Is tooth-ache common, or is caries in the teeth observed? 26. Describe the chief symptoms and course of any disease which is peculiar to the natives. 27. Have you observed any hitherto unknown disease? If so, describe its symptoms and post-mortem appearances if possible.

R. W. F.

No. VIII.—SURGERY.

But little information of a valuable nature, so far as surgery is concerned, can be acquired by a traveller unless he is prepared to sift most carefully any statements which he hears, as to the causes of the conditions that are met with. It cannot be too often insisted on how needful it is that all observations should be accurately recorded at the time they are made. The date and place of the observation in each case should be duly registered. Great care must be taken to distinguish between isolated instances and frequent occurrences, and hearsay evidence separated as far as possible from the results of personal observation.

Accidents.

Observations regarding the general treatment of accidents are much needed. For instance, how far rest and position, as we understand the terms, are considered in the treatment of the patient. Who is the surgeon? Does he undergo any form of special apprenticeship, and what instruments, if any, form his stock in trade?

1. What means are employed for the arrest of bleeding?

2. Does mortification ever ensue after injuries, or after such conditions as snake bite, &c.? How is the condition treated; are the dead parts allowed to separate, or is rough amputation ever attempted?

3. What method is employed in the treatment of ordinary wounds; are any special medicaments made use of? If so, send back specimens, if possible. (For mode of transport, &c., *see* Therapeutics.) Do ordinary wounds heal readily? Is the healing process assisted by bringing the edges of the wound into close apposition? Do erysipelas, pyæmia, tetanus, or other forms of blood poisoning occur?

4. What treatment is adopted with poisoned wounds? Is sucking the affected part resorted to?

5. Are burns of frequent occurrence? How are they treated, and what means are taken to prevent subsequent deformities?

6. Are ulcers of the leg and other parts ever observed? How they are healed? (Under this head *see* "Syphilis.")

7. How are fractures and dislocations treated, and are good or moderate results the exception or the rule?

8. Is any rude plan of trephining adopted? If so, what is the nature of the instrument employed? Bring or send one back, if possible.

Diseases.

1. The occurrence of tumours, innocent or malignant, should be noted; specially with reference to the frequency of cancer, rodent ulcer, lupus, and nævi; also the treatment (if any) adopted by natives for the same.

2. Is surgical tuberculosis ever observed? In other words, is there any evidence of the existence of spinal curvatures (angular) of joint disease in the limbs, etc?

3. Does hernia exist either as a congenital or acquired affection? Mention what variety—femoral, inguinal, or umbilical—is most prevalent, and how is it treated?

4. Is club-foot met with? if so, what variety is commonest Is any attempt made at treatment? Are congenital dislocations ever present?

5. Do rickets, with the usual accompaniments of deformed bones, occur?

6. Do finger deformities, such as web fingers, &c., occur?

7. Is hare-lip ever present?

8. Is goitre ever observed, and is cretinism ever present?

9. The occurrence of rheumatism and its usual resulting deformities should be looked for. Does it attack both young and old?

10. Is there any evidence of other venereal disease than yphilis?

11. Are any operations of a plastic nature practised? (For artificially-produced deformities *see* "Deformations.")

12. Take notice of the condition of the urinary organs.

Is anything of the nature of renal or vesical calculus ever observed?

Do strictures occur: if so, is there any attempt at treatment?

Is there any evidence of enlarged prostate? *It is of especial interest to determine whether enlargement is ever known to occur in eunuchs.*

Is long prepuce common, and is its removal ever undertaken, under ordinary or exceptional circumstances?

13. It is important to obtain all possible information regarding the treatment of Surgical diseases, and the drugs employed for that purpose by natives; whether operations are borne well or are attended by high mortality; and whether any particular Surgical diseases are more prevalent in one than in another race or caste living in the same locality, or affect all races equally.

W. B. C.

No. IX.—THERAPEUTICS.

Travellers in little known or in new countries have many opportunities of benefiting science and mankind by sending home products which are novel, or have a reputation as medicines or poisons. To aid them in doing so, a few directions are here given.

With mineral substances, and with a large number of organic substances met with and used in a dry state, no difficulty is encountered, as it is only necessary that they should be packed in a perfectly dry state, and with such covering as will protect them from moisture.

Difficulties are, however, encountered with many vegetable products. These may possess (A) a botanical, or (B) a medicinal, or what is practically the same, a physiological or toxicological interest.

(A) *Botanical.* The parts of a plant of most value to the botanist are the flowers, fruit, and leaves. The flowers and leaves require merely to be dried, by being pressed between folds of bibulous paper, such as blotting paper. The fruit, if of small size or hard, may be dried by exposure to dry air, natural or artificial; but, if of large size or succulent, it is advisable that at least some specimens should be sent in the natural state, and this may be done by placing them in securely stoppered or corked bottles with a strong solution of sugar or of salt, or with whisky, brandy, methylated or rectified spirit. Other preserving fluids which may be employed are—saturated solution of white arsenic (made by boiling in water), or this arsenical solution with half its bulk of glycerine, or a solution of corrosive sublimate (1 in 500 of water), or a saturated solution of carbolic acid in water; and the preservative properties of each of these solutions will be increased by the addition of methylated or rectified spirit.

It is of great importance that each specimen should be labelled, and for doing this directions are afterwards given.

(B) *Substances of medicinal or toxicological interest.* Of

plants falling under this category, the parts of greatest value are the fruit (including the seeds), the bark of the stem and branches, the root, and the leaves.

The *fruit* may be sent dry, as above described, or moist. In the latter case, the fruit should be preserved in a spirituous solution only, such as whisky, brandy, or methylated or rectified spirit. If the quantity available of either of the latter be limited, water may be added to the extent of one half the bulk of the spirit. All fruits however, which admit of being dried should be sent in that state, as then the large quantities necessary for physiological or chemical examination can more conveniently be sent home. The fruit should be collected when it is fully ripe.

Bark.—Generally speaking, the bark of a medicinal plant is active, the chief exception being when the bark consists largely of cork. When this is the case, pieces of the whole stem or branches should be sent. They, like the bark, merely require to be thoroughly dried; and if the stem or branches are thick, it is advisable to split them before drying.

Root.—The root should be sent in the dry state; if succulent, or possessing any peculiarity of form, several pieces should also be sent in the moist state, preserved in spirit.

The *leaves* merely require to be thoroughly dried, as for botanical examination.

Labelling.—Specimens of each part of a plant sent in a dry state should be placed in a separate package; and of each part sent in a moist state, in a separate bottle. Thus, specimens of fruits and roots, or roots and stems, or branches, &c., should not be placed in the same package or bottle, but the specimens of each part in a separate package or bottle. Each package or bottle should be distinctly labelled, and a list reproducing or amplifying the labels should be enclosed in a letter to the person for whom the specimens are intended. It is advisable that the labels on the packages or bottles should state the name of the substance, the part of the plant, the locality in which the plant grew, and the date on which the specimen was obtained. Besides repeating these facts, the list sent by letter should also state the natural colour of the flower and fruit of the plant, and, in the case of specimens sent in the moist state, the fluid in which they have been preserved. Any information possessed by the sender regarding the uses and reputed proportions of the substance should also be given.

As the physiological examination of a substance can be undertaken only with large quantities of it, as liberal a supply as possible of the part of the plant reputed to have useful or tonic properties should be sent. This becomes all the more important when it is recollected that a chemical as well as a physiological investigation is required before sufficient knowledge of the applicability of the substance to the treatment of disease can be acquired.

It is important also to point out that the examination of the physiological and chemical properties of a part of a plant is eminently unsatisfactory, and the value of the results greatly lessened, if materials are not supplied for the botanical identification of the plant. The parts required for this purpose are the flowers and fruit. When, therefore, these parts are not indicated or suggested on account of the local reputation of the plant, they should be sent on account of their botanical value and interest (*see* A).

Details regarding the mode of preparation and administration of drugs in disease by the natives should be particularly noted, as well as the diseases in which they are used.

T. R. F.

No. X.—NARCOTICS AND ALLIED DRUGS.

1. What narcotics are employed? 2. Are they indigenous? 3. If so, are there any traditions as to their use? 4. If imported, are there any traditions regarding their introduction? 5. Where were they brought from? 6. Were they imported by strangers entering the country, or by emigrants returning home from elsewhere? 7. Do their names appear to be of foreign origin? 8. What is the method of preparing them for use? 9. Are they used in a pure state or mingled

with other substances? 10. What utensils and implements are employed in their preparation? Give a description of them. 11. Are any superstitions connected with their use? 12. Are they employed for religious purposes, or as aids to social intercourse? 13. Are they used during feasts, such as accompany marriage, or at solemnities, such as funerals? 14. Are they employed in the rites connected with purification after certain natural functions or morbid conditions? 15. Is alcohol in use? 16. Whence is it obtained? 17. Are there any peculiarities in the method of its preparation? 18. How is it used? 19. Are any special vessels employed in its use? 20 Are any ceremonies observed when it is made use of? 21. Is tobacco in use? 22. Is any substitute employed in its stead? 23. Is it smoked, chewed, or used as snuff? 24. How is it prepared for use? 25. What are the forms of pipe in use, and of what materials are the bowls and stems made? 26. Are the pipes smoked out by individuals, or passed from one person to another? 27. Are pipes known with a large single bowl, and two or more stems for different smokers? 28. Are any ceremonies connected with smoking? 29. Are any substances, such as Kola, coffee, or cocoa, used to relieve fatigue? 30. Are any substances, such as coca, employed to obviate the effects of exertion? 31. Is the use of any narcotic or similar substance carried to excess? 32. What effects on the moral and physical welfare of the race can be observed from the use of such substances?

G. A. G.

No. XI.—DISEASES OF THE SKIN.

Are affections of the skin (those traceable to, or resulting from, syphilis excepted) common? What features do those most frequently met with present? Are any parts of the body specially or exclusively attacked? Are such as are seen characterized by redness of an inflammatory type, the occurrence of pimples, of watery blisters, of boils or carbuncles, or of dry scales? Are itching, burning, or pain complained of, and in which? Are ulcers or warts prevalent? Do the natives suffer from localised alterations in the colour of the skin, from baldness in limited patches, or from premature baldness diffused over the scalp? Are mother's marks numerous, and how are such accounted for? Have the natives any tradition or theory to explain the origin of these diseases? Can diet, water, habits, or place of residence account for any? Of the kinds met with, which seem contagious? Do they wash much or little, and have they any natural or artificial substitutes for soap?

Are any of the following diseases met with or specially common: Urticaria, Eczema, Herpes zoster, Psoriasis, Ichthyosis, Molluscum contagiosum, Xanthoma, Lupus, Epithelioma, Acne, Alopecia areata, Favus, Tinea tonsurans, Tinea versicolor, Scabies, Pediculosis? If Leprosy be encountered does it present the tubercular, the anæsthetic, or the mixed type? Is it considered a communicable complaint by the natives, and, if so, at what stage and in what manner? What proofs of this can be furnished? Is it looked on as hereditary, and can any evidence of this of a distinct kind and free from the possibility of contagion be obtained? Exact information as to any remedies employed in the treatment of skin diseases, their nature, mode of application, and value.

W. A. J.

No. XII.—DISEASES OF THE EYE.

What is the colour of the eyes? Do any marked differences in colour exist in different individuals? Is there anything striking as to the distance apart of the two yes? What is the usual shape of the lid apertures? Is the sight generally sharp (excluding cases of disease)? Is there any difference in this respect between old and young? Are glass spectacles known? Are spectacles of any other kind (such as small apertures in pieces of wood or shells) used for any purpose? If so, for what purpose? (For instance, for improving near or distant vision or for protecting the eyes from the sun or glare or dust)? Is squinting ever met with? If so, are there any current notions as to the cause of the deformity? Is anything done in the way of treatment? Is there any prevalent form of eye disease? What are the remedies employed? Do they appear to be efficacious? Is any form of ophthalmia (inflammation of the lids) common? If so, to what is it ascribed? What is the probable cause? Is it considered to be contagious, or are there any facts which point to its being contagious? Does it lead to any permanent defect of vision? If so, what appears to be the cause of the subsequent defect? Does cataract occur? Is it correctly diagnosed or confounded with other forms of blindness At what age does it usually come on? Is any operation performed for its cure? Is any other method of treatment other than operative adopted for cataract? Are accidents to the eyes met with? If so, what is the most frequent cause of such accidents? What is the usual treatment adopted? Are all cases treated alike? Are any substances known which act in any way on the pupil? (That is, which cause either dilatation or contraction of the pupil.) Is anything known which has a local anæsthetic action on the eye? Is snow-blindness ever complained of? Under what conditions does it occur? Are measures taken to prevent it? Is night-blindness ever met with? Is it common? At what time of the year and under what circumstances does it occur? Is it associated with any affection of the eyelids? Is anything done for it?

G. A. B.

No. XIII.—DISEASES OF CHILDREN.

What is the mode of treating the new-born infant—as to the umbilical cord—as to clothing—as to suckling?

Give details regarding the artificial feeding of infants, when it is commenced, what food is employed, and how it is prepared. Are there any precautions used by natives in giving water, milk, fruit, vegetables, or cooked meat?

The clothing of infants; give details as to binders and other articles of clothing or mechanism intended for support or constriction.

What are the customs with respect to washing and cleanliness?

What is the average number of children in families?

Observations as to infant mortality should be made in as large a number of families as possible. General statements regarding mortality made on hearsay evidence are of little use. Information should be obtained regarding the important subject of variations in the rate of mortality during the different periods of infant life, and whether the variations are the same in children of European parents as in those of natives.

Observations should be made as to the periods of dentition, and the ailments believed to be associated with dentition.

The following classes of diseases in children should receive careful attention:—

The common ailments of infancy—respiratory and gastro-intestinal catarrhs, convulsions, laryngismus, skin affections, eye and ear affections, bone diseases, especially rickety enlargements of the ends of the bones, bendings of the long bones, beads on the ribs, thickenings of the bones of the head in connection with delayed teething and walking.

It is convenient to remember that a healthy child at twelve months old has twelve teeth and begins to walk and talk.

The common diseases of childhood :—Tubercular diseases of glands, joints, lungs and abdomen ; rheumatism ; purpura ; proneness to hæmorrhage ; anæmia.

Nervous diseases—idiocy, chorea, convulsions, paralysis.

Abdominal diseases—of liver, of kidney, especially noting obscure cases of hæmaturia. Diseases of spleen, with various signs of malaria ; it is important to record the general condition of the very young children in malarial districts.

Parasitic affections, intestinal and otherwise. Notes should be made as to the local distribution and history of parasites. Samples of the parasite to be obtained if possible. Specimens of blood should be obtained, whenever it is possible, in all diseases which may possibly contain bacteria, or be due to micro-organisms. (*Vide* sections on Pathology and Bacteriology.) The excretions should be carefully described.

The prevalence of acute specific diseases, syphilis and exanthemata, should be ascertained, and anything regarding their course or symptoms different from what they usually present should be recorded.

All accounts of diseases should be accompanied by elucidatory and confirmatory descriptions of symptoms observed.

Native names of diseases with accounts of symptoms observed, especially when these form a fairly constant group, are always worth recording, even if no English equivalent can be given. Notes of local remedies and modes of treatment are also useful, and all pathological specimens, coupled with accounts of illness, are worth preserving.

Variations in the symptoms, course, result, or sequelæ of diseases to which the children of Natives and Europeans are alike subject, should be carefully observed, so as to determine, if possible, what part, if any, race and climate may play in the modification of disease.

T. B.

No. XIV.—SYPHILIS.

It is of importance to observe whether syphilis exists in any newly explored country where there had been no intercourse with Europeans, direct or indirect, or where the intercourse had been very limited.

Syphilis may be recognised by the usually painless nature of the local sore, accompanied by hard, multiple, non-inflammatory swellings of the lymphatic glands in the neighbourhood; then within the first six months of the disease constitutional symptoms are seen, eruptions on the skin of a measley-looking or papular character, and loss of hair all over the head and face. Along with the skin eruption, the mucous membrane of the mouth and throat is affected, the patches looking very like snail tracks. Fever and pains in the bones may be looked for before the constitutional symptoms set in.

The later symptoms to be expected, are, pustular eruptions with their resulting crusts, ulcers of the skin, throat, and tongue, diseases of bone, &c.

In any country where syphilis is common, note carefully whether the infants of syphilitic parents are affected by the disease soon after birth. This may be known by the wasted condition of the child, running from the nose, and depression of the bones of the bridge of the nose; cracks round the mouth; eruptions over the body, especially on the buttocks; and enlargement of the ends of the long bones. As the child grows older, note the condition of the permanent upper incisor teeth, whether they are notched at their free edge in a crescentic manner.

The observer should note the existence of late congenital syphilis after puberty, as evidenced by ulcerations; bone disease; eye affections, especially corneitis, followed by ground glass looking corneæ.

What treatment is adopted, 1st, of the disease itself;

2nd, preventive or hygienic treatment; and 3rd, if any inoculations are practised? Any superstitions, regarding syphilis or venereal disease in general, will be of interest.

F. C.

No. XV.—INSANITY.

1. What is the population of the place. Do any trustworthy statistics bearing on the proportion of insane persons per 1,000 exist? If so, state the proportion.

2. In what form (mania, melancholia, dementia) does insanity most frequently show itself? If possible, state figures bearing on the question.

3. Is general paralysis of the insane known to occur.

4. Is intemperance in alcohol, opium, or any other drug, common? If so, is it followed by any well marked series of symptoms?

5. Is syphilis common?

6. Is polygamy a common custom? If so, are there any means of ascertaining whether women of the harem are, or are not, specially subject to insanity.

7. Is suicide a common sequence to insanity?

8. Is any specially well marked type of insanity prevalent in the district: *e.g.* any condition corresponding to the rapidly fatal melancholia of the South Sea Islanders, or the amuk of the Malay.

9. Is idiocy common?

10. What are the statutory provisions for the treatment and protection of the insane? State the general outlines of the Lunacy Laws, or send printed copies. Say how many public asylums exist; how they are managed, and how supported. Do you consider them to be in a satisfactory condition? If not, what are the chief shortcomings? If you consider them well managed, state any special features you

may have observed. If no public provision is made for the insane, state how they are provided for.

Are idiots or lunatics put to death? If so, why and how?

State any superstitions with regard to the cause of insanity or its treatment you can ascertain.

J. B. T.

No. XVI.—BACTERIOLOGY.

It is not sufficient to know that such and such a micrococcus or bacillus has been microscopically observed in the blood of a certain disease, because we are well aware that under conditions of general lowered vitality, it is common to find that certain saprophytic organisms have not only gained ingress to the circulation, but are able to live and grow there more or less abundantly. Such microscopical observations in the past have, to a very considerable extent, only served to burden the science of bacteriology with a store of facts more or less useless, unless coupled with cultivation and isolation experiments. In tropical countries it is no easy task to attempt cultivation experiments, the surroundings in very many cases giving but little hope of success; but while this is so, it is possible for practitioners in such places to collect materials and to send such to bacteriologists, who will be most pleased to experiment with them, especially where full clinical notes of the particular cases are forthcoming. In all cases the following procedure may be adopted:—A drop of blood or lymph is to be placed upon a clean cover-glass, and another immediately superimposed. When the film has spread by capillarity, the one glass is to be slid off the other, and each immediately dried by passing it over the flame of a bunsen burner or spirit lamp. The cover-glasses should then be laid face to face and packed in a pill-box, a small piece of tissue paper being then crumpled up and placed above them so as to revent their being shaken about within the box.

For cultivation experiments it is always necessary that some of the particular blood or lymph should be sent home. Lymph may be taken in ordinary vaccine tubes which have been previously thoroughly sterilized by a heat as near 150 degrees Cent. as possible. This may also be done by placing them in carbolic lotion, 1 in 20, for an hour, and afterwards in absolute alcohol. They must then be heated to a temperature of 120 degrees in a test-tube plugged with cotton wool, in an oven for at least an hour. For blood, this will not suffice, as when coagulation has ensued, it is almost impossible to get any of the contents out again. In such a case the blood should be taken with a vaccine tube, and blown into a small tube containing some sterilized Koch's gelatine, which is then to be sealed up in the flame of a bunsen or spirit lamp. After being thus placed in the tube the gelatine should, by a slight heat, be melted, and the blood mixed up with it by shaking. It is hardly necessary to indicate that all such materials should be carefully labelled.

A. E.

PART II.

ETHNOGRAPHY.

EDITED BY

CHARLES HERCULES READ, F.S.A.

Vice-President of the Anthropological Institute, Corresp. Memb. Soc. Italiana d'Antropologia; Assistant in Depart. of British Antiq. and Ethnography, British Museum.

*** All native names or words should be written at least once in "Roman" type, or in CAPITALS.

PREFATORY NOTE.

It is an obvious fact that to obtain even superficial answers to the queries which form the body of this work would necessitate a long-continued residence among a native race, and that even with the most friendly relations it would be a difficult matter to obtain accurate information upon certain matters, such, for instance, as the significance of quasi-religious ceremonies, of totemic signs, past history of the race, and such like. Some indications as to the most profitable lines of inquiry to be pursued during a short stay among a savage people would seem, therefore, to be a necessary preface to a work of this character. It is, however, by no means an easy matter to point out in what directions observations can be made with the best results during a limited stay. Every student of anthropology would wish a different line to be pursued, according to the direction of his own studies. The best plan seems to be to devote as much time as possible to the photographic camera or to making careful drawings, for by these means the traveller is dealing with facts about which there can be no question, and the record thus obtained may be elucidated by subsequent inquirers on the same spot, while the timid answers of natives to questions propounded through the medium of a native interpreter can but rarely be relied upon, and are more apt to produce confusion than to be of benefit to comparative anthropology. It is almost impossible to make a savage in the lower stages of culture understand *why* the questions are asked, and from the limited range of his vocabulary or ideas it is often nearly as difficult to put the question before him in such a way that he can comprehend it. The result often is that from timidity, or the desire to please, or from weariness of the questioning, he will give an answer that he thinks will satisfy the inquirer. If time serve, these difficulties can easily be overcome by friendly intercourse, and a careful checking of answers through different individuals. The information obtained will probably be more accurate if the examination takes place on the spot to which the questions relate; and the practice of making sketches of obsolete objects or customs, for correction by the natives, is also useful. They will also be found to answer more freely when the interrogator places himself on the same level as themselves, *i.e.*, if they sit upon the ground he should do the same.

The relative importance of particular inquiries is greatly affected by the localities in which they are made, and *some* knowledge of the problems of ethnology should be possessed by the traveller, if he would make the best use of his opportunities. Should he possess no such knowledge, he would do well to put himself in communication with the authorities of the British Museum, or the Museums at Oxford or Cambridge, or any other centre where ethnology is studied. What is needed in this country, with its vast colonial possessions, is a Bureau of Ethnology, such as has now existed for some time in the United States. The value of such an institution for our empire can scarcely be estimated. That its tabulated researches would be of the greatest importance to science will not be doubted; but its strongest claim to existence as a national institution is the immense service it would render, first to the officers governing our distant possessions, and, second, to the central government at home, who would thus have, in the compass of a modest library, a synopsis of the history, manners, customs, and religious beliefs of the innumerable races composing the British Empire. In a word, we should then have at hand the means of understanding the motives which influence the peoples with whom we are constantly dealing, and thus be able to avoid the disagreements arising from ignorance of their cherished prejudices and beliefs.

C. H. R.

ETHNOGRAPHY.

No. I.—CLOTHING.

1. Is any clothing used, or do the natives go entirely naked? 2. Is there any distinction made in the clothing of the sexes. or of persons of various ranks? 3. Is it varied according to the seasons of the year, or for special festivals? 4. Are there any sumptuary laws as to clothing? 5. Are any recognized peculiarities of dress restricted to the subdivisions of tribes? 6. Is any deviation in such peculiaritics considered improper? 7. Are the clothes made by each individual or family? or are there any recognized makers of clothes? 8. How do they rank? 9. Is there any thing which corresponds to what we term "fashion"? 10. Of what materials are the clothes chiefly made? 11. Are they native or imported? 12. Are the clothes much shaped or simple wrappers? 13. How are the latter folded? 14. Is there any difference between the indoor and out-of-door clothing? 15. Are any portions of clothing removed on saluting or visiting a superior? 16. How are the garments put together? 17. If sewn, have the needles eyes? or is the thread passed through a hole previously made? 18. What kind of thread is used? 19. Do clothes descend from parents to children? or are they burned with the individual who wore them, or otherwise destroyed? 20. Is there any uniform garment worn (*a*) by fighting men, or (*b*) by medicine men and priests? 21. Is any addition made to the dress of a man who has killed an enemy or some formidable animal?

Head.—22. Do the natives wear any kind of head-covering? and is it for ornament or protection from the sun or weather? 23. Are there any ornaments attached to their hats, caps, or turbans? 24. Are any sunshades worn (South Seas)?

Body.—25. Are the clothes shaped to the body, or loose? 26. Is the body entirely or partially covered? 27. Is any special garment worn to keep off the rain? 28. Is there any special covering or ornament for the genitals, apart from the waist cloth? 29. Do they wear the *maro* of the Polynesians, the wrapper of the Melanesians, the cases of South Africa, or the string of some tribes in South America? 30. Do the natives attach any ideas of indecency to the absence of such partial clothing? 31. What is the corresponding dress of the women? 32. At what age do the two sexes adopt such articles of dress?

Arms and Feet.—33. Are any gloves worn? 34. Of what materials are they made? 35. Are there any coverings to the feet?

A. W. F.

No. II.—PERSONAL ORNAMENTS.

1. Are any ornaments worn as symbols of rank or station in society, or to denote virginity? 2. Are any especially confined to the principal chief? and is there any penalty on their being assumed by others? 3. Are any special ornaments used by either of the sexes in dances, religious or other feasts, &c.?

Head.—4. In what way is the hair dressed? is it allowed to grow to its full length? 5. Is there any distinction in the mode of dressing it between the two sexes? 5*a.* Is the dressing altered after marriage? 6. Are wigs in use? 7. Is any preparation used to alter the colour of the hair? 8. Is it plaited or twisted into ringlets? 9. What ornaments are worn in the hair, such as feathers, flowers, pins, &c.? 10. Do the natives wear beards or moustaches?

11. Is the absence of these due to natural causes, or are they removed by depilation, shaving, &c.? 12. When a beard or moustache is worn are they allowed to grow naturally, or are they cut into shape? 13. Are any ornaments worn in the ears? 14. Are they passed through the lobe or edge of the ear, or are they pendent ear-rings? 15. Of what materials are they made? and of what forms! 16. Are any ornaments worn in the nose? and of what are they made? 17. Are they worn by both sexes? 18. Do they pass through the septum of the nose or the side? and which side? or are they fixed on the point? 19. Are any ornaments worn in the lips? to which lip are they attached? and what are their forms and materials? 20. At what age are they first inserted? do they increase gradually in size as the wearer grows older, or are they inserted at once of the full size? 20*a*. Can they mend the lobe if it should be broken? 21. Are they easily removable? 22. Are any ornaments worn in the cheeks? how are they inserted? and how kept in their places?

Body.—23. Are any necklaces, collars, armlets, or bracelets in use? and upon what part of the arms or legs are they worn? 24. Of what materials are they composed? and are they easily removable? 25. Is there any difference in such ornaments between the two sexes? 26. Are any pendants worn on the breast? 27. Are any finger-rings in use? of what material are they made? 28. Are they signets? do they indicate rank, marriage, &c.? 29. Are any girdles worn? and do they serve to support weapons or other objects? 30. Are any ornaments worn on the penis?

Legs and Feet.—31. Are any leglets or anklets worn? 32. Are they easily removable? 33. At what age are they first put on? 34. Are any toe-rings in use? 35. How many are worn, and of what forms? 36. What is the effect on the foot? 37. Are weapons or other objects attached to the leglets or bracelets, or worn between them and the body?

[It is very desirable in this class to observe the minuter varieties of ornaments distinguishing cognate tribes, and to obtain a good collection of specimens well labelled. Particular notice should also be taken of any instances in which natural objects worn as ornaments, such as teeth or shells, are copied in metal or other material.]

A. W. F.

No. III.—PAINTING AND TATTOOING.

Painting.—1. Is painting employed in decorating the body? 2. What are the pigments used? 3. How is the painting applied? is it frequently renewed? and by whom is it executed? 4. Do the designs vary according to the sex or rank of the individual? 5. Are any symbolic designs employed by the performers in dances or ceremonies or by warriors? 6. Is any painting of the face employed to heighten beauty, or any application to the eyes to increase their lustre? 7. What are the substances used for this purpose? 8. Is any staining of the nails known? and is it confined to one of the sexes? 9. Is there any coating applied to the body to improve the skin or to keep off insects, or any application to the body in the nature of a thick cake of paint as by the Boobies of Fernando Po? 10. What is considered to be the purpose of the painting? to increase the charms of the individual, or has it a religious meaning? 10*a*. Discriminate between native and imported pigments; any preference for one over the other?

Tattooing.—11. Is tattooing known? and are there any accounts of its introduction, or legends connected with it? 12. Is it confined to one of the sexes? 13. Is it confined to certain parts of the body? and why? 14. At what age is it commenced? and is it done at once or at various periods? 15. Are there any ceremonies connected with it? 16. Is the tattooing made by any professional individuals? and how do they rank? 17. What are the pigments employed and what instruments? 18. Is any special diet observed by the person to be tattooed, or any peculiar vessels for feeding him (New Zealand)? 19. Is tattooing considered indispensable as a sign of manhood? 20. Is it connected in any way with pagan worship? 21. Is the practice dying out, or the contrary? 22. What are the designs employed? and have they any particular significance?

23. Do they vary with the social or family rank of the individual? 24. Are they in any way hereditary? 25. Is the tattooing symmetrical? 26. With what part of the body does it commence? 27. Is the design executed on some preconceived plan? and is any drawing of it prepared beforehand? 28. Is more than one colour employed? [It would be very desirable to obtain drawings of a few characteristic designs with native explanations of their meaning.]

Cicatrices.—29. Is the body ornamented in any way with raised cicatrices? 30. How are they made? and what are the substances rubbed into them? 31. Do they vary according to the tribe or rank of the individual? 32. Is the operation attended with much pain or disturbance to the general health? 33. At what age are they made?

[In the answers to this and the two preceding sections, it would be particularly desirable to obtain photographs or drawings.]

A. W. F.

The following examples have been selected as suggesting points for inquiry.

In India lines are painted on either side the mouth of native women. In Fiji their only tattoo-marks are at the corners of the mouth; and in Easter Island, in the South Pacific, the fleshy parts of their lips used to be tattooed. This is distinctive of marriage amongst the Ainos, where the custom still prevails

In Birmah and Laos, as well as Samoa and Easter Island, it was the practice a short time ago to tattoo the body from the navel to the knee. The marks may be often concealed by the dress, as in the case of the king of Birmah (Crawford). It is desirable, therefore, that travellers should inquire when amongst semicivilized peoples whether they have tattoo-marks beneath their robes, more especially in Arabia and Northern and North-western Asia, where it is known that the custom of tattooing once prevailed.

The following are some further particulars regarding which information is required.

34. Are marks or patterns found more commonly on the face, chest, shoulders, arms, stomach, thighs, or back? 35. In the case of women, are there any patterns about the mouth, breasts, or abdomen? 36. Or on the tip of the tongue, as observed by Captain Cook in the Sandwich Islands? 37. Or under the armpit? 38. Does the custom appear to have prevailed from remote times? 39. Do any marks appear to be personal, *i.e.*, peculiar to or distinctive of the individual tattooed? 40. Do the marks appear to be in imitation of necklaces, armlets, or other articles of dress or ornament? 41. In the case of women, are any marks said to be tokens of marriage? 42. Are they regarded as charms to ward off danger generally? 43. Or as marks of religious dedication? 44. Are the idols or statues of a country ornamented with patterns of the same or a similar character? 45. In the case of young men and women, are the marks or patterns supposed to improve their appearance? 46. Mention especially any instances of the use of a chequered pattern on the forehead or elsewhere. 47. Do women tattoo their own sex? 48. Are additional marks added in after years? 49. Is it the case that very dark races adopt incision and cicatrices only? 50. Are raised scars made by producing "proud flesh"? 51. Is the colour very generally blue or of a bluish tint? 52. When the body is painted, is it in addition to tattooing? 53. When paint is used instead of or in addition to tattooing, is it usually red? 54. When any particular colour is universally employed, is it because the pigment is easily procurable in the country? 55. Is it the custom to paint the body in broad bands of colour? 56. Is there any instance of children being marked with a black pigment except at Mocha? 57. Do any tribes paint their skin black on the death of the chief, like the natives of South Alaska? 58. Or use that colour generally as a sign of mourning? 59. Is the tattoo-mark of the individual ever engraved or painted upon his tombstone, or upon objects belonging to him? 60. Are the tattooed or painted designs related to totemism or exogamy?

J. P. H.

No. IV.—HABITATIONS.

(See also XLVI § Lake Dwellings.)

1. Of what materials are the houses made? 1*a*. Are the beams and rafters fastened with pins or by lashing? 2. What is their form? and is this common to all the tribe? 3. Are any houses built on piles? and if so, only at the shore, or are they found inland? 4. Are dwellings ever built in trees? 5. Does each family have a house? and is it used, day and night, by *all* members of the family? 6. Is there a house for unmarried men? or for travellers? 7. Are houses re-occupied, or destroyed, or left to decay, on the death of the owner? 8. Is the owner buried in his house? 9. Are the houses of the tribe clustered together, or surrounded by a stockade? 10. Do the natives make use of the natural advantages of a position in selecting a site for their villages? 11. Are the houses permanent, or can they be readily taken down and re-erected elsewhere? 12. Is any portion of the floor higher than the rest? and what covering is used? 13. What moveable furniture is there? *e.g.*, stools, hammocks, &c. 13*a*. Are suspended hooks used to hang food or clothes upon? 14. Is any part of the dwelling set apart for sleeping or for eating? 15. Are trophies or sculptured figures placed in a particular spot, *e.g.*, on a shelf? 16. Is there any special place for the fire, and how does the smoke escape? any windows? 17. Is any difference made in arranging the house at night, such as hanging up mats? 18. What is done with the refuse from meals, and from the house generally? 19. Are there any kitchen middens near the dwellings? 20. Are the arrangements cleanly? 21. Are natural shelters or caves ever used for habitation? 22. If so, are they improved by building additional walls? 23. Are any dwellings used only as a refuge in time of war? 24. In selecting a site for a new dwelling, are any acts of divination practised? or is a priest or sorcerer consulted? 25. Or, in felling timber for

the house, are means taken to avert the anger of any spirit? 26. Is any animal sacrificed during the building? and for what reason? 27. When the house is ready for occupation, are any ceremonies performed before it is inhabited? 28. Are the houses built entirely above ground, or is any excavation made? 29. Are there any superstitious observances at the cutting of timber for a new house? 30. Any modes of divination resorted to for determining its site? 31. Any sacrifices of human beings or of animals during the building? 32. Must any part of the building rest upon an animal or upon something once living? 33. Can any reasons be given for those practices? 34. Are any special ceremonies necessary before occupying a new house? 35. Are houses of different construction or material used at different seasons of the year? Describe the varieties? 36. How are the roofs made, and how covered?

C. H. R.

No. V.—NAVIGATION.

(See also LIX, Astronomy.)

1. What forms of boats are in use and are all, or any, of foreign make? 2. Are all or any provided with outriggers on one or both sides? 3. Are canoes made in the form of two or more boats side by side? 4. How are the planks fastened together, by lashing or with wooden pins; and if by lashing, with what material? 5. What material and tools are used for caulking? 6. Are there any dug-outs or boats made of hide stretched on a framework of bark or wattle or of bundles of buoyant rushes? 6*a*. Are special tools used for hollowing out canoes? 7. Are all boats open or decked? 8. Are both sides of the canoe alike, or is one flatter than the other? 9. Are the canoes shaped alike at both ends? 10. Do the natives always sail with the outrigger to windward? 11. Are canoes of a particular kind used by women, or for warlike expeditions? 12. Is the baler of any special form? 13. Do

the natives paddle or row? 14. Is any fulcrum (rowlock) provided in the latter case? 15. How do the men paddle? sitting, standing, or kneeling? 16. Do they keep time, and if so, who gives the time? 17. Does one man steer, and has he a special paddle? is a fixed rudder used? 18. What are the forms of paddles? 19. Are sails used, and if so, of what shape and material are they? 20. How many masts are there and where are they placed, and how are the sails made fast to them? 21. Do the canoes run free, or can they beat up against the wind? 22. Is the mariners' compass known, or do the natives shape their course by sight, either of land or of the heavenly bodies? 23. Do they venture out of sight of land? 24. What is the greatest speed attained in sailing? 25. Do certain canoes belong to the tribe or village, or are they the property of the chief, or of individuals? 26. Is there any special ceremony at the launch of a new canoe? 27. Are there houses for the canoes? 28. Are ornamental figures or charms attached to the mast or any other part of the canoe, *e.g.*, as a protection? 29. Is the sheet or any other rope reeved through a block? 30. Is any part of the canoe set apart for chiefs? 31. Are any parts watertight for provisions? 32. Are any anchors used? what is their form, and of what material are they made? 33. Are any ceremonies practised on the arrival of a canoe from a neighbouring island? if so, describe them. 34. Are rafts made of very light material? or of inflated skins? 35. Is there any process for improving the shape of canoes cut from the solid, *e.g.*, by steaming the wood? 36. It would be of interest to record any special substances used in repairing bark or skin canoes, and the methods of applying them? 37. Is there any arrangement to prevent a canoe from making too much leeway?

C. H. R.

No. VI.—SWIMMING.

1. What is the common method of swimming? 2. Are there any games into which swimming enters? 3. Can the natives swim long distances? 4. Can they swim at a great speed? 4*a*. Is any board or other apparatus used, as described in the surf swimming in E. Pacific? 5. Are the natives expert divers? 6. Do they dive weighted with a stone? 7. How long can they remain under water? 8. Is this considered a feat? 9. Do they dive head or feet first? 10. Do the tribes inland swim as well as the coast tribes? 11. Is swimming *taught*, or is it supposed to be a natural action, like walking?

C. H. R.

No. VII.—WEAVING.

Weaving, like spinning, dates back to a very early period; and the tissues found in the ancient Swiss Lake-dwellings are of more than one kind. The looms used for weaving vary considerably; but the simplest form of complete loom may be thus described:—There is a roll, or "yarn-beam," on which the "warp" of unwoven thread is wound or "beamed," and another roll, or "cloth-beam," on which the woven tissue is received. The "warp," or the threads passing from one roll to the other are kept in a state of tension, and each thread passes through an eyelet-hole in a vertical cord or "heddle." The alternate heddles are attached to two separate frames, so that one set of alternate threads in the loom can be drawn away from the other, either upwards or downwards, and leave a space or "shed" between the two sets of threads, through which a shuttle can be thrown with the weft or transverse thread. This is then beaten up against the thread last thrown in, by means of a "reed," or grating, through the intervals in which the warp-threads pass, and which is fixed in a swinging "batten" or "lay," so as to give weight to the blow. The two sets of warp-threads are of course alternately raised and depressed between each throw of the shuttle, and this is usually done by means of treadles.

For weaving patterns, several sets of heddles are employed. The patterns may be either merely woven, as in diaper, or produced by coloured threads being thrown in, as in figured ribbons. In a still simpler form of loom, such as that in use in India, the reed and batten are dispensed with, a long shuttle like a netting-mesh being used, which first draws the weft into its place, and is then used to beat it up. In other cases, the threads of the warp are stretched in a frame, sometimes by means of weights, and the weft inserted by hand and beaten up with a sort of comb. Sometimes the surface of the tissue is hairy or piled liked velvet, from short threads being woven in.

Articles closely resembling woven fabrics are in some instances made by the simple process of plaiting, like our ordinary rush-matting. Some baskets also present the same texture as if they had been woven. Felting, or the formation of cloth by the entanglement of short fibres crossing each other in every direction, is another process closely allied to weaving. Coloured figures and patterns on cloth may be produced in various ways, either by dyeing portions of both warp and weft of different colours, or by using coloured portions in one of them only; or the tissues may be completed and subsequently printed. The bark-cloth made in Fiji and Tonga is ornamented in this last manner, and is itself a tissue which is neither woven, plaited, nor felted, but consists of the inner bark of the malo-tree dexterously manipulated and beaten. The bast which is used for matting affords an instance of a somewhat similar application of the inner bark of a tree: the outer bark, like the birch-bark so largely employed in North America, is generally used for stiff and not flexible articles.

Another method of ornamenting is by embroidery, or working patterns on a fabric by means of the needle. Looped fabrics knitted from a continuous thread, and knotted fabrics made by tying strings together, may be regarded as varieties of woven fabrics.

The following questions may be of service :—

1. What are the principal materials used for weaving? and how prepared? (*see* No. IX.) 2. What is the form of loom or other appliance for weaving? 3. What kind of shuttle is used? and in what manner is the weft beaten up? 4. In what manner is the warp kept in a state of tension? 5. What is the size of the largest webs that can be produced? 6. Is the weaving plain, or are patterns woven in the cloth? if so, of what character are they? and how produced? 7. Is any process of felting known? and how is it applied? 8. Is any kind of bark-cloth manufactured? if so, describe the process and the mode of ornamentation. 9. Are any tissues or kinds of leather or bark ornamented by embroidery? if so, with what materials, and with what kinds of pattern? 10. Is any process of knitting known? 11. Are plaited fringes or other articles of personal clothing or ornament manufactured from cord or strips of leather? 12. Is the pattern made entirely from memory or is a model set up before the weaver?

J. E.

No. VIII.—BASKETWORK.

The process of basket-making is closely allied to that of weaving (*ante*, VII.), and in like manner dates back to a remote period. Baskets made of esparto have been found with hatchets and other instruments of stone in Andalusia; and our ancient British ancestors were renowned for their skill in basket-making, the Latin word *bascauda* being a mere derivative from the British.

Basketwork is either stiff or flexible; the stiff variety is generally made by wattling fine withes over others rather more rigid which form the ribs of the structure, while the flexible kind is usually made by plaiting or weaving flat strips together; occasionally, however, rush-like stems are used for this kind of fabric. So closely are some of these baskets woven, that they are perfectly watertight, like the milk-baskets among the Kaffirs.

Basketwork of a coarse kind is sometimes employed in the construction of huts and stockades, and for the manufacture of boats or coracles covered with skin.

Bark of trees is in many countries employed as a substitute for basketwork of various kinds, and is even used as a material for boats (No. V.). Articles of clothing, such as hats, and other objects for personal use, such as fans, are frequently made of basketwork. The following questions may serve as hints to the traveller :—

1. What are the materials principally used in basketwork, and how are they prepared? are any plants specially cultivated for basket-making? 2. What are the chief articles manufactured in this manner? If possible, describe the process. 3. What are the principal forms of baskets? and in what manner are they wrought, and to what purposes applied? 4. In what manner are they ornamented? 5. What other articles besides baskets are made in the same manner? and what are their forms and uses? 6. Are strainers or colanders made of basketwork? and if so, for what are they used? 7. Are special forms of baskets used for special purposes? are they kept, or are they thrown away after having been once used? 8. Are baskets or other articles made from the bark of trees, without any plaiting? what are their forms, and how ornamented? 9. Are waterproof baskets in use? and is any material applied to render them waterproof? 10. Are baskets used as moulds for pottery? 11. Are the shells or rind of any fruits or vegetables used as substitutes for basketwork? 12. When the ornament is formed by plaiting in different colours, what are the patterns? representations of animals or plants, or only geometrical forms? 13. Do these patterns appear upon any other objects than basketwork? 14. Are vessels of other material covered with basketwork, e.g., pottery, eggs, gourds, &c.? 15. Are any parts of dress or defensive armour made of basketwork, shields, cuirasses, head gear, or sandals? 16. Is plaited decoration much used for weapons or utensils? or are plaited

sheaths in use? (For further details as to methods of plaiting, see O. T. Mason, Basketry in Smithsonian Rep. for 1884. For colours used in plaiting see No. XII.—DYEING.)

J. E.

No. IX.—STRING.

The art of making string from vegetable fibre has been known from a very early period, and was practised by the occupants of the Swiss Lake-dwellings at a time when cutting-instruments were formed of stone and not of metal. The use, however, of animal fibre for ligaments of various kinds probably dates back to a much more remote period, as needles formed of bone have been found in caves of the first stone age, or what is known as the Palæolithic period. String or twine composed of long fibres is usually twisted, but sometimes also plaited. Thread made of finer and generally shorter fibres is usually spun either by hand or by means of a wheel; such spun thread is generally used for weaving. In some cases, split vegetable stems (such as rattan), strips of skin, or the intestines of animals, are employed for binding purposes without being twisted. The following questions are suggested:—

1. What animal or vegetable substances are employed for the manufacture of rope, string, or thread? 2. Are they subjected to any preparation before or after manufacture? 3. Are they used in strips or twisted, plaited or spun? 4. To what purposes are each of the principal varieties applied, as, for instance, for binding, netting, making bow-strings or fishing-lines, plaiting into articles of clothing or for weaving? (No VII.) 5. In the case of animal fibres being used, what are the parts thus employed? and how they are prepared? 6. Are the bands of these materials used wet, so as to tighten in drying? 7. In spinning thread for weaving, what process is employed? 8. Are any domesticated animals kept for the purpose of supplying materials to be spun? or are any plants

cultivated for the sake of their fibre? is silk known? 9. How are articles sewn? are needles employed, or awls to bore holes, or tweezers to draw through the thread? 10. What is the process of netting, and the form of the needle and mesh? 11. Are knotted ropes or strings used as aids to the memory? 12. In the case of silk being known, what is the process of preparation? 13. Are cords in any way used as measures of length? 14. Are the string and thread usually dyed? (No. XII.) 15. Are spindle-whorls used in the manufacture of thread or string? 16. Does the twisted string consist of two or three or more plies?

J. E.

No. X.—LEATHER WORK.

The preparations of the skins of animals, so as to render them fit for use, for clothing, and for hundreds of other purposes to which they are applied, has always been one of the most important occupations of savage life. Even among civilised races the part played by leather has but little diminished in importance.

Skins with the hair on are frequently merely dried, the inner part being dressed with some antiseptic preparation, and sometimes curried or shaved.

Leather, more properly so called, is usually tanned or prepared with bark, like shoe-leather—tawed, or prepared with alum, &c., like kid-leather for gloves—or dressed with oil, like chamois or wash leather.

For each kind the skins pass through several processes, one of the principal being usually the steeping the hides in lime-water, so as to loosen the hair and prepare the substance of the skin for receiving the final dressings. The uses to which skins and leather may be applied are so multifarious that it would occupy too much space to attempt to enumerate them. The following questions may suggest to travellers some points towards which their attention might be directed:—

1. What are the animals the skins of which are principally prepared for use? is any fish-skin used? 2. In what manner are they removed from the animals? and what instruments are employed for the purpose? 3. Which of them have the hair left upon them? and in what manner are they prepared or dressed? is the hairy side dressed, or treated in any particular manner? 4. If the hair is removed, in what manner is this effected? and how are the hides tanned or prepared: 5. What are the ingredients used for dressing them? and how administered? 6. Are the inner sides of the skins scraped or curried? and if so, with what kind of instruments? 7. Is any beating process employed so as to render the leather supple? 8. Is the preparation of leather the work of the men or the women? 9. Is the leather dyed, or its surface in any way ornamented or varnished? (In the case of shagreen, this is done by means of hard seeds being incorporated in the body of the leather. In the case of morocco leather, the grain is produced by crumpling the leather.)

10. Are any skins used for holding liquids, like wine-skins? if so, what are they? and how prepared? 11. Are raw hides used, either whole or in pieces or strips? and how applied? (No. IX.) 12. For what purposes are the different kinds of leather chiefly used? and are they dressed in any way for the sake of preserving them while in use? 13. Are any portions of the human skin, such as scalps, prepared in any way by drying or otherwise? and if so, how and under what circumstances?

J. E.

No. XI.—POTTERY.

1. Is pottery made by the natives? or, if imported, from whence? 2. Are there any traditions as to its origin? 3. What are the kinds of clay employed? 4. Are any other substances mixed with the clay? 5. Are the vessels turned on the wheel? 6. Are any moulds used to fashion the bases of the vessels, *e.g.*, baskets, gourds? 7. How is a vessel made? by the addition of small pieces of clay to an existing

base? or is a mass of clay sufficient for the whole vase taken at once and moulded? 8. What are the most common forms of vessels? Give drawings. 9. What are the tools used in fashioning the vessels? 10. Are there any scorings or impressed ornaments? and of what patterns? 11. How is the pottery burnt? 12. If in holes in the ground, is the smoke allowed to permeate the ware? 13. Is any kind of painting employed? and what are the pigments? 14. Is any painted decoration applied before the pottery is burnt? if so ascertain the nature of the pigment, and obtain specimens. 15. Is any kind of glaze, either of lead or salt, in use, or any varnish? and of what is the latter composed? 16. Is any porous pottery made to serve as cooling vessels? 17. Are any figures of men or animals made of clay? and how are they fashioned? 18. Is the making of pottery the work of any particular class or sex? or does each family prepare its own vessels? 19. Is the pottery exported to any other tribes? 20. Are different qualities used for different purposes? 21. Are earthen vessels made especially for funereal purposes? and if so, are they of different materials from those in ordinary use? 22. Is broken pottery buried in graves or beneath landmarks? 23. What substitutes for pottery are used, such as gourds, shells, &c.? and have they given the form to any of the earthen vessels? 24. Are there any traditions as to the introduction of pottery making? and what are they? 25. Is congealed blood formed into drinking-vessels? and by what process?

A. W. F.

No. XII.—DYEING, &c.

The use of colour for ornamental purposes is almost universal throughout the world, but the number of colours, their nature, and the purposes for which they are applied vary greatly in different countries. There are, broadly speaking, two distinct methods by which colour is applied:—(A) dyeing, when the colouring-matter is used in a state of solution, and penetrates the pores of the object to be dyed; and (B) painting, when the pigment is mixed with some medium or vehicle to fix it when dry, and is applied to a part or the whole of the object to be painted by means of some kind of brush.

Dyeing is usually practised in connexion with animal and vegetable fibre and tissue, such as leather, thread, and cloth; but sometimes also the process is applied to wood and bone. Painting is more commonly applied to wooden objects. Both processes are occasionally employed with the object of rendering the human form either more terrible or more beautiful.

Dyes.—1. From what substances are these prepared? and how are they applied? (If possible procure specimens of the materials used, and an account of the method of preparation.) 2. What are the articles usually dyed—skins with the hair on, leather, twine, cloth, &c.? 3. Is any mordant or solution used, either to prepare the object for receiving the dye, or for rendering it permanent after it has been applied? 4. What are the favourite colours? (Their arrangement and proportions will come under No. XXIV. ORNAMENTATION.) 5. Are any portions of the human body dyed, such as the teeth, nails, hair, or skin?

Painting.—6. What are the principal pigments used, and how prepared? (Obtain specimens if possible.) 7. In what manner are they ground or precipitated? and what is the medium employed to fix them? 8. Is any subsequent process of varnishing or lacquering employed? and if so, how is the varnish made? 9. What are the objects usually painted? and what kind of brushes are used? 10. What colours are most in vogue? and are they transparent, like dyes, or opaque, like body-colours? 11. Is any process allied to gilding known? 12. In painting patterns, in what order are the colours applied? and is the outline first painted and the colours subsequently filled in? or is the pattern roughly sketched in the first instance, and the outline completed as the final process? 13. Are any mechanical means, such as compasses or stencilling-plates, used? or any printing process? 14. Is paint employed on the human body or hair? and if so, on what occasions, and in what manner is it applied? (*See* TATTOOING, No. III.) 15. What are the colours used for these purposes? and with what ingredients are they mixed? 16. Is any colour regarded as especially sacred, and reserved for sacred purposes?

J. E.

No. XIII.—STONE IMPLEMENTS.

The study of the stone implements of modern savages is of interest as a means of explaining the uses and mode of fabricating those of prehistoric times.

1. What is the mode of cutting stone when metal is not employed? is sand-string or another stone employed for this purpose? 1*a*. Is heat employed to break up large pieces? 2. In what manner are holes bored in stone, and with what materials? 3. Describe the mode of grinding or polishing the surfaces; and of what materials are the rubbers employed for this purpose? 4. Describe the implements used in flaking, and the mode of holding the stones whilst flaking them. 5. What means are taken to procure long thin flakes? are the stones pressed against the thigh whilst flaking them, or are they bound round tightly so as to increase the line of least resistance to the blow of the flaker? 6. What are the uses of the different forms of stone implements employed? 7. In what manner are they hafted? and with what materials are they bound on to their handles? 8. What materials are employed for the different kinds of stone implements? and where are they procured? 9. What length of time do they take in fabricating the several implements? 10. How long do they continue in use? 11. What becomes of them when they are disused? 12. Are any of them used in the hand without handles? 13. Note and describe the effect of wear upon their edges, and the marks of abrasion where the handles have been fastened on; and observe the manner in which these marks are produced. 14. Note the length of time taken

to fabricate the different objects with stone implements. 15. Are there special workers of stone implements, or does each man make his own? 16. Are there any implements which are valued as specimens of the skill of the fabricator? 17. Are small flakes chipped off by pressure or by striking? 18. What is the use of serrated edges? 19. How are scrapers made? 20. Are arrow-heads used as knives in carving? 21. In cutting bone or wood, are flakes used with a sawing or cutting motion? 22. How are small holes, such as the eyes of needles, bored with flint? 23. Are flints used for striking lights? and are any particular forms of flints carried for this purpose? what other materials are used with the flints for this purpose? 24. Are flints or stones kept in water before working them? or do they undergo any other process before they are worked into implements? 25. Are the natural forms of stones and flints ever used as implements? 26. Give the native names of all the different parts of implements and materials employed. 27. Is the form of a knife or an arrow-head much influenced by accidents of fracture during fabrication? 28. To what extent are the different forms designed for special purposes, or merely the result of fashion? 29. Do the several forms of implements pass into one another by varieties, or are the different types well marked and distinct? 30. Are stone implements left as heirlooms? 31. Are there any superstitious usages associated with any of them? 32. Since the introduction of metal, are stone implements still used for religious purposes, mutilations of the body, or any other purpose? 33. Are metal implements made in imitation of the stone ones formerly employed? 34. Are stone implements found in the earth? and are they of similar forms to those of stone or metal now in use? 35. Are stone implements used as a medium of exchange in lieu of money? (See also No. XLVI., Archæology.) 36. Are they regarded as thunderbolts, and supposed to have fallen from the skies? 37. Are they used as amulets? 38. Are suitable pieces for implements ever produced by heating a stone and shivering it by dashing cold water upon it?

A. L. F.

No. XIV.—METALLURGY.

1. What metals are in use? 2. What are their native names? 3. Are they produced in the country or obtained from elsewhere? 4. To what uses are the metals put? 5. Are any of the metal articles, such as bars, ornaments, &c., made for the purposes of barter, or used as currency? 6. From what ores are the metals obtained? 7. Are the ores found in the beds of streams or dug out of the ground? 8. What are the native names of the ores? 9. If ores are smelted describe the process of smelting, noting the quantities of the materials put into the furnace and of the metal and products obtained, and the time required for the operation? 10. Is the ore submitted to any preparatory treatment before smelting? 11. Is any material mixed with the ore and fuel for smelting? 12. What kind of fuel is used; note the shape and size of the furnace used in smelting, and give sketches, if possible? 13. What kind of bellows is used? is more than one kind in use? Make sketches, if possible, of the bellows; also of the tools used in smelting, and give their dimensions? 14. Is the product of the smelting process a metal ready for use, or is it subjected to any subsequent treatment before use? 15. Describe any process of purifying or refining practised? 16. Is the art of casting practised? Describe the furnace used for the operation? 17. Are crucibles used; if so, describe them? 18. Give a description of the moulds into which the metal is poured? 19. Are the moulds made of sand, clay, stone or metal? 20. Are the castings subjected to hammering or chiselling, or to both? 21. Is any process of hardening practised in making cutting implements or weapons or sonorous instruments? 22. In forging is welding known? 23. What kind of forge and bellows is used by smiths? 24. Is soldering practised? 25. Is wire of any metal in use? 26. Is it made by the natives? 57. If so, is it made by simple hammering or by drawing the metal through apertures?

Gold.—28. Do the natives wash the sands of rivers or of the beach to obtain gold? 29. Is it obtained in the form of "dust" (coarse or fine flaky powder) or of nuggets (small irregular shaped pieces)? 30. Are articles made by melting the gold dust? 31. Are any made by hammering the nuggets? 32. Are any superstitious beliefs held regarding the origin of gold dust?

Silver.—33. Is silver found native (*i.e.*, as metal)? 34. Is it obtained by smelting ores? 35. Are lead ores smelted to obtain silver? 36. If so, describe the process used for separating it from the lead?

Copper.—37. Is copper found native (*i.e.*, as metal), or is it always obtained by smelting ores? 38. Is the ore burnt in heaps or in any way before being smelted?

Iron.—39. Is cast-iron made by the natives? 40. Do they make any distinction between wrought-iron and steel? 41. If iron ores are smelted, are both steel and cast-iron obtained at the same time in the smelting process?

Bronze.—42. Is any bronze alloy in use? 43. Is it made by smelting the metals copper and tin together, and what are the proportions? 44. Are copper ores and lead ores smelted together, and is the alloy of copper and lead so produced in use?

Brass.—45. Is brass (alloy of copper and zinc) known? 46. Is it made in the country or imported? 47. Is it made by heating metallic copper with zinc ores?

48. Describe any methods practised for mending broken metal articles? 49. Describe the processes and tools used for ornamenting metal utensils, weapons, personal ornaments, &c.

In all cases specimens of the metals, ores, &c., should, if possible, be obtained and be carefully labelled.

Descriptions of furnaces, tools, &c., are most valuable when accompanied with sketches and dimensions.

W. G.

No. XV.—MACHINERY.

The use of machinery, even in its simplest form and moved by manual power, may be regarded as a sign that the people employing it have already emerged from the lowest stages of civilization. The transition, for instance, from the use of a pair of rubbing-stones or "saddle-quern" to that of a pair of millstones, one of which revolves and is driven by hand (the ordinary quern), is a great step in advance; but machinery can hardly be said to have been thoroughly introduced into a country until some of the forces of Nature, such as those of wind and water, have been utilized as motive power. The windlass, the common pump, the potter's wheel (No. XI.), the revolving hand-mill, the spinning-wheel (No. IX.), the turning-lathe, and some forms of looms (No. VII.) may however, be regarded as machines, as they are mechanical means of economizing human labour.

The earliest and simplest application of hydraulic power appears to have been for purposes of irrigation, and in some countries the use of water-power appears to be almost restricted to this purpose. The following questions are suggested:—

1. Are revolving millstones in use? if so, describe their form, the manner in which driven, and the purposes to which applied. 2. What kind of stones are used for this purpose? and of what materials are the pivots and bearings formed? 3. Are pebbles with a conical socket in them used as bearings for the pivots, or are the pivots made of stone? 4. Are any pounding-mills in use, or any mechanical means employed to assist the motion of pestles in mortars? 5. Are any forms of rolling-mills employed for crushing purposes? 6. Is any form of turning-lathe in use, and of what kind? is the rotary motion continuous or alternate? 7. How are the turning-tools applied? and what is their character? 8. What articles are turned? 9. Is the common windlass in use? and for what purposes? 10. Is any form of pump in use? if not,

and wells exist, in what manner is water raised? 11. What form of bellows is in use? (No. XIV.) 12. Are any water-wheels or other hydraulic machines known? if so, for what purposes are they applied, and in what manner? 13. Is any form of windmill known? 14. Is the drill known? 15. What system is employed? the bow drill, or pump drill or any other? 16. Is the drill provided with a fly-wheel?

J. E.

No. XVI.—FIRE.

As a general rule, all tribes both preserve and produce fire. There are statements as to fireless tribes which should be carefully examined when met with; most of them have broken down under close inspection. The history of the practical art of fire-making is interesting; and the place of fire in social and religious ceremony gives valuable information as to the constitution of family and tribal life, the idea of moral purity, and several points of theology.

1. By what means is fire produced? 2. If by friction of wood, what is the exact instrument used, whether the stick-and-groove, the simple fire-drill twisted between the hands, or some improved form. 3. Is this ruder instrument still kept up in religious ceremonies? 4. If the fire is made by striking flint on pyrites or iron, is it remembered if this art was learnt from foreigners? 5. Are any other instruments used, such as the fire-syringe, burning-lens, &c.? 6. How is fire kept up and carried about? 7. What fuel is used? 8. Are there legends of the discovery of fire or invention of fire-making! 9. If so, do they seem to be myths personifying the fire or the fire-drill itself?

10. Is the household fire symbolic of family ties? 11. Is it held sacred, placed in charge of any particular person? is there any family worship connected with it? and by whom performed? 12. Is there a council-fire or other fires on special occasions or in special buildings?

13. Is a sacred fire kept up, or kindled on special festivals? and is its extinction unlucky? 14. Has such fire particular reference to the course of the sun, the solstices, year, seasons, &c.? 15. Are the fires put out and kindled from newly produced fire on such occasions, and by whom? and is the new fire made by friction of wood, or otherwise? 16. Is the kindling of the new fire a religious ceremony? and what is its meaning?

17. How is fire regarded in religion? 18. Is there any custom against wounding or polluting fire? 19. Are sacrifices given to it or consumed by it? 20. Is the fire itself a living divinity receiving worship and devouring the offered food? or does it act as a means of conveying sacrifice to deities and the dead, at funerals, and how? 21. Is there a fire-god to whom all particular fires belong? 22. Is fire a means of driving away evil demons?

23. Is fire a means of purification from uncleanness, blood, death, moral guilt, &c.? and how is it applied? 24. Is new fire made for such purification? 25. Is its making in any way connected with moral, especially sexual, purity?

E. B. T.

No. XVII.—INVENTION.

Among nations capable of historical record, account is to some extent given of the invention of particular arts, the introduction of new laws, the change of customs, &c. All such accounts should be preserved, although, more often than not, they are but fables invented to account for the facts. Otherwise our information as to new inventions, &c., must be derived from inspection of the arts themselves. Thus some instruments show that they must have been derived directly or indirectly from earlier and ruder forms, as the cross-bow from the long-bow. Some arts are judged to have grown up among a particular tribe because no neighbouring tribe possesses them--like the use of iron pyrites for striking fire among the Fuegians. The best general advice to observers is, that in cataloguing the details of art and customs, they should carefully look for symptoms of native invention and modification.

1. Are there any arts used which are not common to most or all tribes of the district? 2. If so, are they such as the people themselves probably invented? 3. Are there any tools, weapons, &c., used which seem as though they had been improved or modified by the people? 4. Are any such arts connected with plants or minerals specially belonging to the district, so as to show that they were no doubt brought into use by direct discovery or invention there? 5. Do the people themselves claim to have invented any such art, &c.? and if so, is the alleged inventor a mythic personage or divine ancestor, or does he belong to actual history?

E. B. T.

No. XVIII.—VARIATION.

Every slight variety which distinguishes the art and custom of a tribe from those of its neighbours is worth study, as affording evidence of the course of development into new forms. This is well shown by weapons, &c., all the varieties of which should be noticed, and drawings of them preserved. Many of the connecting links between existing forms have no doubt been lost, but might be discovered by inquiring of the older natives, or by examining the relics deposited in the graves.

It is obvious that these remarks apply to arts and customs in general.

Are, then, variations of this kind noticed which seem to have arisen in the tribe, as to social customs, penalties, and course of judicial procedure, religious doctrines, ceremonies, &c? Can reasons be assigned for these changes taking place, and especially are they improvements? Do the tribe tell any myths, &c., slightly altered from the form in which they are current among neighbouring tribes?

E. B. T.

No. XIX.—NATURAL FORMS.

In the infancy of the arts mankind must have availed themselves of the natural forms of the objects met with; and as the process of adapting and modifying them to their wants has been slow and continuous, traces of the forms of nature have been preserved in those arts which are indigenous and have remained isolated. When, on the other hand, they have been derived from civilized races, or have degenerated from a more advanced state, the more complex forms of the higher civilization become conventionalized, and are frequently retained in an altered condition after the knowledge of their original uses has been lost. It is desirable, therefore, to pay attention to the forms of the objects constructed by savages, with the view of ascertaining to what extent they approximate to the natural forms of the materials employed, and to note those objects in which the natural forms have been little or not at all changed.

1. Do the clubs and other weapons approximate to the natural forms of the stems, roots, or branches of trees? 2. Are the curves the natural curves of the branches? and do they follow the grain of the wood? 3. Are the natural forms of stones employed as hammers, mace-heads, or for other purposes? 4. Are gourds, shell-fruit, sea-shells, human or other skulls employed as drinking-vessels? 5. Are the forms of these closely imitated in pottery? 6. Are gourds, reeds, bones, skulls, sinews, and root fibres employed in musical instruments? 7. Are the skins of animals or bark of trees much altered in clothing? 8. Are the skins of animals flayed off the body with only one incision employed as water-vessels, bagpipes, pouches, or bellows? 9. Are the head-skins of animals, with the ears and mane, employed as head-dresses, or the skins of horned or prickled fish? 10. Are any of them copied in artificial head-dresses? 11. For what purposes is the bamboo used—tubes, drinking-vessels, baskets, rings, &c.? 12. Are shells, teeth, claws, seeds, bones, beetles' wings, vertebræ of snakes, and other natural objects

employed as personal ornaments? 13. Are any of these copied in metal for the same purpose? if so, give drawings of them. 14. Are the defences of animals employed in artificial defences—tusks or horns as spears? saw-fish blades as swords? teeth, claws, split reeds, or blade of the sting-ray as arrow points? crocodiles' backs as breast-plates or shields? scales of the pangolin as scale-armour? 15. Are any of these copied in metal? if so, give drawings. 16. Are the thorns or spines of trees employed as barbs, awls, pins, needles, or for other piercing purposes? 17. Is a plough used, consisting of a tree-stem, with a branch as a share? 18. Are trees or skins used as boats, the people sitting outside? 19. Are caves, rock-shelters, or tree-tops used as dwellings? 20. Can the use of these be traced in the architecture of the people? 21. Are leaves used for roofing?

A. L. F.

No. XX.—CONSERVATISM.

The indisposition of most men to change of habits is to be studied for its immense practical effect as a barrier to improvement in art and reformation in society, while also, to a great extent, it tends to preserve existing art and knowledge from decay. Among its results, one has special value to anthropologists as a means of tracing the history of civilization. This is "survival," which takes place when old arts and fashions, though superseded for ordinary purposes, are kept up under special circumstances, especially on state occasions and in solemn ceremonies, as may be exemplified in our official retention of garments otherwise disused, or in the making of fire for religious purposes in India by the almost forgotten process of friction of wood. These "survivals" prove that the people keeping them up had them in ordinary use at some earlier period, information which history often fails to give.

1. Is there a general attachment to ancestral habits and

dislike to change and reform? 2. Does this refer to all the proceedings of life, or especially to matters of state, magic, religion, &c.? 3. Are weapons, houses, &c., made in a way which is practically unreasonable, and only intelligible as the keeping up of ancient ruder practices? 4. Are any rude arts or inconvenient customs kept up as matters of ceremony while disused for ordinary purposes? 5. Do any of the usages at festivals, peculiar dishes and customs, &c., appear to be relics or "survivals" from an earlier state of civilization?

E. B. T.

No.. XXI.—ENGINEERING.

In most countries, even those now highly civilized, there are earthworks of various kinds belonging to some prehistoric period, and of which, in many instances, the purpose and method of formation are unknown; observations of similar works of more recent construction in other countries may perhaps throw some light upon the history of the more ancient examples.

The prevention of floods by means of *levées* thrown up along the banks of rivers, the construction of artificial islands to serve as places of retreat or safety, the damming up of streams so as to form lakes, the formation of artificial channels either for irrigation or communication by means of boats, the throwing up earthworks and making palisades for protection in time of war or for hunting purposes, the construction of bridges, all require a certain amount of engineering skill, and the processes employed are all worthy of study.

It will be well to note any works of this kind, and where possible to give an approximate idea of their antiquity. Where such works are being carried on at the present day, it will be well to state their object and describe the means employed.

1. If earthworks are being constructed, how is the material

procured, and how is it transported? what tools are used for digging and carrying? give approximate sections and an estimate of the number of men, women, and children employed, and the amount of work done in a given time. Are there other materials than earth employed? 2. Is any piling employed? and, if so, how driven? 3. If palisading is used, how are the trees prepared and fixed in the ground? what is the mode of entrance and its defence?—What is the usual manner of constructing bridges? (*See* COMMUNICATIONS, No. LXVIII.)

J. E.

No. XXII.—WRITING.

The expression of ideas by graphic signs has two bearings on anthropology: first, the use of marks, pictures, &c., for record and communication preserves stages in that course of development which leads through full picture-writing to phonetic and alphabetic writing; second, when an alphabet of any kind is in use, it usually shows resemblance to that of other districts, proving that they all must have had a common origin; and it is an essential element in the history of any tribe or nation to discover from what country it obtained its alphabet. With the alphabet, it is probable that it derived other and not less important parts of its civilization.

1. Do any methods of the nature of writing exist? 2. When it is desired to send a message to a distance, to recruit a war party, to record numbers, to preserve the name and feats of a dead warrior, &c., does any method exist of tying knots in a string, making notches in a tally, figures on wood, bark, or stone? 3. Do such marks exist on the rocks in the neighbourhood, as if made for the purpose of record? 4 Are pictures or carvings made for the purpose of communication or record, as distinct from mere ornament? 5. If so, does the picture simply indicate an object such as it represents, *i.e.*, is the system one of picture-writing? 6. Or is any

trace to be found of the picture representing not the object itself, but the sound of its name, *i.e.*, is any rudiment of phonetic writing noticeable? 7. If pictures or other characters are used for phonetic purposes, what is the system of their use? 8. Is there a system of signs for syllables or letters? 9. Is any mixed system of picture-signs and sound-signs used, as in the Egyptian hieroglyphics? 10. Is the syllabarium or alphabet apparently of pure native invention, or suggested by the sight of some civilized alphabet? or is it directly borrowed from some other country? 11. Is there any record of the time and circumstances under which a foreign alphabet was introduced? 12. Is printing of any kind from stamps, blocks, or types in use? 13. Give drawings of any owner's marks upon arrows, weapons, tools, &c. 14. Draw mason's marks, cattle-brands, ciphers, and secret signs.

E. B. T.

No. XXIII.—DRAWING AND SCULPTURE.

Great difference is observable in the capacity for drawing shown by different races. Thus the Esquimaux are comparatively skilful draughtsmen, whilst the Australians, as a rule have but little knowledge of it. Amongst the relics found in the caves of Périgord, in France, life-like representations of animals have been discovered, whilst the rock-engravings of South America represent figures so grotesque as scarcely to be recognized. Care should, however, be taken to distinguish between true representative art, however rude, which is the best attempt of natives to depict the objects truthfully, and conventionalized symbols, which are merely based upon the forms of nature. These, although of the utmost interest, come more properly under the head of writing or ornamentation, and must not be confounded with the former. The three branches, *drawing*, *writing*, and *ornamentation*, spring from a common centre; and the traveller should make it his best endeavour to classify the rock sculptures, carvings, and drawings of savages under one or other of these headings, assigning to each its true signification.

1. Have the natives a natural aptitude for drawing? 2. Do they draw animals in preference to other subjects? 3. Are the most conspicuous features, such as the head, nose, &c., generally exaggerated? 4. Have they the least knowledge of perspective? 5. Are the more distant objects drawn smaller than those nearer? 6. Are the more important personages or objects drawn larger than the others? 7. Do their drawings represent imaginary animals or animals now extinct? 8. Do they evince a tendency to introduce uniformity into the representation of irregular objects, such as trees, so as to produce a symmetrical pattern? 9. Are the drawings:—*a*, historical (XLV.); *b*, religious (XXVII.); *c*, obscene; *d*, symbolical or hieroglyphic (XXII.); *e*, ornamental (XXIV.); *f*, badges or tribal marks, heraldic (LXIX.); *g*, copies from nature; *h*, imaginative designs; *i*, topographical; *k*, scribbles to occupy idle time, without any definite meaning? 10. Are events of different periods depicted in the same drawing? 11. Have they any conventional modes of representing certain objects? 12. Do they draw from nature, or copy each other's drawings? 13. Do they, in copying from one another, vary the designs through negligence, inability, or other causes, so as to lose sight of the original objects, and produce conventional forms, the meaning of which is otherwise inexplicable? if so, it would be of great interest to obtain series of such drawings, showing the gradual departure from the original designs. 14. Do they readily understand European drawings? 15. Do they show any aptitude in copying European designs? 16. What are the materials usually employed for drawing? and with what tools are the carvings and engravings made? 17. What colours are employed, and how are they obtained? 18. Have they special artists to draw for the whole tribe, or does each man draw his own designs? 19. Is there much difference in the degree of talent shown by men of the same tribe? 20. Is drawing more practised in some tribes of the same race than others? and if so, does this rise from inclination or traditional

custom? 21. Do they draw maps or plans? 22. Do they understand European maps? 23. Have they any notion of drawing to scale? 24. Do they improve much by practice? 25. At what age do children commence drawing? are they encouraged to draw at an early age? (A series of native drawings by children of different ages, from five or six upwards, would be interesting as a means of comparison with the development of artistic skill in Europeans.) 26. Have they any knowledge of shading? with what colours are the shadows made? and are they correctly placed?

A. L. F.

27. Do they carve bas-reliefs, or sculptures, in the round? 28. What materials are used for these sculptures—stone, wood, &c.? 29. Do they represent natural objects, such as men and animals? 30. Are they naturalistic or purely conventional? or both? and if so, why is the distinction made? 31. Are the carved figures representations of gods or ancestors? (XXVII.) of totems; (XL.) signs of taboo (XXXVII.)? 32. Are these figures kept in special houses or temples? or does each household have one or more of its own? 33. Are there any ancient carvings or statues of which the natives can give no account?

C. H. R.

No. XXIV.—ORNAMENTATION.

Nothing is more persistent than the various patterns of ornamentation in use by the different tribes and races of mankind, and nearly all have some historical continuity by means of which they can be traced in their varieties to different nations. Nearly every uncivilized nation has a pattern of its own, or some two or three patterns, which are repeated continually in all their ornamental designs with but slight variation. These may be classed under three heads:—1st, incised lines and geometrical patterns ; 2ndly, coils and scrolls and 3rdly, conventionalized representations of animal and vegetable forms applied to ornamentation. Thus the ornamentation of Australia is confined chiefly to incised lines, punch-marks, and geometrical patterns, which also prevail over the greater part of the Polynesian Islands. The continuous looped coil is much used in Assam and Cochin China, but is unknown in China, where it is replaced by lines of broken coils and frets ; and broken coil patterns constitute a prevailing feature in the ornamentation of New Guinea and New Zealand. The continuous looped coil was the principal ornament of the bronze age in Scandinavia, and is used at the present time on the west coast of Africa, where it is an exception to the prevailing geometrical ornamentation of the African continent. The continuous coil ornament developed into the wave pattern and into the fret, which is used in Europe, China, and Peru, and in a modified form is still seen in the designs from South America and Marquesas. On the other hand, certain designs of the New Irelanders may be taken as an instance of the third class of ornamentation, consisting of an infinite variety of patterns, all derived from the representation of a human face ; or that of the north-west coast of America, where patterns derived from the head and beak of the albatross monopolize the entire system of ornamentation amongst the Ahts and neighbouring tribes. In order to trace the history of the patterns, it is desirable that travellers should delineate as accurately as possible all the varieties of ornamental design amongst the races visited, especially those by which a sequence can be determined. Instances in which forms originally serving a useful purpose have survived in ornamentation are extremely common ; such as, the binding of a spear or arrow-head represented by painted spirals, representations of strings used to carry vessels, or the parts of an extinct form of weapon or tool retained in the ornamentation of those which succeeded it. These should be figured wherever they are found, and their origin shown, as they afford useful links in tracing the development of the arts.

The following are some of the principal forms of ornamentation employed by savages :—

1. Circular dots or punch-marks 

2. Elliptical punch-marks 

3. Bands 

4. Chevrons 

5. Herring-bone 

6. Parallel incised lines 

7. Cross lines or chequer 

8. Crosses 

9. St. Andrew's cross 

10. Egyptian cross 

11. Lines of triangles, which may be filled with any of the foregoing ornaments 

12. Lozenge pattern 

13. Double triangle 

14. Pentacle 

15. Fylfot 

16. Contiguous or detached circles 

17. Concentric circles 

18. Plain coil 

19. Reversed coil 

20. Loop coil 

21. Continuous loop coil 

22. Fret derived from 21 

23. Broken or branching coils derived from 21

24. Broken frets derived from 22.

25. Wave pattern derived from 21 

26. Scrolls 

27. Plait ornament or guilloche 

28. Basketwork ornaments 

29. Rope pattern or spiral 

30. Impressions produced by twisted cords or thongs 

31. Note any of the foregoing that are not known, or any that are omitted here, and give the varieties of each.

32. What combinations of colours are used? are tertiaries (citrine, russet, olive), secondaries (orange, purple, green), or only primaries (yellow, red, and blue) employed? and in what proportions? 33. Are white, black, or neutral grounds used? 34. Is colour used to assist light and shade? 35. What is

their idea of contrast, proportion, and harmony? 36. Are the details of ornamentation subordinate to the general forms and outlines? 37. Are conventionalized representations of flowers, trees, and branches employed? 38. Do the lines and curves radiate from a parent stem? 39. Are the junctions of lines and curves tangential to one another? 40. What is the effect aimed at in the ornamentation? 41. What objects are ornamented—houses, weapons, clothes, furniture, &c.? 42. Is filigree work used? 43. Is enamelling known? if so, describe the process (enamel is a vitreous substance fused *in situ*).

A. L. F.

No. XXV.—FOOD.

Articles of Food.—1. What are the substances chiefly used as food? 2. What are the principal varieties of fish, flesh, fowl, vegetables, and fruit so employed? and are they derived from wild or domesticated animals, and from wild or cultivated plants? 3. Are corn or any other cereal, bark, or other substances made into bread? 4. Is any pith so employed, or any roots, such as cassava, &c.? 5. Is milk in use, and from what animal is it obtained? 6. Are any preparations of milk employed, such as curds, butter, cheese, &c.? 7. For what class of food is there a marked preference? and are there any especial delicacies? 8. Is marrow much sought after? and how is it extracted? 9. Is blood utilized as an article of food? and how is it prepared? 10. Are any kinds of food, usually eaten elsewhere, forbidden for religious or sanitary reasons? 11. Are there any seasons during which the use of special articles of food is forbidden? and does it depend on custom, taboo, or special enactment? Are the seasons fixed or dependent on the will of the chief or the priesthood? 12. Are such restrictions due to the desire to increase the stock of such article of food, or to superstitious or sanitary causes? 13. Is the use of certain articles of food restricted to men, women, or children, or to chiefs and persons of rank?

14. Are individuals or families prevented from eating certain animals and plants for superstitious reasons, such, for instance, as their being the totems of the individuals or family? 15. Are there any storehouses for food? and are they public or private property? How are they constructed? and how protected from the ravages of animals? Are they the property of individuals, families, or villages? 16. In seasons of scarcity or famine are any unusual substances used as food, such as bark, clay, &c.? 17. When going long journeys or undergoing hard labour, is any kind of substance of a peculiarly invigorating nature eaten? 18. Are any oils used in cooking? are they expressed from vegetable or animal substances? and how are they made? 19. Are any, and what, spices in use? and are they native or imported? 20. Is salt used? and whence is it obtained? or sugar, honey, or other sweetening substance? 21. Are any whets to the appetite in use? 22. Is there any marked difference in the food of the chiefs or rich men and that of the poorer classes? 23. Is the eating of earth known? what is the nature of the earth? what effect has it on those who eat it? and what is the reason for eating it?

Mode of Cooking.—28. Are any articles of food other than milk, vegetables, and fruit used raw? and are any kinds of fish, flesh, or fowl so used? 29. Is the food preferred high or fresh? 30. Is any mode of preparation by smoking, salting, or drying in the sun employed? and if so, is the food consumed without further preparation? 31. Are roasting or broiling, baking, boiling, stewing, or frying in use? and what are the methods adopted in each? 32. In roasting or broiling, are spits or other utensils employed? 33. In baking, are the ovens simply pits in the earth, or built up? are they permanent, or constructed for the occasion? are they lined with leaves? and are hot stones placed with the food? 34. Are any vegetables cooked with the meat? 35. Are hollow trees, ant-hills, or such like used as ovens? 36. In frying, what grease or oil is preferred? 37. In boiling, is the use of hot stones known? 38. What are the forms and materials of the cooking-vessels and implements? and are they cleaned after use? 39. Are rings of clay or other material employed to keep the cooking vessels upright? 40. Are any vessels suspended over the fire? and how are they hung? 41. Are broths and stews made with vegetables? is any kind of farinaceous pudding known? 42. Is the cooking carried on in the dwelling-house or in a separate building? 43. Is it performed exclusively by men or women? and are there any ceremonies or superstitions connected with it? 44. Is the food for men and women cooked together or separately? 45. When cooks are a separate class, do they rank high or low in the community? 46. Do the natives prefer the meat slightly or well cooked? 47. What kind of rubbers or instruments are used in converting the grain into flour? 48. Is it made into bread or cakes? and how? 49. Is any leaven, yeast, or similar substance employed? 50. When poisonous plants or animals killed by poison are used as food, how are the noxious qualities extracted? 51. Is there any mode of preserving fruit or vegetables by cooking it with sugar, fermenting it, pickling, &c.? 52. Are there any traditions as to the origin of the art of cooking? 53 Are there in the country any ancient heaps of refuse or kitchen-middens, containing shells, bones, &c.? and what do they contain? 54. Do the present inhabitants form such heaps? and do they adjoin their permanent habitations? or are they at a distance, near a spot where there is a supply of food, such as shell-fish, &c.?

Manufacture of Drinks.—55. What drinks are chiefly in use? and what are their native names? 56. Is beer known? from what grain is it made? 57. Is the grain used raw or malted? if the latter, how is it turned into malt? 58. Are any ingredients employed, such as hops, to flavour the beer or make it keep? 59. Describe the mode of brewing and fermenting: how is the fermentation checked? 60. How is the beer stored? and how long will it keep? 61. What are the utensils used in making, storing, and serving out the beer? 62. Is beer-making a distinct vocation, or does each family brew for itself? 63. Is any wine made? 64. Is it prepared from the juice of fruits, the sap of trees, or any other substance? 65. How is it made and stored? and how long will it keep? 66. Are any drinks made by mixing substances with water, such as mead, kava, or chicha? 67. Are any ardent spirits known? are they of native manufacture or imported? 68. If native, from what substances are they made? and how? 69. Describe the still and other appliances. 70. Is any flavouring employed? 71. Whence was the art of distilling imported? 72. Are any infused drinks known, such as tea, coffee, or any substitute for them? 73. Are they of native growth or imported? 74. Is the substance simply infused or boiled? 75. Are any drinks known, not coming specially under any of these heads?

Meals.—76. Are meals at set times, or dependent on the accidental supply of food or individual inclination? 77. Are they common to a household or village, or does each person eat separately? 78. Does all the household eat together, or is there a distinction of ranks, sections, or ages? 79. Is there any particular sequence in the order of the dishes? 80. Are there any ceremonies used at the commencement of meals, such as offerings to the divinities, &c., or any religious rites connected with them? 81. Are there any great feasts held? and if so, on what occasions? 82. Are there any drinking-festivals, such as the kava-drinking in the South Seas? 83. Are there any attentions paid to invited guests or strangers? 84. Is the food ready cut up, or does each help himself? 85. Is there any order observed in helping the persons present or in giving drink? 86. What are the implements used at meals? and what are their native names? 87. Are there any peculiarities in the mode of eating or drinking? 88. Are men and women allowed to have their meals together? and if not together, are they allowed to have them in the room or building? 89. In times of temporary scarcity (*e.g.*, on a journey) are any means employed to deaden the pangs of hunger?

A. W. F.

No. XXVI.—CANNIBALISM.

1. Does cannibalism prevail? 2. If it no longer prevails, are there any traditions as to its once having been known? 3. Is it frequent or exceptional? 4. Are any reasons assigned for it? 5. Is it the result of a craving for animal food, or to show victory over a deceased foe, or for the purpose of acquiring part of the valour of the person eaten? 6. Are the victims generally men, women, or children? 7. Are they enemies slain in war, captives taken in war or by deceit, or slaves, or other persons selected for the purpose? 8. Are any special ceremonies observed in cannibal feasts? 9. What parts of the body are eaten, or are any parts considered delicacies? 10. What is done with the bones? 11. Are any of them used for implements or ornaments? 12. Is any religious idea connected with it? and are the victims considered sacrifices to the gods? 13. Has the cooked human flesh any name of its own, euphemistic or otherwise? 14. Is it prepared in the usual cooking-places, or are there special cooking-places set apart or constructed for the purpose? 15. Are any special vessels or implements used for cannibal feasts (Fiji)? 16. Is the use of human food confined to any class or sex? 17. Does it form part of the regular food of the people? 18. Do the natives seem ashamed to confess their cannibalism? 19. Is an individual considered unclean after joining in a cannibal feast? (*i.e.*, is there a distinction between a dead body in the ordinary sense and one intended to be eaten?)

A. W. F.

No XXVII —RELIGION, FETISHES, &c.

(See also TOTEMISM, XL.)

It is often a matter of difficulty to obain precise information as to the religion of an uncivilized people, who conceal their doctrines for fear of ridicule, and will purposely put the inquirer off the track. After long and friendly intercourse, however, a clue may generally be obtained ; and when something is known, it serves as a means of raising further questions. It is especially desirable to watch for religious ceremonies, such as prayer, sacrifice, festivals, &c., as the native religion may be more easily learnt from the explanations of these acts, than by an attempt to obtain answers to questions on abstract doctrine. It is now difficult to find any religion which has not borrowed ideas from the civilized world ; all that can be done is to ascertain, so far as possible, whether these have been introduced within the memory of the relater. Information should be obtained from as many sources as possible, so that the peculiarities of individuals should not be mistaken for the general doctrine of the nation. The accounts of missionaries are of the greatest value ; but the impartial inquirer should be careful not to be led away by their descriptions of heathen deities as "devils," and their tendency in other matters to view native religions as essentially products of imposture and wickedness, instead of representative stages of theological and moral development in the course of civilization.

There is great difficulty in determining how far religions exercise a moral influence over the ordinary lives of believers. In many religions, the moral element seems hardly to enter at all ; in others the strict performance of ceremonies seems held to atone for selfish and wicked lives ; a fair way of classing religions as high and low is according to how far they inculcate morals, promise divine favour to the just and good, and threaten divine punishment against evildoers. The influence of each religion on morals in every nation demands careful and unprejudiced observation.

Souls.—1. Is something of the nature of a human soul believed in? 2. What is its name? is it associated with the breath, shadow, &c.? 3. Does it depart when the body dies? 4. Does it go away from the body in sleep, trance, &c.? 5. Are any ceremonies performed to bring back the soul when the patient is sick or dying from its absence? 6. What is the soul considered to be? what is its form, substance, voice, power, &c.? 7. Is there more than one kind of soul; has an individual several souls? 8. Are souls ever driven away by beating, &c., shut up, let out at holes, &c.? 9. Can souls appear in more than one shape? 10. How are all the phenomena of dreams and visions accounted for? 11. Is there any belief in wraiths, *i.e.*, apparitions of men seen at a distance at the time of their death?

12. Are the lower animals considered to have souls? and are these of the same nature as human souls? 13. Are animals treated and talked to as if human? 14. Does any idea prevail of animals having human or even superhuman intelligence? 15. Are animals sacrificed at funerals? and if so, is there a notion of their souls being transported, with their master's, to the world after death? 16. Are plants considered to have life and consciousness like animals? 17. Have plants souls? 18. Is there any notion that objects, such as food, clothes, weapons, &c., have anything of the nature of souls belonging to them, or phantoms separable from them, which continue to exist after the natural object is destroyed? 19. What are the images of objects supposed to be which are seen in dreams, such as clothes, weapons, &c.? 20. Are any funeral offerings given, that the souls of the dead may in any way become possessed of the objects or their phantoms? 21. Do the native notions of souls seem genuine, or have they adopted civilized ideas?

22. What becomes of the soul after death? 23. Do some souls survive after death, but others perish? 24. Can a surviving soul die a second death or be destroyed? 25. What reason do the people give for believing that the soul does not

perish with the body? 26. Do they think that the souls of the dead visit the living? 27. When the figures of the dead are seem in dreams or as apparitions, are these souls? 28. Can only one person in a company see them, or all? 29. Are survivors in fear of ghosts of the dead? and do they take any means to get rid of them or keep them off?

30. Do ghosts of the dead haunt houses or burial-places? 31. Does it matter whether the body was properly buried or not? 32. Is food set out for the souls of the dead? 33. Are there annual feasts in honour of the dead? 34. If so, are the souls considered to consume the food? and how, materially or spiritually?

Future Life.—35. Is there any doctrine of transmigration of souls? 36. Are the souls of the dead supposed to be re-born in children? 37. Do men live successive lives in different human bodies? 38. Do souls transmigrate into animals, vegetables, inert bodies? 39. Is there moral reward or punishment in such transmigration, the good man going up and the bad man down in the scale of existence? 40. If transmigration is believed in, what do the people give as their reason for belief in it? 41. Is there a special locality where the souls of the dead live in the future life? 42. Are there stories of men going thither and returning to give an account of it? 43. Is it a material or phantasmal region? 44. Is there any particular road or starting-place where the souls set off? 45. Is any connection to be noticed between the West or Sunset and the Land of the Dead? any myth of a divine personage (such as Odysseus) descending into Hades and returning, like the Sun? 46. Is the Land of the Dead in some distant country, mountain, or island? has any water to be crossed? and how, by boat, or bridge, or swimming? 47. Is there an under-world or Hades? is it a cavernous region, gloomy, or fiery? 48. Are volcanoes the mouths communicating with it? 49. Is there a heavenly region of the dead in or above the sky?

50. What is the fate of souls after death? 51. Is life in the next world much like this, with land, houses, and occupations? 52. Is it looked forward to as dismal or beautiful? 53. Is there a difference in men's conditions in the next life?

54. If so, what determines a man's happiness or misery? do nobles fare better than plebeians? have warriors a glorious life? what becomes of those who die by violence? 55. Is there a moral retribution? *i.e.*, are good men happy and bad men unhappy after death? 56. If so, what qualities of virtue and vice constitute a good or bad man—*e.g.*, bravery, hospitality, fidelity, chastity, temperance, kindness, &c., and their opposites? 57. Do the priests claim authority as to the fate of men, and require sacrifices, gifts, austerities, &c. to secure future welfare? 58. Is there a tribunal or judge to decide on the fate of the soul? 59. Is there a special place of punishment? 60. Is this of the nature of a purgatory? and are souls, when purified from sin, transmitted to a happy region? 61. Does the expectation of the future life affect men's conduct in the present? and how? 62. How far do these notions of the future life seem original and genuine? and how far do they look as though adopted from foreign religions?

Manes-worship.—63. Are the souls of the dead, especially of ancestors, looked on as demons or divinities? 63*a.* Are figures of ancestors carved and placed in the houses, or at the tombs, or carried on the person, for the purpose of worship? or are their skulls preserved for this purpose? 64. Are they worshipped with prayer, sacrifice, &c.? 65. Is there any recognized means of communicating with them? and is this done by any one, or specially by priests, &c.? 66. Are the divine manes of a kindly or unkindly disposition? do they treat all men alike, or favour their kinsfolk and worshippers, and do ill to others? 67. Are they looked on as causing the good and ill fortune of the living? 68. Do they act, fight, give counsel, &c., among men, or influence events in some spiritual way? 69. Are they the principal gods of the nation? 70. Is the primitive ancestor of the tribe worshipped under the form of, or in connection with, some sacred animal or other object, as a totem or clan-deity?

Obsession and Possession.—71. Are some or all diseases regarded as caused by demons? 72. Do they enter into the patient or afflict him from without? 73. Are fever, delirium, trance, hysteria, epilepsy, mania, or other diseases specially ascribed to demoniacal influence? 74. Are nightmares considered real spirits? 75. Are erotic dreams caused by visits of demons (incubi and succubi), who have sexual connection with women and men in their sleep? 76. Are there stories of women thus becoming pregnant? 77. Are there vampires or such spirits who suck their victim's blood in sleep, and cause them to waste away and die? 78. Is exorcism practised as a cure? and who are the exorcists, priests, sorcerers, or doctors? 79. What are the processes of exorcising spirits from patients? 80. Can disease-spirits be conjured into objects or animals, and the patient be so released? 81. Is the possessing spirit considered to speak through the patient's voice or by "ventriloquism"? 82. Does the intruding spirit give its name? 83. Are hysterical and epileptic fits, &c., encouraged or artificially brought on to obtain oracles from deities through possessed mediums? 84. Are patients of morbid constitutions selected as mediums, prophets, or oracle-priests?

Spiritualism.—85. Are other proceedings, of the nature of those carried on by modern "spiritualists," known in the nation? 86. Are the souls of the dead summoned to be conversed with? 87. Are *séances* or assemblies held for the purpose? and if so, in light or darkness? 88. Are there persons who act as "mediums"? 89. Are the spirits said to appear visibly, to speak, move objects, &c.? 90. How do they answer questions! 91. Are rappings and other mysterious noises and actions reported? 92. Do mediums rise in the air? 93. Are they supernaturally loosed from bonds?

Fetishism.—94. Do spirits or deities enter into or attach themselves to objects, such as sticks, bones, ornaments, &c.? 95. Are such objects of supernatural power? and are they kept sacred or carried as vehicles of spiritual influence? 96. What sort of spirits can be conjured into such objects? and by whom, and how? 97. Are relics of the dead, as bones, mummies, &c., so inhabited by their former souls? 98. Can ghosts be "laid" in objects? 99. Do possessed objects move, dance about, give oracular answers, &c. 100. Are objects inspired or inhabited by gods worshipped? 101. Are blocks of wood stones, &c., considered such habitations of deity and worshipped? 102. Are they prayed to? sacrificed to? have they temples and priests?

Idolatry.—103. Are images made to represent demons, and deities? 104. Do they receive worship by prayer and sacrifice? 105. Have they temples and priests? 106. Do they consume food, give oracular answers, speak, nod, wink, bleed, walk about, and act otherwise? and how do they do this? 107. Are idols mere representations of spiritual beings? 108. Are the images treated well, or beaten and abused, according to their supposed behaviour to their worshippers? 109. Is there difference of opinion among priests and worshippers as to the nature of the idol, whether it is to be adored as a symbol only of the deity, or as itself divine?

Spirits and Demons.—110. Is the world full of spiritual beings? 111. Are some good and some evil? 112. Does this mean that they are kind to friends and hostile to enemies? 113. Have some men, and not others, the gift of seeing spirits? 114. Do animals see them when men do not? 115. Are persons often troubled by apparitions of demons? 116. Do they come especially in the dark? and is fire or light a means of driving them away? 117. Are they driven away from houses or villages by priests or with ceremonies? and is there a periodical ceremony? 118. Have any persons familiar spirits? and what do they do for them? 119. Have some or all men guardian-spirits who attend them? 120. Is each man specially attended by a good or evil spirit? 120*a*. Are disease and death thought to be caused by spirits?

Nature-Spirits. Worship of Plants and Animals.—121. Are there spirits especially attached to natural objects? 122. Are there spirits of mountains, rocks, &c.; are there spirits of pools, wells, springs and streams, rapids and cataracts, &c.? 123. Do they drown men? 124. Are offerings given to them? 125. Are there spirits of trees? if so, are they like souls of the trees, or spirits who dwell in them? 126. Are groves and woods favourite places of worship or sacrifice? if so, is the worship given to tree-spirits or to deities who inhabit the forest? 127. Are there special spirits of each tree, each wood, each kind of tree, or a god of the forest? 127*a*. Are any offerings placed beneath trees? 128. Are any beasts worshipped? 129. If so, are they creatures actually dangerous or powerful, as tigers or elephants, or many sorts of reptiles, birds, and beasts? Are sacred animals incarnations of a deity, or under its protection? 130. Is it unlawful to eat them? and to whom? 131. Are there tribes named after particular animals? 132. Is such an animal considered to represent the ancestor, totem, or patron deity of the tribe? 133. Are individuals of the tribe known by its name as a clan-name or totem? 134. Has each species of animals a patron deity. (TOTEMISM, No. XL.)

Polytheism and Monotheism.—135. What are the gods worshipped? are any of them distinctly the great powers of nature? 136. Is there a heaven-god? if so, is he the sky itself, or a being dwelling in or above it? or does he partake of both characters? 137. Is there a rain-god? 138. Is there a thunder-god? 138*a*. Are thunder and lightning considered the same or separate deities? 139. Are the winds considered deities, independent, or controlled by a wind-god. 140. Is there an earth-god? 141. Are there great river-gods, a sea-god, a water-god, or gods representing celestial bodies? 142 A fire-god? 143. What special ceremonies are performed for these gods, such as turning to the east in sun-worship, worshipping the moon at new and full, &c.? 144. What other great deities are known? are their special deities concerned with agriculture, war, &c.? is a divine ancestor of Man a god of the dead? 145. Are there other deities of importance, whose natures are other than those mentioned, or whose character and functions are of a mixed kind, not easily accounted for? 146. Do any deities seem borrowed, in name or character, from the religions of other nations! 146*a*. Are the gods of other nations recognized as being real and powerful? 147. Are there two hostile deities, one good and the other evil? 148. If so, what other functions have they? and is either of them one of the previously mentioned deities, heaven, sun, &c.? 149. Is there a Creator of all things? 150. Is any one of these deities the supreme deity above all others? 151. Is there a supreme deity distinct from all other gods? and is his nature that of a soul or spirit of the universe? 152. Is he active in the world and the affairs of men? or does he remain unmoved, seldom or never interfering, and leaving the conduct of the universe to deities of lower order? 153. Is the divine government of the universe regarded as having any moral element? are deities believed to reward good and punish evil? do they favour only certain individual nations or their own worshippers?

Worship. Priests and Temples.—154. Are particular persons set apart as priests? 155. Are they chosen as children and specially educated? 156. Are they at the same time sorcerers? 157. Are they spirit-mediums, giving oracles in trances, &c.? 157*a*. Are they epileptic or otherwise nervous persons? 158. Do they instruct youth? 159. Have they political influence? 160. Is the same person often both priest and chief? 161. Do they appear sincere in their beliefs, or imposters? 162. Do they practise austerities, observe chastity, &c.? 163. Are there several orders of priests? 164. Are there priests and priestesses? and what are the social conditions of the latter? 165. Is any special building set apart for worship? Is it built in a particular position, as facing the east, &c. 166. Is the deity supposed to reside there or to come thither? 167. Are idols kept there? 168. What rites are performed in the temple? 169. Are all the rites public? or are any of the nature of mysteries or orgies? 170. Are mysterious objects kept in the sanctuary and miracles performed there? 171. Is the temple kept inviolate and only accessible to persons in a state of ceremonial purity? 172. Is it respected in time of war?

Festivals.—173. What festivals of a religious character are performed? 174. What do they consist in—processions, games, dances, banquets, &c.? 175. Which are at regular periods, and which occasional? 176. Are there annual religious festivals marking the months, seasons, equinoxes, solstices, seed-time, first-fruits, harvest, &c. 177. Is there an annual feast of the dead? 178. Are festivals held in honour of particular gods? 179. Are festivals performed by particular families, classes, or castes? 180. Are these festivals with relation to war, victory, or such events? 181. Are there festivals at the puberty of the young men and girls or their initiation into the duties of life? 182. Do families celebrate private festivals of a religious kind, as at birth of a child, manhood, marriage, &c.? 183. Do the priests take part in such festivals? are sacrifices offered, &c.? 184. Are there festivals at which marriageable youths and girls mix and matches are made? 185. Are any festivals specially connected with sexual relations? if so, what are the social consequences? 186. Do any festivals commemorate mythical or historical events with significant ceremonies, &c.? 187. Are any at once political and religious? do they afford means of moral teaching? (INITIATORY CEREMONIES No. XXXIX.).

Prayer.—188. Are formal prayers offered to souls of ancestors or other divine spirits? and in what terms? 189. Is prayer offered by private persons, chiefs, or priests? 190. Is prayer a private or public ceremony, offered in the house, temple, or elsewhere? 191. Is prayer solemnly made in times of emergency or distress? 192. Are only temporal benefits asked for, as aid against enemies, safety, abundance of food, children, &c.? 193. Are the gods asked to promote virtue or goodness in the worshipper or others?

Sacrifice.—194. Is sacrifice offered? and to what deities? 195. Is it a private or public act? 196. May anyone, or only priests, sacrifice? 197. Is sacrifice made in temples? What is offered? 198. Is an altar used and the offering placed on it? 199. Does the offering consist principally of food? 200. Is it exposed, destroyed, or consumed? 201. Is the deity considered to consume it or to become possessed of it? and how? 202. Is it fraudulently removed under the pretence of the deity having taken it? 203. Does the deity consume the essence or spirit of it, leaving the material part? if so, what becomes of this? do the priests or worshippers consume or remove it? 204. Is incense used? and with what motive? 205. Do people sacrifice objects that the deity may be pleased to obtain them?

or is there a notion that there is merit in the worshipper giving them up? 206. Are human sacrifices made? if so, are the victims captives or slaves, or the sacrificer's own children, or who? 207. Are the bodies burned or exposed or eaten? 208. Are the souls of the victims considered to go to the deity? 209. Are substitutes in sacrifice used, such as part of an animal, an effigy, or imitation? 210. Do worshippers sacrifice parts of themselves, such as hair, tips of fingers, drops of blood, &c.? 211. Are oblations and libations usual at meals? and to whom? (FOOD No. XXV.).

Austerities.—212. Do priests, devotees, or the whole nation perform religious austerities, such as fasting, flagellation, exposure, &c.? 213. What are the motives? Are spiritual communications ever obtained by dreams, visions, &c. 214. Does the suffering of the worshipper give pleasure to the deity? 215. Is it a self-imposed punishment for offences? 216. Are austere devotees considered holy? and are they respected and supported by the people? 217. Is public penance and mortification done on any solemn occasion? 218. Can the divine anger be thus averted?

Purification.—219. Are ceremonial purifications practised? 220. Are any persons at any time impure or unclean, and requiring purification, as after child-birth, during menstruation, after bloodshed or funeral, &c.? 221. Do they purify themselves, or is it the priest's office? 222. What is used for lustration—water, urine, herbs, fire, smoke? 223. Does any kind of baptism exist? how soon after birth, and connected or not with the naming? 224. Is there an understood distinction between physical, ceremonial, and moral purification? 225. Are disease, ill-fortune, contamination by contact with the dead, violation of religious ordinances, and moral wickedness capable of being removed by purification? 226. Is the cleaning of the household and lighting of new fire a part of the purification? 227. Is unchastity, &c., connected with ceremonial impurity? and how is it atoned? 228. Are the same words used to denote bodily cleanness and moral purity?

Special and Miscellaneous Ceremonies, &c.—229. Are there other religious ceremonies connected with birth, marriage, burial, &c.? 230. Is new fire made on special occasions? and by whom and how? 231. Is it customary to turn to the east or west, to sleep in this direction, or to bury corpses so? 232. Are religious dances, pantomimes, processions in masks or disguise, &c., in use? 233. Are games practised with a religious significance? 234. Is the installation of a chief or king a religious act? 235. Is any religious ceremony used in treaties or alliances?

E. B. T.

No. XXVIII.—MYTHOLOGY.

The collection of mythic stories among the lower races may be conveniently carried on with a view to several points of interest. It is desirable to take them down verbatim from the lips of a skilled storyteller, as they thus form specimens of the language in its best form, exhibiting native metaphor, wit, and picturesque diction. They should be copied out with an exact translation between the lines or on the same page. As to the subject-matter of mythic legends, they contain the ideas of the people on religious subjects, names of gods, &c., often in more original and exact forms than those used in common conversation. Real traditions of historical events and names often appear in them, and mentions of old arts, customs, and states of society, which are historical material of high quality; incidental remarks in them show the moral and social state of the people, often with curious contrasts between old times and new. The episodes, jests, &c., in mythic legends should be particularly noticed when they correspond to those known in the legends or folk-lore of other races, for such evidence throws light on the connection or intercourse in former times between the two races. For this end it is especially desirable to separate all matter which might have been borrowed from the religious and other traditions of the Christians, Moslems, Buddhists, &c., so as to leave the native mythology as pure and genuine as possible. It would thus be a serious mistake to suppose the mythology of the lower races of little scientific value. Few studies throw more light on the early history of the human race and the human mind.

1. Are mythic legends, fairy tales, &c., told habitually? and is any special class of priests, bards, &c., concerned especially in preserving them? 2. How far are they seriously believed and stand in the place of history and religious teaching? and how far are they told as nursery tales and popular jests, for mere amusement? 3. Are the personages who figure in them considered to be real and historical? and are there other traces of such heroes, chiefs, &c., having really lived?

4. What stories come under the heading of nature-myths, being told of the sun, moon, stars, rivers, &c., as personal beings? 5. Do any of the heroes or heroines bear names which suggest such origin? or do their feats seem to be suggested by natural phenomena? 6. Are there, for example, myths relating to the sun, his birth, course, and death; day and night; eclipses; the changes of the moon? are stars and constellations imagined to be living beings? are there stories of rainbows, thunder and lightning, winds, whirlpools, rivers, volcanos, &c., as being animated beings? 7. Are there any native riddles in connexion with such subjects?

8. Are stories which seem myths told to account for events, such as peculiar customs, the invention of arts, the prevalence of certain plants or animals, &c.? in short, are fanciful tales told to account for all sorts of things in nature and life? 9. Are there eponymic heroes, *i.e.*, names of a mythic chief or ancestor, devised to account for the names of tribes, like Danaos as the ancestor of the Danaoi or Greeks, or Albion of our own countrymen? 10. Are stories told to explain etymologically the names of places or objects? 11. Are there geological myths accounting for large fossil bones, as relics of giants, or for shells on mountains by legends of a deluge, or other philosophical myths of this class? 12. Are there stories of men being descended or developed from apes or apes from men, of transformation of men into animals, of monstrous tribes of men, one-eyed, great-eared, tailed, giants and dwarfs, &c.? 13. If so, is there reason to suppose these

stories told metaphorically or exaggeratively of real tribes of men? 14. Are beast-fables told, *i.e.*, stories of talking birds and beasts, and their adventures? 15. Are any stories, allegories, or parables, told in order to teach some moral lesson?

16. Do any of the native stories contain episodes which seem as though they might have been learnt from modern Europeans, *e.g.*, mentions of guns or of writing, stories of devils with horns, fragments of Æsop's fables, or other European notions, familiar Scripture stories, &c.? 17. Are there any similar touches which betray contact with Mohammedans or Buddhists? 18. Apart from these, are stories current which have a resemblance to well-known classical or folk-lore mythology, but may have a distinct or independent origin? 19. Are there episodes which resemble 'Jack and the Beanstalk,' 'Red Riding Hood,' &c.? 20. Are there traditions of a river of death, a bridge across the sky where souls pass, a universal deluge? 21. Is there any legend current of the origin of Man, the introduction of language, houses, war, civilization? 22. Are the gods of old time related to have come on earth and had dealings with mankind? 23. Do the legends of the people go back to a golden age or divine-human period, when wonders happened which have now ceased, and when the ancestors of men had knowledge, powers and happiness now lost?

E. B. T.

No. XXIX.—SUPERSTITIONS.

Superstitions are customs and beliefs of an absurd or harmful kind. They often belong to the class of "survivals," being old-fashioned habits and ideas retained after their original sense has vanished. But, especially among the lower races, they to a great extent still carry their original meaning and purpose, which may be ascertained best from the old people. When thoroughly analyzed, they can be referred to their proper heading, such as Magic, Religion, Custom (Nos. XXX.,

XXVII., XXXV.) : but it is convenient to keep Superstition as an open class for the collection of a number of obscure and puzzling usages.

1. Do any superstitions prevail as to touching fire, drinking water, handling particular objects, &c.? 2. Any ideas of lucky and unlucky objects and acts? 3. Prejudices connected with sneezing, yawning, spitting, whistling, talking, and any other actions? 4. Any curious fancies as to animals? 5. Are animals treated as rational, and talked to? 6. Are exaggerated stories told of their sagacity and habits? 7. Are special places considered lucky or unlucky, and visited or avoided? 8. Are houses or villages ever abandoned or destroyed on account of sickness, death, or other cause? 9. Are there any peculiar ideas as to east and west, north and south? 10. Any remarkable notions as to sun, moon, and stars? 11. Are storms, thunder and lightning, or darkness the subject of any special prejudices? 12. Is there any objection to crossing water, going by particular paths, &c.? 13. Any peculiar customs as to cutting hair and nails, leaving articles of clothing about, &c. 14. Any superstitions about human excreta or urine? 15. Any superstitious usages as to birth and naming of children, period of manhood and womanhood, marriage, divorce, sickness, death, and burial? 16. Any other superstitions not included in these classes? 17. Are dreams regarded? Do they give information of the past, and prophecy or omens for the future? 18. How are dreams interpreted? are they direct visits or communications from spirits? are their scenes taken symbolically—as when to dream of a knife or blood is an omen of war? do they ever go by contraries? 19. Are dreams sought by fasting, narcotics, &c.? 20. Are the words of men in a state of ecstasy specially regarded? or the talk of madmen and children, words accidentally heard, &c.? Are omens taken from such words? 21. Are there any reported cases of second sight? 22. Are cries of animals and birds taken as omens, by way of augury? 23. Is meeting a particular animal ominous? 24. Are omens taken from accidents, such as stumbling, &c.?

E. B. T.

No. XXX.—MAGIC AND WITCHCRAFT.

Magic includes the results of two principles. On the one hand it may seek the aid of spiritual beings, in which case its theory forms part of that of religion; on the other hand it deals in sympathetic and symbolic hurts and cures, discoveries and communications, supposed to take place by the way of cause and effect, so that it is here a misdevelopment of natural philosophy. In all cases it is desirable to describe not only the magical method used, but its supposed motive and action.

1. Are magic arts held lawful or unlawful? or is there both a "black magic" and a "white magic"? 2. Are they practised among the people at large? or is the craft set apart to special sorcerers, witches, &c.; 3. Are these priests, or connected with religion? or is there jealousy or hostility between the priest and the sorcerer? 4. What manner of people are the magicians? what lives do they lead? do they follow useful occupations, as rude herbalists or surgeons, &c.? 5. Are they largely rewarded, applied to in times of calamity? and is it usual for the mob to fall on them in times of misfortune, so that they seldom die a natural death?

6. Are spirits or demons called on to give oracles, disclose secrets, do good or harm? 7. Are they propitiated or influenced by sacrifices, prayers, charms, symbolic rites, &c.? 8. Have magicians the aid of familiar spirits? 9. Do they associate these with particular objects or fetishes, such as images, pictures, odd stones, or bits of wood, claws, seeds, and other things? 10. Are objects regarded as possessed or influenced by spirits to give magical omens, discover thieves, &c.? 11. Are drums, rattles, &c., used in such incantations? 12. Are particular songs or charms connected with these rites known?

13. Is the effect of the evil eye believed in? Is cursing or ill-wishing dreaded as a practical means of doing harm? 14. How are these supposed to act on the victim? 15. Is he allowed to know of the curse? and does he actually fulfil it

by dying of fear? 16. Is it usual for the sorcerer to operate through objects belonging to the victim or intimately connected with him, such as his cut hair or nails, morsels of his food or clothing or property, so that he may be harmed by what is done to these objects when they are burned, &c.? 17. Are names considered to give a hold to the sorcerer? and are the real names of people ever concealed from fear of this? 18. Is any object hung up or placed in the path of the victim to "take his soul away," *i.e.*, kill him?

19. Are symbolic arts of magic common? Are pictures or figures practised upon to produce an effect on the objects they represent, as when an image is wounded in order to act likewise on the person it stands for? 20. Are dice, lots, sticks, &c., thrown that they may indicate by their fall or position an answer to the question? 21. Are there any other mechanical divining instruments, as swinging-rings, &c.? 22. Are death-charms or love-charms made with symbolic objects, such as a dead man's bone to produce death, knots to fasten love, &c.? 23. Is the idea of curing a wound by salving the weapon, &c., known?

24. Is haruspication or examination of entrails used? 25. Are the stars noticed as giving prophetic information? 26. Are there any distinct rules of astrology?

E. B. T.

No. XXXI.—CRIMES.

Even the rudest communities have something approaching an unwritten criminal code. The administration of justice readily conforms itself to system, and unconsciously crime and punishment fall into relation with each other. Inquiry will be made under this head as to what acts are regarded as criminal—(α) against person, (β) against property, (γ) against the state, (δ) against religion; and the reasons why they are so regarded. The procedure in the administration of justice and the punishments inflicted, come under No. XXXIV.

(α) 1. *Homicide.* Whether considered criminal at all? under what circumstances excusable? 2. *Suicide.* Whether considered criminal or praiseworthy? 3. *Maiming.* 4. *Rape.* 5. *Abduction.* 6. *Seduction.* 7. *Abuse of children.* 8. *Assault.* 9. *Adultery.* Are all these offences which may be revenged by the party injured? or must he appeal to the chief or others for redress? or are they or any of them looked upon as mere venial offences? 10. *Unnatural offences.* Does any sense of criminality attach to these? Under each head of crime, inquire as to the extent to which it prevails.

(β) 11. *Arson.* 12. *Trespass.* 13. *Theft.* 14. *Fraud.* Are these recognized as offences against the community, or only against the person injured?

(γ) 15. The *crimen læsæ majestatis*, including treason, rebellion, and all offences against the chief of the state. Are his dignity and person protected by any special sanction?

(δ) 16. Offences against the persons of priests or the ceremonies of religion. 17. Dissent from the prevailing religion. 18. Are either or both of these esteemed criminal? and in what degree? 19. Does there exist a criminal class? 20. Does Thuggism prevail, or any organized system of crime? if so, give statistics.

E. W. B.

No. XXXII.—MORALS.

The imperfection of our accounts of morals among savage and barbarous peoples is in a great measure due to travellers supposing the particular system of morals in which they themselves were educated to be the absolute system; thus they have merely approved or condemned what corresponded with, or opposed their own notions, but have scarcely ever appreciated the fact that every tribe has its own system of morality, based on its own principles of right and wrong. It is necessary to place ourselves at the point of view of the particular tribe, to understand its moral scheme. The leading ideas to be borne in mind are especially the following:—That every tribe makes a distinction between right and wrong, but hardly two tribes exactly agree on what acts are right and what wrong; in fact, there is hardly any act considered wicked and abominable by some men, that is not somewhere or other looked on as harmless or virtuous, *e.g.*, infanticide, treachery, &c. Next, that in all peoples, civilized or not, there exists an ideal high standard of morals, while public opinion tolerates or approves a lower practical standard: it is desirable to obtain a definition of both. Also the moral standard varies from age to age, as our own has changed in the last thousand years; all records of such variations are important. Lastly, the moral standard differs, as between members of a family, members of a nation, or tribe, or alliance, and aliens and enemies; among many nations it may be held right and even glorious to cheat, plunder, illuse, or even murder a stranger, or foreigner, or one of another religion, but wrong to act thus towards a kinsman, fellow-citizen, or co-religionist.

1. What words are used to express right and wrong virtuous and vicious? 2. Do terms such as good and bad also denote this distinction when a man is described as good or bad? what characters correspond to this description? 3. Are there well-known precepts as to what acts are right or wrong? are these taught to children, or inculcated in any ceremonial act by elders or priests? 4. Do popular legends, &c., set up heroic ideals of virtue? 5. What is the practical judgment of public opinion as to what conduct is admirable and glorious? what is required of every man on pain of public disapprobation? and what conduct is held wicked, vile, despicable? 6. What distinction is drawn between punishable crimes and wrong acts only to be visited by public reprobation? 7. What acts of oppression or cruelty may be done by the father in his family or the chief in his tribe, without its being any one's place to condemn him? 8. What acts are considered wrong when done against a tribesman,

but right when done against an alien (*e.g.*, theft, deceit, &c.)? 9. Is any moral code ascribed to an ancient lawgiver, hero, or deity? 10. Is religious influence brought to bear on moral conduct? are gods or spirits considered to punish certain acts by afflicting the doer or his family? 11. Is any moral or immoral conduct considered to affect the state of a man's soul during life or after death?

12. Is it wrong to do harm to the person or property of a non-tribesman or member of a hostile tribe? are there exceptional cases? 13. Is wanton ill-treatment of wives, children, and slaves wrong? and who may protest? 14. Is hospitality inculcated toward tribesmen or all men? is it wicked to refuse it and mean to stint it? 15. Is giving away or sharing of food and other property a duty or a virtuous act? what is the notion of liberality and generosity? 16. Is covetousness condemned? and is the accumulation of property regarded as an avaricious act? 17. Is it wrong to steal from one's friends and tribesmen? 18. Is it wrong to rob strangers? 19. Is cheating approved or condemned? and what difference does it make whether the person cheated is a friend or stranger? 20. Is lying wrong in itself, or under particular circumstances? 21. Is the breaking of solemn engagements or oaths condemned? and what is the usual judgment as to treachery? 22. Is abstemiousness in eating, and temperance in, or abstinence from, use of intoxicating drink approved? 23. Are gluttony, laziness, dirtiness, gossipping, tale-bearing, &c., condemned? 24. Is reverence to the aged a duty or virtue? and is its neglect condemned?

25. Is general courtesy and kindness inculcated and rudeness condemned? 26. What are the rules of right and wrong as to unchastity in either sex before marriage? 27. After marriage, are acts of unchastity offences which public opinion takes account of as wrong? 28. Is adultery a personal injury, or an offence against morals, or both? 29. How does public opinion judge of unnatural crimes? 30. Is selfishness considered a vice? 31. How is cowardice judged of? 32. Are bravery, ferocity, tenacity of revenge, endurance of pain and hardship, and other warlike qualities looked on as the chief

virtues? 33. How are such warlike virtues accounted of in comparison with the milder virtues of kindness, generosity, &c.? 34. Can offences against public feeling be atoned for by courageous acts?

E. B. T.

No. XXXIII.—COVENANTS, OATHS, ORDEALS.

Solemn covenants are made by all nations; oaths and ordeals are rare among the lower tribes, and worthy of careful study when they occur. The question of principle usually involved in them is this, whether a personal spirit or deity is called on to witness the covenant or decide the truth, punishing the offender, or whether the operation is merely symbolical. The ceremonies and formulas used should therefore be carefully described.

1. What forms of covenant are used, as in settling tribe-rights, making peace, &c.? 2. Do they appeal to any personal being, as to Heaven or Sun, to punish breach of faith? 3. Is anything of the nature of an oath taken by an accuser, witness, &c.? 4. If so, is it accompanied by any symbolic form, such as swearing on a bear's head or sitting over a pit, with the idea that the breaker of covenant will be killed by a bear or fall into a pit? 5. Is the blood of the parties mixed as a sign of covenant, each party drinking it? 6. Is eating and drinking together of any particular food a form of covenant? and does it confirm friendship? 7. How is this supposed to act? is a deity considered to execute the punishment, or does it come by a magical connexion? 8. Does any thing of the nature of an oath enter into the marriage ceremony? 9. Do sorcerers or priests superintend covenants or oaths? and is their breaking looked on as a civil or a religious offence?

10. Are any ordeals in use, such as plunging into water,

passing through fire, drinking poison, &c.? 11. May they be done by deputy? 12. Are they religious acts, as may be known by their depending for their efficacy on deities and being administered by priests? 13. Is the truth ascertained by this means when the accused denies or there is conflict of testimony? 14. Does the ordeal act symbolically, as when a weapon is touched with the idea that such a weapon will slay the guilty? 15. Does it act directly, as when food is taken into the mouth, with the idea that it will choke the guilty? 16. Are ordeals fraudulently used by chiefs and priests, so as to save their friends and ruin their enemies?

E. B. T.

No. XXXIV.—LAWS.

α. *Land.*—1. Are there any territorial divisions? 2. Does the whole of the land belong to the chiefs? 3. Is there a separate class of landowners? 4. Whence are titles to land derived? 5. Is there any means of conveyance? 6. May females hold land? 7. May infants? 8. What remedy is there for encroachments on rights of property? 8*a*. Are any stones or posts placed to mark a boundary? 8*b*. Is it an offence against the community to move one of these? or is the individual only injured?

β. *Game.*—9. Is it preserved? 10. Are rights in it restricted to privileged classes? 11. How are those rights maintained? 12. What is the punishment for infringing them? (See XLVIII.)

γ. *Inheritance.* (see XXXVI.)—13. To how much of the property and rights of the father do eldest sons succeed? 14. To how much are youngest sons entitled? 14*a*. Is the youngest child entitled, as such, to any property? 15. Have daughters any right of inheritance? 16. Is there any testamentary power? 17. Generally how far and in what degrees are relationships traced, and the devolution of property or rights of jurisdiction ascertained. Specially enquire as to right of inheritance in mother's brother, or other laws ignoring succession through the father.

δ. *Administration of Justice.*—18. Are courts held for the trial of offenders? 19. Are there any officers appointed for the purpose of administering justice? 20. Is there any recognized principle of procedure? 21. Must the accused be present? 22. Is he subjected to torture? 23. Must a confession be obtained before conviction? 24. Is there any ceremony analogous to the taking an oath by witnesses? 25. How is perjury dealt with? 25*a.* Is the evidence of all classes held to be of equal value? 25*b.* Do secret societies exist whose office it is to punish crime? and are they independent of the more regular tribunals?

ε. *Punishments.*—26. By what authority inflicted? 27. By what means executed? 28. Death: for what crimes? how suffered? 29. Is taliation ("an eye for an eye, and a tooth for a tooth") acted upon? 30. Mutilation: for what crimes? and how inflicted? 31. Flogging. 32. Mulcts or penalties: for what offences? how recovered? to whose benefit applied? 33. Imprisonment: how enforced? for what periods? with what consequences? 34. Other punishments, if any? 35. Is private revenge permitted? 36. Generally, is justice administered with severity or with clemency, with caprice or with regularity? are the laws respected? are they undergoing improvement? and what is their influence on the character of the people?

37. Can the prisoner appeal to another court for mitigation of sentence? (*e.g.*, from the sentence of a chief to a priest).

E. W. B.

No. XXXV.—CUSTOMS.

The distinction between a law and an authoritative custom may be best drawn with reference to the manner in which society compels obedience to it. If a judge or tribunal declares the rule, and punishes its infraction, it is a law; if it is left loosely to public opinion to practically accept the rule, and to with those who disobey with blame, insult, and social exclusion, it is a custom. Many customs are mere habits without authority. Many exist whose original meaning is hardly known or doubtful. All customs should be recorded, and, not least carefully, the obscure ones, in the expectation that close examination and comparison with those of other districts will disclose their real meaning. The ethnological principle is daily growing more certain, that all customs soever had originally a real and rational meaning; they may have now lost or altered this by passing into "survivals," but when analogous examples have been collected from several districts, it is usually possible to trace the common cause to which all were originally due.

1. What customs prevail as to salutation, by bowing, prostration, touching and shaking hands, kissing, rubbing noses, &c.? 2. Do salutations differ according to rank and relationship? 3. Do members of a family greet in the morning? do husbands greet wives, &c.? 4. How do friends and relations meet after long absence or danger--with shouting, weeping, &c.? 5. What are the forms of meeting between strangers and enemies in truce? 6. What are the rules of politeness in the household and between strangers? 7. Are there special phrases of compliment? what rules of precedence? 8. How are guests served? 9. What are the rules of right conduct and politeness between men and women? 10. Do they eat together and associate? 11. Are women consulted and honoured, or treated roughly and contemptuously? 12. How are the aged treated? 13. Are they honoured and cherished, or neglected? 14. Are the hopelessly infirm old people and the mortally sick abandoned or put an end to?

15. What are the rules of hospitality as recognized between kinsfolk, neighbours, strangers, and enemies? 16. What are the rules of propriety? 17. Are the young reproved for being forward and impudent? 18. Is respectful demeanour inculcated? 19. What are the rules of decency? what acts and

exposures are considered indecent? 20. Is coarse conversation disapproved of between the sexes or with the young? 21. Does great licence prevail among unmarried or married? 22. Is drunkenness approved, tolerated, or condemned? and how with reference to age and sex! 23. Is drunkenness usual at public feasts?

24. Do any remarkable ceremonial customs prevail? 25. Are old-fashioned customs used on state occasions? 26. Are ancient habits observed at feasts, &c., such as old dishes and ways of cookery? 27. Any special forms of address, healths, &c., at feasts? 28. Any remarkable customs at funerals, festivals on birth of children, harvest festivals, family gatherings, &c.

29. Are peculiar forms of language in use? 30. Are certain words used or avoided in addressing certain people? 31. What forms of address are usual between common people, chiefs, kings? 32. Are old-fashioned terms and expressions used ceremonially or officially? 33. Are there othe remarkable customs not otherwise classed? (See also XXIX. SUPERSTITIONS; XXVII. RELIGION; XXX. MAGIC; XXXVII. TABOO, &c.).

E. B. T.

No. XXXVI.—GOVERNMENT.

a. The Head of the Government.—1. What is his title? 2. How is he appointed? 3. If by election, with whom does the election rest? 4. If by succession, what are the limits of the succession? 5. May females succeed? 6. May minors? 7. Who will be his probable successor? 8. What is the extent of his power? 9. How does he exercise it? 10. Are his people well affected to his rule? 11. How long has the present system of government been maintained? 12. Are there frequent revolutions? and have they affected only the individual ruler, or extended to an alteration of the system?

β. Inferior Officers.—13. *Petty Chiefs:* have they independent jurisdiction? 14. Does their power act as a check on that of the head? 15. To what extent are they accountable to him? 16. Are they appointed by the king or superior chiefs, elective, or hereditary? 17. Does the power of each inferior chief extend over a sept personally attached to himself? 18. Has it territorial limits? 19. Do quarrels arise between chiefs? and are they settled by reference to the head, or by war, or how otherwise? 20. What is the extent of their power over their subjects? 21. Have their subjects any right to appeal to the head or to any other authority? 22. How does the system work? 23. What are the number of inferior jurisdictions? and are there any distinctions of rank between them? 24. Do the inferior chiefs ever meet in council?

25. *Counsellors or Ministers:* how are these appointed? 26. Have they any authority independent of the will of the head? 17. What offices do they hold? 28. Have they any direct power over the people? and how do they exercise it? 29. Is the head virtually ruled by his counsellors? or does he exercise an individual will? 30. Is he ruled by favourites? 31. Is he ruled by women? 32. Is there any machinery of government, or any established constitution? 33. What is the revenue of the chief and the other rulers and officers? 34. How is it raised? 35. Are there annual or more frequent feasts at the capital town for the payment of dues or tribute?

E. W. B.

No. XXXVII.—TABOO.

Ceremonial prohibitions of eating certain food, touching or even looking at certain persons or things, mentioning certain names, are very frequent among mankind, and though not reducible to one common principle, are in various ways instructive as throwing light on early and rude ideas. In taking down the details of these prohibitions, it is well to inquire their reason, as this may sometimes be the true one, or at least afford a clue to its discovery.

1. Is any particular food, animal or vegetable, forbidden though obtainable and wholesome? 2. Do the whole people abstain from it, or only certain families or individuals, or persons under some special circumstances? 3. Is the prohibition religious, or referred to custom and propriety? 4. Is there a distinction between young and old, male and female, as to these prohibitions? 5. Is the animal or plant abstained from in any way regarded as divine, a tribe-fetish, the incarnation of a local deity or personal guardian-spirit, or the soul of some ancestor? is it the animal after which the tribe or family has its name? 6. If the food is abstained from at certain times only? 6*a*. Are these occasions, puberty, menstruation, pregnancy, the period after child-birth, mourning after a death, time of purification after manslaughter, times connected with hunting and war, time of preparation for observance of religious rites, &c.? 7. Does it seem that the abstention has to do with fasting, and that it prepares the abstainer for spiritual intercourse? 8. Is the idea that the food contains a spirit or deity, or is holy, so that persons in a state of uncleanness must not defile it by eating it? 9. Or, on the other hand, is the person in a state of sanctity, and would the food defile him? 10. Is there any thing symbolical, as where the flesh of slow or cowardly animals is abstained from by warriors, lest they should become slow or cowardly? 11. Is there any particular caste or tribe, or member of family, who may eat what others may not, or may not eat what others may? and why? 12. Are any persons under any circumstances not allowed to eat with others? 13. Do men and women take their meals apart? and is this a ceremonial usage, or a matter of inferiority? 14. Are persons ever forbidden to feed themselves or touch their food with their hands? (See also No. XL., TOTEMISM.)

15. Do any persons object to eating with, touching, speaking to, looking at, or calling by name, other persons? 16. Do these prohibitions apply to persons of different ranks, occupation, or caste? 17. Are they between relations, as between parents-in-law and their children-in-law? 18. If so, what appears to be the motive? is the one holier than the other? is there an idea of magical harm, or is it a mere question of social separation.

19. Are the names of chiefs, of dead persons, &c., avoided in conversation, and even excluded from the language? and if so, why? 20. Are any specials words or subjects considered improper or indecent?

21. Are any places or objects sacred or taboo? 21*a*. Are any paths taboo to women, but not to men? 22. Is this with a religious idea, as in case of temples, idols, sacred pipe, &c.? 23. If so, who may enter or touch with impunity? 24. Is there a special prohibition to women and children? 25. Does the touch of any person defile or sanctify an object, so that its owner may not touch it? 26. Is a place or object made taboo with the idea of keeping it safe? and is it considered that magical evil will befall the unlicensed toucher? or is the place or object made sacred to the gods, who will punish violation?

27. In general, whose authority is appealed to as such prohibitions? and is their infraction punished by divine or magical vengeance, by law, or by public disapproval?

E. B. T.

No. XXXVIII.—CIRCUMCISION.

The practice of circumcision prevails, or has prevailed, in parts of Asia, Africa, and America, being confined chiefly to the equatorial and southern regions of the globe. It is undoubtedly of great antiquity, and was described as an ancient custom even in the time of Herodotus. So peculiar and painful a custom appears less likely to have arisen independently in different centres than others for which ordinary causes can be assigned; and it will therefore be of interest to trace all the varieties of the custom as it is practised amongst different tribes and races, and to record the reasons given for it at the present time or in the past history of the people.

1. Does the custom prevail at the present time? or is it known to have existed in times past? 2. Is it known, though not practised? and is it spoken of as a barbarous custom when practised by others? 3. Is it performed upon males or females, or both? 4. At what age is it performed on males and females? 5. Does the custom in regard to males and females appear to have the same or a different origin? 6. Who performs the operation on the different sexes—old women, priests, or midwives? 7. Is the position of circumcisor considered especially honourable? 8. Is it illegal after a certain age? 9. Is the operation performed with any special instruments? 10. What is the part cut off in males? ditto in females? 11. Is it fully performed? or is it only a vestige of the custom? 12. Are any other incisions made upon the body at the same time? what is their meaning? Give drawings of them. 13. Does this apply to males and females alike? 14. What is done with the parts cut off? 15. Any special custom with respect to the blood? 16. Is any godfather or godmother appointed? 17. Is a name given to the person at the time or subsequently? 18. Is any particular dress worn on the occasion? 19. Is the person to be circumcised led upon a horse, ass, or mule? 20. Is anything done to heal the wound? 21. For how long is the circumcised person exempt from labour? 22. With what other ceremonies does it appear to be especially connected? 23. Are any lustration practices especially associated with it? 24. Is it considered a religious duty, a law, or only a custom? 25. Does happiness in a future state depend on it? 26. Is there any tradition respecting it? 27. Can its origin be traced to any other tribe, race, or locality? 28. What is the recognized name for it? 29. Is it ever performed after death? 30. Is there any reason to suppose it was established as an offering of part of the organ

of generation to the deity? 31. What is the reason now assigned for it? 32. Is it supposed to prevent disease, or to preserve cleanliness? 33. Is it effectual for this purpose? 34. Is it considered to render marriage prolific? 35. Is any special seat set apart for the operator or the circumcised, or for an imaginary personage or deity? 36. Is the operation ever dispensed with for fear of deterring proselytes? 37. Is it performed by all classes alike? 38. Is it in full force or dying out? 39. Is it in any way connected with Phallic worship?

A. L. F.

No. XXXIX.—INITIATORY CEREMONIES.

Among most uncivilised races, the period when lads cease to be children, and take their definite position in the community as responsible members of it, is marked by ceremonies in which the chief actor is usually the boy whose entry into the tribe has occasioned them. With girls analogous ceremonies are observed, usually on their attaining the marriageable age. As a rule, a part of these ceremonies is performed in great secrecy, and only those are permitted to be present who have already passed through the ordeal. A new name is generally given to the youth; and, in addition to instruction from the elders in the moral code of the tribe, some form of mutilation is often practised, such as circumcision, or, among the Australians, knocking out one of the teeth. Abstinence from food, or from particular kinds of food, is a frequent and essential part, or a result, of the initiation, and may be either a test of endurance, or may have some less obvious reason.

These ceremonies are at times intimately connected with TOTEMISM (No. XL.), and questions which could well be entered here will be found under that head, as well as under those of CUSTOMS (No. XXXV.), and TABOO (No. XXXVII.).

Where the ceremonies are performed in secret, it will obviously be difficult to obtain a full account, or to witness them, but much insight into their purpose may be gained by judicious and persistent enquiry.

1. Are any ceremonies of initiation performed? (*a*) for boys? (*b*) for girls? 2. At what age, or period of life, do they occur? 3. Is there any visible sign borne by those who have undergone the ordeal? (mutilation, addition to dress, or ornament, tattooing, &c.) 4. Are the ceremonies secret from all but the initiated? 5. Are women permitted to be present at the initiation of boys? 6. Or men at that of girls? 7. What preparation is exacted from the candidates? (fasting, isolation, &c.) 8. Do the ceremonies take place at a particular time of the year or month, and why? 9. How long do they last? and are they continuous, or separated by intervals? 10. Where are the ceremonies performed? in the village, or at a special place apart? 11. Are any special dresses or disguises worn by the performers? Describe them. 12. Are any implements used on these occasions which are obsolete in daily life? (*e.g.*, stone implements among an iron using people). 13. Is the name of the individual changed on his initiation? and does the name then given last during life? 14. Is it thought unlucky, after initiation and change of name, to mention the name previously borne? 15. Is any special or cryptic form of language taught to the initiated? or are words not in the ordinary language used at the ceremonies? 16. Have the initiated any pass words or signs? 17. Do these signs extend beyond the tribe? (*e.g.*, to a neighbouring tribe having similar, but not identical, ceremonies). 18. Are there grades of initiation? 19. Do these indicate distinctions in social rank? or can an individual of low rank pass through all in the course of time? 20. During the ceremonies, is there any pretence of putting the candidate to death? and what reason is assigned for this? 21. What ordeals has the candidate to undergo? 22. Is he isolated from the tribe for some period after his initiation? 23. Is this to prove his ability to pro-

vide for himself? 24. Is there any restriction placed upon certain kinds of food? and why? 25. How long does this taboo last? is the release gradual? 26. Is there any ceremony on the raising of the taboo from any particular animal? 27. What are the privileges of the initiated? 28. Is initiation essential before marriage in both men and women? 29. Are any phallic symbols carried or worn during the ceremonies? 30. Is there any suggestion of Phallic worship?

C. H. R.

No. XL.—TOTEMISM.

Totemism is the name given to a religious and social system which has been found amongst savages in many parts of the world, especially Australia, North America, and Africa. A totem is a sacred object, generally an animal, less often a plant or inanimate object, of which the whole species is revered by a tribe or clan. The tribe or clan generally takes its name from the totem. Thus if the totem is a wolf, the tribesmen or clansmen call themselves Wolves, and they will not kill or injure wolves or eat wolf's flesh. Often the clansmen think that they are descended from the totem, but sometimes they explain their connection with the totem in other ways. Where totemism exists in full force, a man may not marry a woman of the same totem as himself; thus if he is a Wolf he may not marry a Wolf, but may marry a Bear, &c. Where this rule of exogamy (*i.e.*, marrying out of the clan) exists, we necessarily have two or more totem clans existing side by side; generally there are many different totem clans living together. In some clans the children are of their mother's totem; thus, if the father is a Wolf and the mother is a Bear, the children will be Bears. In other clans children are of the father's totem; thus, if the father is a Raven and the mother a Dog, the children will be Ravens.

3. Deformities of the face, &c., such as supernumerary auricles, hare lip, cleft palate, cleft tongue, cleft cheek (macrostoma), abnormally small mouth (microstoma), and any peculiarities of the teeth.

4. Deformities of the extremities, *e.g.*, supernumerary fingers or toes, webbed fingers, imperfect development, or absence of one of the bones of the forearm, hypertrophy of the limbs, club hand, club foot.

5. Deformities of the genitals, *e.g.*, abnormal length of the labia, imperforate hymen, undescended testicles, cleft penis epispadias or hypospadias, cleft scrotum with the testicles in what appear to be labia, absence of the anterior wall of the bladder, extroverted bladder.

6. Does excessive development of fat about the haunches, buttocks, *steatopyga*, or labia occur? Can any causes, artificial or otherwise, be assigned for the occurrence?

7. Note any deformities or malformations which may occur in the region of the umbilicus, and state how the cord is treated at birth.

8. Are any of the above deformities more common than usual, or any one of them frequently met with? Are there any of hereditary nature? How are they regarded and treated?

J.B. Revised by J. W. B. H.

No. V.—DEFORMATIONS.

(*Artificial* Deformities.)

The practice of artificially producing deformities in the human subject appears to have existed from the most remote times of which we have any record, and to have prevailed at one time or another in all parts of the world. In the investigation, therefore, of the ethnographical characters of a people, considerable interest attaches to observations respecting artificial "deformations," as the practice in question has been termed; for it is very possible that important information may thence be derived with regard to the relations between

be free to marry a woman of any other totem? or are there certain other totem clans beside his own into which he may not marry? Enumerate as many of these prohibitions of marriage as you can ascertain. 6. If a man may not marry a woman of the same totem as himself, is he allowed to have sexual intercourse with her, either generally or at stated times? If at stated times, what are these times? and what reason do they give for this license? 7. What do they think would happen to them or to their children if they married or had sexual intercourse with, women of a forbidden totem? Does the tribe punish such breaches of tribal law? and if so, how? 8. How does a man ascertain whether he may marry, or have intercourse, with a stranger woman, especially when they speak different dialects? 9. Are the tribes, clans, castes, and their subdivisions, distinguished from each other by badges, or by differences in dress, the mode of wearing the hair, tattooing, chipping or filing the teeth, &c.? Distinguish carefully the national badges (*i.e.*, the badges worn by *all* the people) from the tribal or clan badges (*i.e.*, the badges worn by different subdivisions of the people, namely, the tribes, clans, &c.) Do the tribal or clan badges ever consist of representations of totem tattooed, painted, or carved? Does a man wear the skin of his totem animal? 10. Are any special ceremonies observed by each totem, tribe, or clan, at the birth of a child? Describe such ceremonies. 11. Are any initiatory rites performed on boys or girls at puberty, to admit them to the full position of tribesmen and tribeswomen? (XXXIX.) Describe such rites fully. Is there any pretence of killing the boys and bringing them to life again? 12. During and for some time after these initiatory rites are the lads forbidden to see women? If so, why? 13. What is the relation of children under puberty to the totem? May they eat the totem animal or plant? Are they absolved from the other restrictions which are imposed upon grown members of the clan in regard to the totem?

14. Have the ceremonies at the death and burial of a member of a totem tribe any reference to the totem? Describe such ceremonies. What is supposed to happen to

the spirit or soul of a member of a totem tribe at death? is it thought to transmigrate into the totem?

15. Are omens drawn from the appearance, motions, cries, &c., of the totem? 16. Is the totem supposed to help the tribe or clan in any way? 17. Is food offered to the totem animal? Is it caught and kept in captivity? 18. Is the totem ever treated like a human being, dressed in clothes, prayed to, &c.? 19. Is constraint ever placed on the totem, in order to compel it to grant the wishes of the tribe? 20. Is the totem animal ever killed as a solemn ceremony? If so, is this killing or sacrifice occasional or periodic? If occasional, what are the occasions? if periodic, what are the periods? When the totem is so killed, do the members of the totem tribe or clan partake of its flesh as a solemn rite? is its blood sprinkled upon them or upon the houses? If its flesh is not eaten, what is done with it? what is done with the bones? what with the skin? What is the object and efficacy of this rite? Is the slain animal regarded as a scapegoat to take away the misfortunes and sins of the people? Is it supposed to come to life again immediately after it is killed? 21. Are there totem dances? *i.e.*, do the members of the totem tribe or clan dress up in the skins of the totem animal and represent its movements and cries? On what occasions, and with what object, are such dances performed?

22. Does each tribesman or clansman revere all members of the totem species equally? or does he suppose that he has a special connection with one particular individual of the species? *e.g.*, if he is a Wolf, does he respect all wolves equally? or does he think that one particular wolf is his special friend; and that his fate or life is bound up in that particular wolf so closely that if it dies or is killed he must himself die at the same moment?

23. In addition to the tribal or clan totem, has each man a totem of his own? *i.e.*, an animal, plant, &c., which he specially reveres and with which he conceives that his fate is bound up? how does he acquire his personal totem? is it chosen for him at his birth by his parents or the priest? or does he choose it for himself, and, if so, how and with what

ceremonies? Does he take for his personal totem a whole species of animals or plants &c. (as all eagles, all turtles) or only one individual of the species (as a particular eagle or turtle)?

24. Has each sex a totem? that is, do all the men revere one kind of animal, plant, or other natural object, and do all the women revere another kind of animal, &c.? what is supposed to happen if a man kills a woman's totem, or *vice versâ?* how do the men act towards the women in such a case, or the men to the women?

25. Have the subdivisions of the tribes and clans also totems? if so, what is the relation of the totem of the subdivision to the totem of the clan or tribe? what allegiance does a man owe respectively to the totem of his clan and the totem of his subdivion? how do these totem subdivisions arise? are their totems always different from those of the clan? or does one of the subdivisions bear the same totem as the clan? are the totems of the subdivisions sometimes parts of the clan totems? thus, if the clan totem is the bear, will the totem of one subdivision be the bear's head, that of another the bear's foot, &c.?

26. Are there any traces of the transition of totemism into a more advanced worship? *e.g.*, are there any gods worshipped in human form with the heads of animals, or in animal form with human heads, &c.? are gods in human form supposed to have certain animals or plants specially connected with their worship? do these animals or plants appear to have been once the totems of tribes or clans?

J. G. F.

No. XLI.—MUSIC.

The music of every nation has certain characteristics of its own. The progressions of intervals, the modulations, embellishments, rhythmical effects, &c., occurring in the music of extra-European nations are not unfrequently too peculiar to be accurately indicated by means of our musical notation. Some additional explanation is therefore required with the notation. In writing down the popular tunes of foreign countries on hearing them sung or played by the natives, no attempt should be made to rectify anything which may appear incorrect to the European ear. The more faithfully the apparent defects are preserved, the more valuable is the notation. Collections of popular tunes (with the words of the airs) are very desirable. Likewise drawings of musical instruments, with explanations respecting the construction, dimensions, capabilities, and employment of the instruments represented.

Vocal Music.—1. Are the people fond of music? 2. Is their ear acute for discerning small musical intervals? 3. Can they easily hit a tone which is sung or played to them? 4. Is their voice flexible? 5. What is the quality of the voice? is it loud or soft, clear or rough, steady or tremulous? 6. What is the usual compass of the voice? 7. Which is the prevailing male voice—tenor, baritone, or bass? 8. Which is the prevailing female voice—soprano or alto? 9. Do the people generally sing without instrumental accompaniment? 10. Have they songs performed in chorus by men only, or by women only, or by both sexes together? 11. When the people sing together, do they sing in unison or in harmony, or with the occasional introduction of some drone accompaniment of the voice? 12. Is their singing in regular time, or does it partake of the character of the recitative? 13. Have they songs for *solo* and *chorus*, or with an air for a single voice and a burden (or refrain) for a number of voices? 14. Describe the different kinds of songs which they have (such as sacred songs, war songs, love songs, nursery songs, &c.) with remarks on the poetry.

Instruments.—Describe, with drawings, the construction of all instruments; the most minute details may be of value. 15. What are their instruments of percussion (such as drums, castanets, rattles, cymbals, gongs, bells, &c.)? 16. Have they instruments of percussion containing sonorous slabs of wood, glass, stone, metal, &c., upon which tunes can be played? if so, write down in notation or in letters the tones emitted by the slabs. 17. Have they drums with cords, or some other contrivance, by means of which the parchment can be tightened or slackened at pleasure? 18. Have they drums with definite tones (like our kettle-drums)? and if so, what are the tones in which they are tuned when two or more are played together? 19. (*a*) Any open hand-drums with one parchment only, like our tambourine, or (*b*) are any drums provided with a membrane at both ends? 20. Are the drums beaten with sticks or with the hands? 21. What wind-instruments (trumpets, flutes, &c.) have they? 22. Any trumpets with sliding-tubes (like the trombone)? 23. How are the flutes sounded? is there a plug in the mouth-hole? 24. Any nose-flutes? 25. What is the number and the position of the finger-holes on the flutes? 26. What tones do the flutes yield if the finger-holes are closed in regular succession upwards or downwards? 27. If the people have the syrinx (or Pandean pipe), ascertain the series of musical intervals yielded by the tubes, and whether the intervals are the same in several examples. 28. Do the people construct wind-instruments with a vibrating reed, or some similar contrivance, inserted in the mouth-hole? 29. If they have a reed wind-instrument, observe whether the reed is single (like that of the clarionet) or double (like that of the oboe). 30. Have they a kind of bagpipe? 31. What musical instruments have they which are not used by them in musical performances, but merely for conveying signals, and for such like purposes? 32. Have they stringed instruments the strings of which are sounded (*a*) by being twanged with the fingers, (*b*) twanged with a plectrum, (*c*) beaten with sticks or hammers (like the dulcimer), or (*d*) played with a bow? 33. If there are stringed instruments with frets on the neck (as is the case with our guitar), note down the intervals produced by the frets in regular succession. 34. What are the strings made of (gut, wire, &c.)? 35. Is there any particular contrivance on some of the instruments in the arrangement and situation of the strings? 36. Are there stringed instruments with sympathetic strings (*i.e.*, strings placed under those strings which are played upon : the sympathetic strings merely serve to increase the sonorousness)? 36*a*. To what order of intervals are the sympathetic strings tuned? They will be found to vary, and in India are tuned to the intervals of the Râga, or melody type, employed at the time. 37. What are the musical intervals in which the stringed instruments are tuned? 38. Describe, and give the native name of, each instrument, with illustrations or photographs on as large a scale as possible; these should show the front, details of fret, bridge tailpiece, &c., as well as the side view. 39. Give some account of the woods, metals, hide, gut, hair, and other materials used; of their tools, &c. 40. What are the usual adornments and appendages of the musical instruments?

Compositions.—41. On what order of intervals is the music of the people founded? Is it the diatonic major scale (like *c*, *d*, *e*, *f*, *g*, *a*, *b*, *c*), or the diatonic minor scale (in which the third is flat, thus *c*, *d*, *e flat*, *f*, *g*, *a*, *b*, *c*), or the pentatonic scale (in which the fourth and the seventh are omitted, thus *c*, *d*, *e*, *g*, *a*, *c*), or some other order of intervals? 42. Is the seventh used sharp (*c–b*) or flat (*c–b flat*)? 43. Does the superfluous second occur in the scale? (In the example *c*, *d*, *e flat*, *f sharp*, *g*, *a flat*, *b*, *c*, the steps from the third to the fourth and from the sixth to the seventh are superfluous seconds.) 44. Does the music contain progressions in semitones or chromatic intervals? 45. Are there smaller intervals than semitones, such as $\frac{1}{3}$ tones, $\frac{1}{4}$ tones? If you have sufficient technical knowledge, describe how the temperament employed differs from equal, or mean temperament, or just intonation. State how you arrive at conclusions. 46. Are there peculiar progressions in certain intervals which are of frequent occurrence in the tunes? if so, what are they? 47. Do the tunes usually conclude in the tonic (the key-note, or the first interval of the scale)? or if not, on what other interval? 48. Do the tunes contain modulations from one key into another? if so, describe the usual modulations. 49. Are there certain rhythmical peculiarities predominant in the music? if so, what are they? 50. Is the time of the music generally common time, triple time, or irregular? A regular rhythmical method often exists. Find out how they construct their rhythms. 51. Are there phrases or passages in the melodies which are of frequent reoccurrence? Melodies are often constructed of several different parts, which in performance cannot be easily distinguished. Care should be taken to ascertain whether their melodies are constructed to any rule of musical form. 52. Have the airs of the songs reoccurrences of musical phrases which are traceable to the form of the poetry? 53. Have the people musical compositions which they regard as very old? and do these compositions exhibit the same characteristics which are found in the modern ones? 54. Are the compositions generally lively or grave? 55. Describe the form of the various kinds of musical compositions. In all cases try to study national music from the native standpoint, and if possible with a native teacher.

Performances.—56. Have the people musical bands (or orchestras)? 57. Which are the instruments (*a*) generally used in combination? or (*b*) commonly used singly? 58. What is the number of performers in a properly constituted band? 59. Is there a leader of the band? How does he direct the performers? 60. Does the band play in unison or in harmony? 61. If vocal music is combined with instrumental music performed by the band, is the instrumental accompaniment in unison (or in octaves) with the voices, or has it something of its own? 62. Is the *tempo* generally fast or slow? 63. Are there sudden changes or gradual changes in the *tempo?* 64. Are there changes in the degree of loudness? 65. Do the musicians, on repeating a piece, introduce alterations or variations of the theme? 66. Do they introduce embellishments *ad libitum?* 67. Mention the occasions (religious ceremonies, social and public amusements, celebrations, processions, &c.) on which musical performances take place. 68. Is music employed to facilitate manual labour (*e.g.*, paddling)? 69. Are there songs or instrumental compositions appertaining to particular occupations or trades?

70. Have the people a national hymn or an instrumental composition which they perform in honour of their sovereign, or in commemoration of some political event? 71. Any war-dances, dances of defiance, &c.? 72. Any dances in which they imitate the peculiar movements and habits of certain animals, &c.? 73. Are their dances accompanied by musical instruments, by singing, or merely by rhythmical sounds, such as clapping of hands, snapping of fingers, reiterated vociferation, &c.? 74. Endeavour to ascertain whether the rhythm of the music accompanying the dance is suggested by the steps of the dances, or *vice versâ*.

Cultivation.—75. Do the people easily learn a melody by ear? 76. Have they a good musical memory? 77. Are the children taught music? and if so, how is it done? 78. Are there professional musicians? 79. Any minstrels, bards, reciters of old ballads? 80. Any professional improvisators? 81. Are there professional musicians of different grades? 82. Who composes the music? 83. Do the musicians follow other professions besides music? 84. Have the people some kind of musical notation? 85. Have they written signs for raising and lowering the voice in singing, for giving emphasis to certain words or phrases, or for similar purposes? if so, describe the signs. 86. Do they possess treatises on the history, theory, &c., of music, instruction books for singing and for playing musical instruments, &c.? if so, give a detailed account of their musical literature. 87. How do the people appreciate their own music? 88. What impression does the music of foreign countries produce upon them?

Traditions.—89. Are there any popular traditions respecting the origin of music? 90. Any legends or fairy tales in which allusion to music is made? if so, what are they? 91. Any tradition about the invention of certain favourite musical instruments? 92. Any tradition or historical record respecting the antiquity of stringed instruments played with a bow? 93. Any records respecting their sacred music? 94. Is music believed to possess the power of curing certain illnesses? 95. The power of enticing and taming wild animals? 96. Are there popular tunes, or certain rhythmical figures in the tunes, which, according to tradition, have been suggested by the songs of birds?

C. E.

No. XLII.—ETYMOLOGY.

Local names, as of mountains, rivers, towns, &c., afford important evidence as to previous inhabitants of a district, as in the familiar case of Keltic local names in England. Well-known geographical names, belonging to the actual language of some little-known tribe, are also interesting to philologists as easily remembered examples of their language and its structure; while the rapid extinction of many languages leaves local names as their principal relics. It is therefore desirable to draw up a full geographical list for each district, with the etymology of each name stated carefully when known.

1. What words, such as hill, river, rock, wood, &c., enter into the composition of local names, corresponding to such English forms as Black-*down*, Sand-*wich*, Bex-*hill*?

2. Are the names of rivers, mountains, villages, &c., mostly intelligible to the present inhabitants, and belonging to the language at present spoken in the district? 3. Do any words show old but still intelligible forms of the present language? 4. Are there local names not intelligible in or belonging to the present language? if so, is it known to what language they belong and what they signify?

5. What kind of names are given to—

a. Men?
b. Women?
c. Families?
d. Tribes?
e. Animals?
f. Gods?
g. Towns?
h. Rivers?
i. Wells or Springs?
k. Hills?
l. Rocks?
m. Mounds?
n. Caves?
o. Ruins?
p. Islands?
q. Tombs?
r. Trees?

E. B. T.

No. XLIII.—LANGUAGE.

The only really satisfactory method of treating a language for anthropological purposes is to have a complete grammar and dictionary drawn up. As to the compilation of such, in savage languages, two suggestions are worth making. First, that the dictionary should be printed with the grammar prefixed, otherwise neither will be properly available; second, that specimens of native compositions, such as folk-lore tales, poems, traditions, prayers, &c., should be taken down *verbatim*, and published with an accurate translation, with the grammar and dictionary. Where it is impossible to deal with the language in this thorough way, the fullest vocabulary possible should be drawn up, and sentences carefully taken down and translated word for word. The practice of judging of the affinities of a language by means of a short vocabulary of isolated words, without a guide to the grammatical structure, is to be condemned as loose and misleading. The missionary alphabet of Professor Max Müller and the phonetic alphabets of Mr. A. J. Ellis and Mr. Melville Bell may be used; the former is here inserted (p. 171) for the use of travellers. (See 'Outline Dictionary for the use of Missionaries, Explorers, &c.' Trübner and Co., Ludgate Hill.) Whatever alphabet is used, the one essential point is to use each character for one sound, and one only, defining the pronunciation of each by examples from well-known languages. For special sounds not represented in the alphabet, combined or modified letters may be used.

1. What sounds are used in the language? and which differ from those of European languages? and what sounds are they unable to pronounce? 2. What expressive interjections are in common use? and how are they like or unlike our own? 3. Does the meaning of words and sentences depend much or little on tone, accent, or emphasis? 5. Can a sentence, such as an interrogative or affirmative, be roughly written with musical notes to show rise and fall of tone? 6. Are there

words which are direct imitations of noises, cries of animals, &c., like *puff*, *mew*, *rat-tat*, &c.? and does such imitation of sound prevail largely in the language? 7. What is the grammatical structure of the language? are roots or crude forms, &c. clearly discernible in it? and by what arrangement of particles, inflexions, &c. are these built up into words? 8 Are particles, such as prepositions, pronouns, adverbs, &c., combined in the words, or do they stand separately? 9. Are prefixes or suffixes used? 9*a*. How are plurals formed? by suffixes? and if so, has this suffix an independent meaning? 10. Are changes of vowel or consonant usual in inflexion, &c.? 11. Are compound words usual, and how formed? is there a tendency to contract compound words into shorter forms in which the original words are mutilated? 12. Are there diminutive or augmentative words? and do changes of sound cause such changes of meaning? 13 How are genders indicated? and do they relate to difference of sex or to the difference between animate and inanimate? 14. Are there forms of number and case in nouns and adjectives? 15. What are the numerals? and do they show any traces of derivation from reckoning by fingers and toes, such as the words hand, foot, man, to indicate 5, 10, 20, &c., or their compounds? (See No. LX. ARITHMETIC.) 16. How are the moods and tenses of verbs indicated? 17. What are the rules of syntax? are the relations of subject, object, predicate, indicated by grammatical inflexions or by their place in the sentence, or both? 18. Is the language a dialect of some well-known family? and if so, where does it principally differ from well-known languages of that family? 19. Are there neighbouring dialects of the same stock? and if so, are they mutually intelligible, or at least recognized as allied, by the tribes speaking them? 20. What traces are there of words having changed within the memory of man? 21. Are words to be noticed as borrowed from other languages? 22. Are there any unusual sounds in the language such as the Kafir click, strong gutturals, &c.?

E. B. T.

Missionary Alphabet of Professor Max Müller.

a	America.	o	philology.
a	psalm.	*o*	note.
v	bought all.	ö	könig (Ger.).
ä	väter (Ger.).		peu (Fr.).
ai	aisle.	oi	oil.
au	proud.	p	pat.
b	bid.	q	(*see* k).
c	(*see* k).	r	true.
ch	(see *k*).	*r*	car
d	dock.	s	sin.
d*h*	this.	*s*	sharp.
e	debt.	t	tan.
e	date.	t*h*	thin.
f	fat.	ü	unc (Fr.).
g	gate.		für (Ger.).
g	gin.	u	full.
h	hand.	*u*	fool.
‘h	loch.	*v*	but, birch.
’h	tage (Ger.).	w	wine.
i	knit.	‘w	whine
i	neat.	x	*i.e.* ks.
	(see *g*).	y	yet
k	kite.	’y	ich (Ger.).
k	church.	z	zeal.
l	let.	*z*	pleasur
l	William.		
m	man.		
n	not.		
n (or ñ)	new		
N	bon (Fr.).		
ng	sinking.		

XLIV.—POETRY.

The poetical compositions, which in some rude form appear among the rudest tribes, should be taken down carefully as to words, and also as to the musical intonation with which they are chanted. It has to be ascertained, if possible, whether the poem or song is one handed down from former generations, or a modern or extempore composition. Old records of national and personal history, and mythical and religious ideas, are often handed down in such old compositions, which also frequently preserve ancient words and forms of speech which have been disused in ordinary conversation.

1. Are poetical compositions common, old and new? 2. Are they repeated in precise unaltered form, and known to the people generally? 3. Are poetic compositions still often made? is there any thing like an order of bards? and do they receive rewards for making or singing them? 4. Are old historical events or personages commemorated in songs? 5. Are there special chants for religious purposes, prayer and praise of gods, &c.? 6. Are such chants sung at religious and other festivals? and by whom? 7. What are the rules of melody in chants? 8. Do they follow any definable rules of rhythm or metre? and are particular words used in order that they may suit this? (See XLI.) 9. Are any peculiar, mystic, or ancient words used in poetry? 10. Are choruses in use? and how far do they consist of intelligible words, and how far of nonsense-syllables? 11. Are there any performances of a dramatic nature, commemorating religious legends, wars, &c.? and if so, is the dialogue in set forms handed down by tradition? (See LXVII.)

E. B. T.

No. XLV.—HISTORY.

While remembering that all ancient history and tradition, and especially that of savage tribes and barbaric nations, is in large measure fabulous, travellers will do well to take down oral legends and procure written documents where they exist. Beside the mention of really historical events and persons, much may be learnt from details thus incidentally given as to relations with other people, manners and customs, arts, &c. Even the evidently mythical parts, as showing connexion with the legends of other nations, may afford important evidence as to the history of the tribe or nation which possesses them. It is desirable to have such documents in the exact words of the narrator or scribe, with verbatim translations. Care should be taken as far as possible to distinguish really native matter from that obtained from foreigners, such as the borrowed Hindu legends repeated by the hill-tribes of India, or the ideas which so many tribes have taken up from the Bible or the Koran.

1. What means exist of preserving the memory of past events? 2. Do the old people habitually relate them, as at feasts? are they handed down in songs or chants? have such repetitions any religious character? are they specially attended to by any class, as of priests or bards? 3. Is picture-writing, or staves of special form, used as a record, or any other method, such as the use of beads or knotted cords? 4. Do written or pictorial records of any sort exist? and if so, are such records held sacred, and where are they kept? 5. Have they any definite chronology? and is there evidence to how many years back they remember or record known events, such as visits from Europeans, &c.

6. What account do they give of themselves, and their connexion with other nations, wars, alliances, &c.? 7. What names does the tribe, nation, or race go by? and which are

native names used by themselves, and which terms given by other people? 8. Do they trace their descent from a first ancestor or chief, or several? Do they derive their name from his? and does it appear that he is an eponymic personage, invented to account for the existence of the tribe or race? 9. Do families trace their descent from a single ancestor? and does he appear to be real or mythic?

10. Do the people believe themselves indigenes in their land, or to have come from elsewhere? 11. Do they consider other tribes, related to them by language, as having branched off from them, or *vice versâ*, or all from some other national source? 12. What have they to say of former migrations? 13. Do they believe their nation was once poorer and smaller? and has increased and improved, or that their ancestors were a greater and wiser and happier nation than themselves? 14. What do they say as to the invention of their arts, the origin of their customs and laws, &c.? 15. What are their traditions of national heroes? do they seem historical or mythic? 16. What have they to say as to the introduction and changes of their religion, invention of new ceremonies &c.? 17. Have they traditions to account for monuments, such as old graves, mounds, sites of villages, &c., in their district? 18. Any traditions of great floods?

E. B. T.

No. XLVI.—ARCHÆOLOGY.

Much information is wanted respecting the archæology of savage and barbarous countries. Most of the stone implements received from Australia and the Pacific Islands are of recent manufacture, and but little evidence has yet come to hand to throw light on the origin and duration of the stone period of culture in those regions. In New Zealand, however, something has been effected in this direction by discoveries in ancient deposits. In Japan, evidence of a stone age corresponding in its forms to our neolithic period has been discovered. From China we have received specimens of both stone and bronze implements; but detailed evidence on the subject is wanting. From the Asiatic Islands stone and bronze implements have been received. In Birmah stone and bronze implements have been discovered. In India three periods have been recognized, corresponding to our palæolithic, neolithic, and bronze periods. From Central and Northern Asia information is wanted respecting both stone and bronze implements. Stone implements of neolithic forms have been found at the Cape of Good Hope and in Western Africa. Palæolithic forms have also been found at the Cape of Good Hope and in Egypt; but we have no conclusive evidence of their being of the palæolithic period. In North and South America relics of the stone age are more abundant, and a bronze period is recognised in the central regions of America. When it is considered that the palæolithic implements of Europe have only attracted the attention of archæologists during the last thirty years, it is not surprising that in uncultivated countries so little should be known of the relics that are hidden beneath the soil. It is very desirable that, when opportunity offers, the river-drifts and cave-deposits should be examined for the relics of a past age, and that the attention of travellers should be directed to the *débris* scattered on the surface and in the surface-soils turned up by cultivation for the vestiges of a more advanced stone period. The ancient tombs and tumuli should also be examined, and their relics preserved whenever it can be done without offending the superstitions of the people.

Palæolithic Period (*River-drift.*)—1. Notice any evidence that may exist of the erosion of valleys by their rivers. 2. Do terraces exist on the sides of the valleys? how many, at what heights above the existing rivers, and at what distances from their present courses? 3. Do such terraces and drift-deposits consist of gravel, sand, or other alluvial matter? and are the deposits stratified as if by the action of running water? 4. Are the materials all derived from the present area of drainage? 5. Do they contain freshwater or marine shells, human or other animal remains, or stone implements? if so, preserve them carefully. 6. Label each specimen with the locality at once, and give sections to scale showing the exact depth beneath the surface at which the remains were found: note the thickness of the various stratified layers above them, and obtain as nearly as possible the height above the existing river. 7. What is the growth of timber upon the terraces? and is there any marked difference in the flora of the different terraces? 8. What is the excavating power of the river at the present time, as shown by the damage caused by floods? how high do the floods of the river rise at present? is the present bed of the river rising or sinking? 9. Should opportunity occur, look for implements chiefly at the bottom of the gravels between the river-drift and the subjacent rocks, in the positions shown by a + in the following imaginary section across a valley. 9a. Note whether the

Fig. 1.

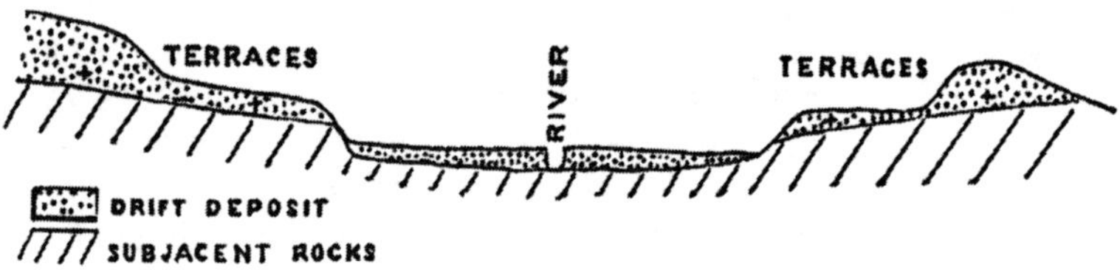

stone of which the implement is made is a local rock? 10. The following, amongst many varieties, are the two principal types which have been found in Europe, in the drift-gravels, associated with the remains of elephant, rhinoceros, hippopotamus, and other extinct animals: these illustrations are contributed by John Evans, Esq., F.R.S.

Fig. 2.

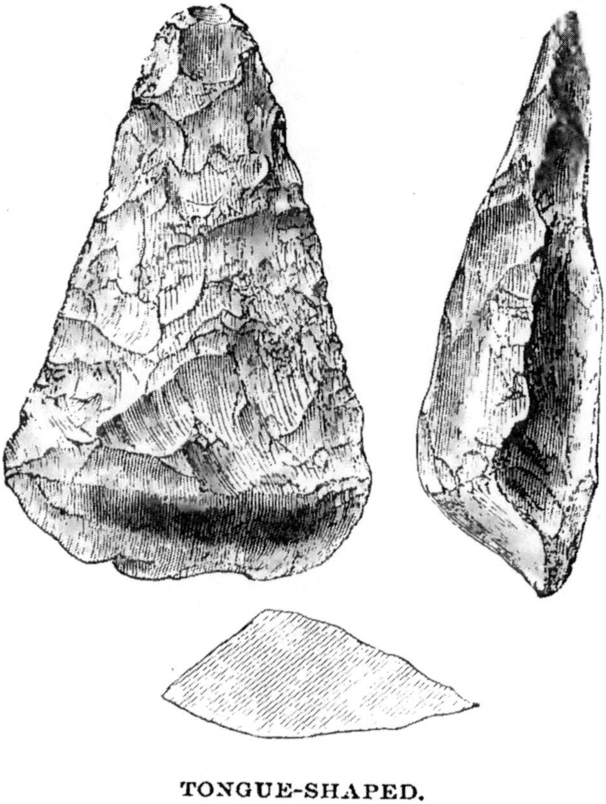

TONGUE-SHAPED.

Fig. 3.

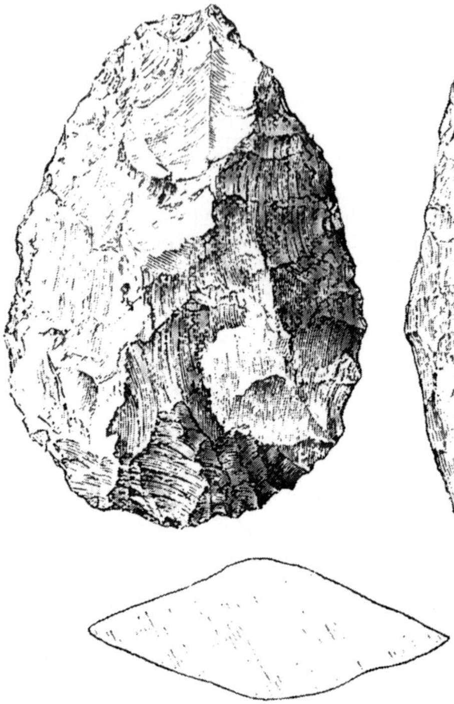

OVAL.

Caves.—11. Examine the floors of caves by cuttings from the surface as far as the solid rock; take sections of the deposits and note the relics discovered in each stratum. In limestone caverns, note the thickness of any stalagmite coating upon or beneath the floors. 12. It must be remembered that strata representing vast periods of time may be represented by deposits only a few feet or even inches in thickness, and that a very false impression might be conveyed by any error in labeling or describing the position of the specimens. Animal remains should be preserved for examination at home, and for submission to a comparative anatomist, especially if the traveller is not one himself. 12*a*. Pebbles showing any bruises or signs of wear should be brought away, as well as more obvious relics. 13. Note the elevation of the mouths of the caverns above the existing watercourses, and give plans and sections when practicable.

Neolithic (*Surface*) *Period.*—14. Implements of neolithic type are likely to be found in soil turned up by cultivation, or where the surface has been removed by rains, on the borders of plateau-lands overlooking a valley, near the margins of ancient forests, or in any place suitable for an encampment near water: attention may be drawn to such spots by observing the flakes, which are always abundant in places where stone implements have been fabricated. 15. Note what class of pottery, if any, is found, with flakes and implements on the surface. 16. Notice whether the implements have been formed by chipping or by grinding; if by grinding, look for the concave rubbing stones on which they were ground. 17. Notice any evidence that may exist of metal having been little used at the same time or subsequently to the stone implements. 18. Preserve any bone implements or other relics found on the spot. 19. Should any implements be found with holes bored through them, notice whether the holes are cylindrical or enlarged towards the outside, from having been bored from the two sides. 20. Preserve as many specimens as possible, and *label them all at once*, by writing with ink (or preferably lead pencil) upon the stones if possible; take measurements and make outline drawings of any that cannot be carried away, and notice what animal remains are found with them. 21. The following illustrations of some of the principal types of neolithic implements found in this country are contributed by John Evans, Esq., F.R.S.

Fig. 4.

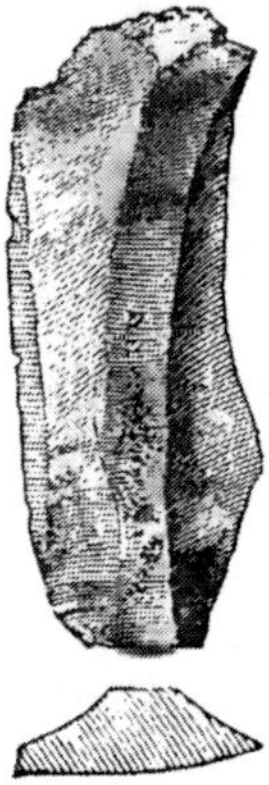

FLAKE.

Fig. 5.

CHIPPED CELT.

Fig. 6.

FLINT BORER.

Fig. 7.

FLINT HAMMER-STONE.

Fig. 8.

CORE.

Fig. 9.

SCRAPER.

Fig. 10.

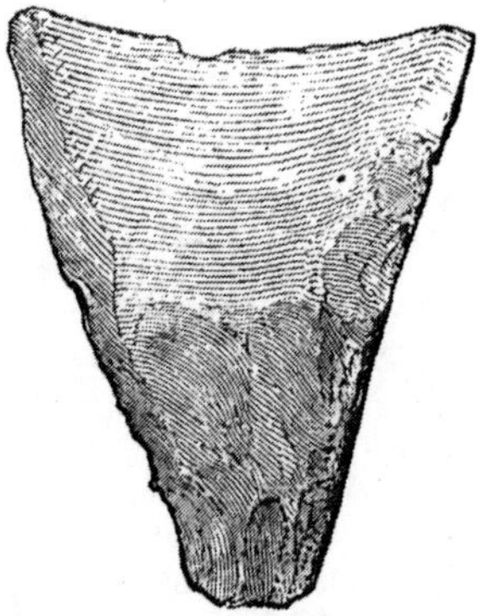

CHISEL-SHAPED ARROW-HEAD.

Fig. 11.

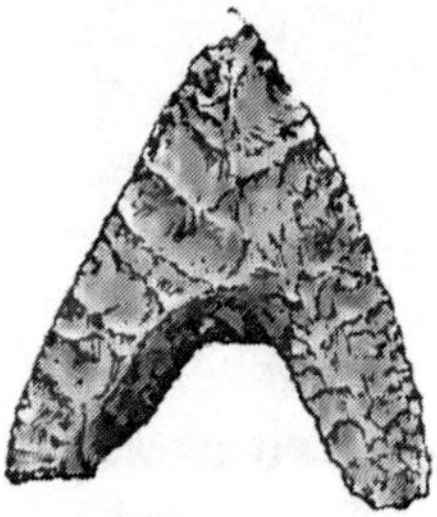

TRIANGULAR
ARROW-HEAD.

Fig. 12.

LEAF-SHAPED
ARROW-HEAD.

Fig. 13.

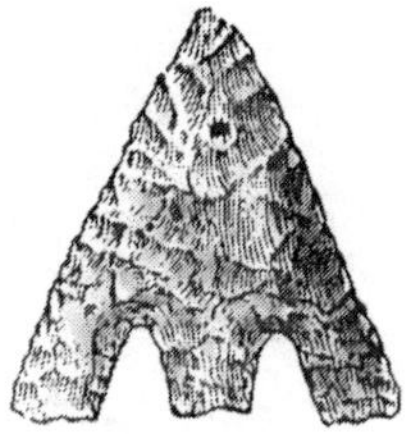

BARBED
ARROW-HEAD.

Fig. 14.

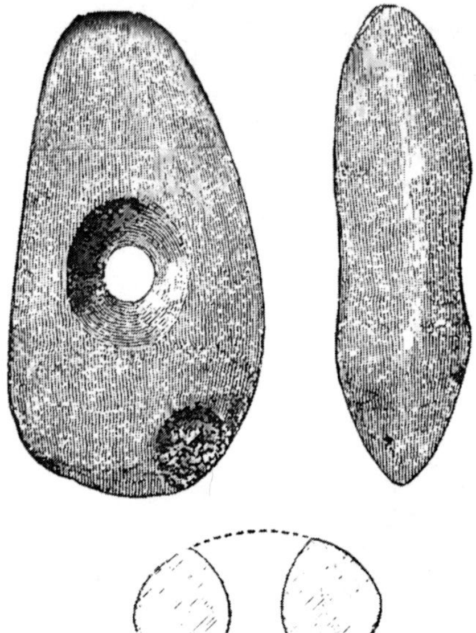

PERFORATED STONE HAMMER.

Fig. 15.

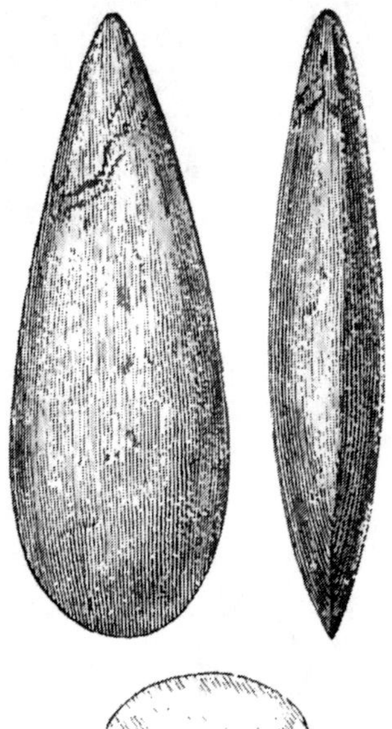

GROUND CELT.

Fig. 16.

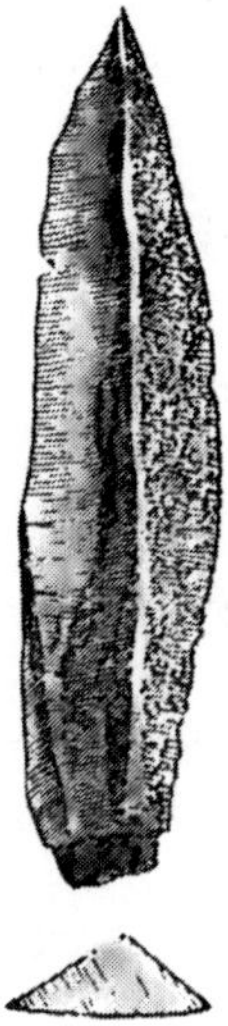

FLAKE.

Fig. 17.

FLINT SAW.

Fig. 18

LOZENGE-SHAPED ARROW-HEAD.

22. The traveller before starting should make himself thoroughly acquainted with these forms from original specimens at the British Museum or elsewhere, and also with the appearance of stone flakes, bulbs of percussion, facets, &c., and he should be able to distinguish the drift-types from the surface-types as they are known in this country.

Megalithic Monuments.—23. Dig between the uprights of megalithic monuments to ascertain if they have been used as burial-places, taking care not to overturn the stones. 24. Take plans, marking the uprights in lines and the cap-stones in dotted lines, noting the compass-bearings, and be particular in stating that they are compass-bearings, when such is the case, and not true bearings. 25. Are holes bored in the uprights? and are there any superstitious observances in the country connected with these or similar holes? 26. Note the topographical position, whether situated on hill-tops, on the terraces of river-valleys, and so forth. 27. Note the age of any trees growing within or upon these or similar monuments. 28. Is there any evidence of the stones having formerly been covered by a tumulus? 29 Describe all the varieties that exist, and ascertain, if possible, whether the varieties of form are due to original design or to subsequent dilapidations. 30. What is the greatest observed size of single stones? Is the stone used found close to hand, or has it been brought from a distance? 31. Are they ever daubed with red or any other colouring matter? 32. Recount any traditions of the inhabitants respecting these monuments. 33. Are votive offerings still made at these monuments? and have the superstitions connected with them been incorporated into the religion of the period?

Tumuli.—Burial-places.—34. Take sections of the surface of tumuli, when possible, before excavating them; drive in a peg in some spot where it is not likely to be covered by the excavated material, and let this be a standard of reference for the levels of all objects discovered in the tumulus. 35. Cut a trench from the outside towards the centre at least one half the width of the tumulus, throwing back the earth; be careful to reach the undisturbed soil everywhere; look out for holes in the undisturbed soil, and examine their contents carefully; when the central interment is reached, dig downwards over it from the top. 36. Note the levels of any layers of charcoal that may occur, also animal remains. 37. If the tumulus has been used as a place of interment subsequently to its original construction, distinguish carefully the primary from the secondary interments. 38. For relics deposited with the dead *see* No. LVIII. 39. Take the compass-bearings of all interments, preserve the skulls, if possible, with the lower jaws, and even any fragments of skulls, and measure the bones; make sketches of the relative position of the bones.

Ancient Intrenchments.—40. (XLVII., WAR.) Cut into the ditches of ancient intrenchments in search of any relics which may have accumulated at the bottom and become silted over.

Lake Habitations.—41. Examine small islands near the shores of lakes or rivers, to see if they have been inhabited at a former period; see if piles of wood have been driven in round the margin, and whether there has been a communication with the shore by means of a causeway; preserve all relics found on or beneath the surface, and make a plan of the locality.

Inscriptions.—42. (See No. LXXVI.)

Ancient Habitations.—43. Examine the floors of ancient habitations as far as the undisturbed soil, and further, for burials or other relics of a past age; take plans (See No. IV., HABITATIONS.)

A. L. F.

No. XLVII.—WAR.

The arts of peace and war have at all times progressed simultaneously. No nation has ever achieved warlike renown without some corresponding progress in the industrial arts; nor has any nation survived which has neglected the art of war. It is necessary, therefore, to study the warlike institutions of a people, in order to form a true estimate of their culture.

Organization.—1. Does any custom equivalent to enlistment exist? 2. Are all adult males warriors or are any of them reserved for other duties during war? and at what age do they begin to serve? are tallies or musters kept of the warriors? 3. What are the functions of the women during war? 4. Is there any permanent organization for war during peace, or is it extemporised on the outbreak of hostilities? 5. Have they sham fights during peace? and if so, describe them? 6. How are the warriors brought together preparatory to war? and how is war proclaimed—by heralds or others? 5. How are war-councils composed?

Discipline.—8. How are the leaders appointed? 9. Are they identical with civil governors, priests, and doctors? 10. Have they any distinctions of dress (give drawings)? 11. Are they the strongest and most courageous? 12. Have they any subordinate leaders, and how are they appointed? 13. Have they any rewards for warlike achievements, or punishments for offences in war? 14. Is the religion conducive to warlike prowess? 15. Have the chiefs any aids, or runners, or criers, to carry messages? and what authority do these possess?

Tactics.—16. Do warlike expeditions set out by word of command? 17. How is the march of a party conducted? do they move in a body or in detached parties, with a broad front or in column? 18. Do they send forward advanced parties, or parties to guard the flanks? 19. Any specific order or custom with respect to encampments on the line of march? by whom are the encampments regulated? how are the horses tethered? any orders as to fires? how are the huts and tents made and placed? 20. Are battles planned beforehand? 21. Have they any disposition or order of battle? do they stand in closed or open files, and how many deep, in line or in disorder? and how many under the command of one voice? do they keep step? how do cavalry and infantry support each other when these exist? how are the camp-followers and baggage disposed of? 22. How do they change from the column of route to the line of battle? 23. Are they courageous? and are the young and the weak placed in front or in rear? 24. Have they any war-songs, cries, or dances? 25. Have they any recognized cries or commands for moving to the right or left, advancing or retreating in battle? 26. Are any portion of the warriors kept in reserve, and if so, at what distance, and in what number? 27. Have they any knowledge of turning an enemy's flank? 28. Any regulated method of carrying, holding, or using their weapons? 29. Do they rely chiefly on missile or hand-weapons? and have they any special disposition for these arms? 30. Do they employ noise as a means of encouragement, or do they preserve silence in combat? 31. Do they stand and abuse the enemy before fighting, or boast of their warlike achievements? 32. Any knowledge of the advantages of ground or position in battle? under what circumstances do they quit a masked wood or defile, and take to the open? 33. Have they rallying-points in rear in case of defeat? 34. Do they employ treachery, concealment, or ambush? and what is their usual mode of proceeding in this respect? 35. Any superstitious customs or omens in connexion with war? 36. Do they especially preserve chastity during or before war? and is there any superstition with respect to this custom? 37. Do they make night-attacks? 38. Any stratagems for concealing their trail from the enemy? 39. Are dogs employed in war? 40. Are the horses well reared, trained, and treated? what is their speed and endurance? give any details respecting farriery, mode of riding, &c. 41. Do they form alliances with other tribes? and if so, to what extent do they act in concert, and under what leadership? 42. Do personal combats take place between men of the same tribe? and how are they conducted?

Weapons.—Describe minutely all the varieties of their war weapons. 44. Are the same weapons used in war and the chase, or as tools? 44*a*. Are their weapons home made or made by other tribes? if the latter, do they make any alteration before using them? 45. Describe their defensive armour, and its capabilities for defending the body. 46. Are special weapons used by particular tribes? 47. Do the weapons vary in the same tribe? and what have been their varieties in times past? 48. Do they use the amentum, the throwing-stick, or any other means of accelerating the flight of the javelin? 48*a*. Are the spears provided with a spud at the butt? and for what reason? 49. Do they employ sinews, whalebone, or any other means of giving additional spring to the bow? 50. Are the arrows furnished with a foreshaft of hard heavy wood, and tipped with stone, glass, bone, or metal? 51. Are feathers used with the arrows? how many? are they set on spirally, or are the heads twisted to give a spin to the arrow? 51*a*. Are the arrows notched at the butt to fit the bowstring? 52. Describe the ingredients of any poison that may be used, its effects, and the cure employed. 53. Is the bow drawn to the shoulder or the chest? is it held horizontally or vertically? are the feet used in shooting? 53*a*. How is the butt of the arrow held by the fingers when drawing the bow? 54. What is the range, accuracy, and penetration of these missile weapons? 54*a*. Is any guard worn to diminish the blow of the bowstring on the left hand? 54*b*. Is any apparatus worn on the right hand to draw the bow?

[*Note.*—It appears desirable that some test of accuracy should be established. If the natives can be induced to shoot at a target, the distance of each shot from the point aimed at should be measured, added, and divided by the number of shots. The figure of merit obtained by this means would enable a comparison to be made with the shooting of other races conducted under similar conditions. If no measure is at hand, tie a knot in a string for each shot, and divide the string into as many equal parts as there were shots fired. A target composed of grass bands covered with paper might be used, not less than 6 feet in diameter. Misses should be scored with a deviation of 4 feet; distances, 50, 100, 150, and 200 paces of 30 inches (LXXII., STATISTICS).]

55. Have they any regular system of training to the use of weapons? and at what age do they begin? 56. Are the women trained to the use of weapons? or have they special forms? 57. Are weapons handed down as heirlooms from father to son? 58. Are the same forms of blades used for different weapons, as the axe-head, spear-head, sword, &c.? 59. Are the points of wooden implements hardened in the fire? 60. Are stones thrown by hand in war? and if so, with what degree of force and accuracy? 61. Is there anything resembling a standard? and what is its history? 62. Describe the manner in which European blades are hafted by the natives? 63. Any use of slings, clubs (straight, curved, or mushroom-headed), crossbow, blowpipe, boomerang, holy-water sprinklers, knouts, glaives, bills, spears, pikes, gisarms,

halberds, two-handed swords, serrated weapons, partisans, daggers, &c.? 64. Are the swords single or double edged, used for cutting or thrusting? 65 Are the heads of the arrows constructed to come off in the wound? any use of harpoons? 66. Do they throw their axes, daggers, or other weapons at the enemy? 67. Any use of sickle or concave edged swords? 68. Are ogee-sectioned blades used for spear-heads, swords, &c. (blades sunk on alternate sides)? 69. Describe all the varieties of shields. Are the shields used for parrying darts by twisting them in the hand? are plain sticks or clubs used for the same purpose? 70. Describe the meaning and use of all the marks and grooves on the metal blades. 71. Describe the mode of hafting, holding, and using all weapons. 72. To what extent have the natives adopted civilized weapons and abandoned their own? do they take readily to European weapons? have they altered their forms in any way? 73. Careful drawings to scale of all the varieties of weapons are very desirable, with the native names for them. 74. Describe the horse-equipment used—bits, saddles, spurs, cloths, and horse-armour.

Fortifications and Outposts.—75. Give plans and sections to scale of any defensive works. 76. Plans and sections of any pitfalls used for war. 77. Any knowledge of inundations for defensive purposes? 78. Any stakes, palisades, stockades, abatis, or thorn-hedges for defence? 79. Do they employ caltraps (small spikes of wood or metal fixed into the ground to wound the feet)? 80. Do they ever build on raised piles for defence? 81. Do they fortify the villages in which they usually reside? or have they strong places in the neighbourhood to resort to in case of attack? 82. Are their fortified posts arranged to support each other for the mutual defence of a large district, or constructed for isolated and independent defence? 83. Do they occupy naturally defensive positions, such as hill-tops, promontories, &c.? 84. Are their defensive posts selected with a due regard to water-supply? are there cisterns? 85. Do they take in stores for prolonged defence, and make a protracted resistance? 86. Do they man the whole line of their entrenchments, or only defend the gateways? 87. Give plans of any special defences for the gateways, drawbridges, &c. 88. Any knowledge of second and third lines, keeps, or advanced works? 89. Any arrangements for cross-fire, flanking defence, &c.? 90. Are loopholes used? 91. When earthworks are employed, do they stand *on* or *behind* them? 92. Do their entrenchments command the whole of the ground on the outside within range of their weapons, and have they a good command of view? 93. Do their entrenchments run in a straight line, or do they conform to the defensive line of the ground? 94. Is the size of the fortress regulated by the number of its defenders, or solely by the features of the ground? 95. Any knowledge of mines or fougasses? 96. Do the defenders roll down large stones on the enemy? and do they take in a store of them? 97. Any knowledge of fire-balls, fire-arrows, boiling oil, &c.? 98. How is the attack usually conducted? 99. Do they sit down and invest the place? 100. Any knowledge of escalading or breaching? and how is a breach defended? 101. Do they operate on the supplies of a fortified place? 102. Any lines of circumvallation or countervallation, saps, or breastworks against the place? when stone walls are used are they covered by earthworks in front? 103. Have they scouts or outposts? 104. Do they employ special men for this duty, or do all take it in turn? 105. Are outposts are arranged on any regular system? 106. Have they any special signals for war?

Supply.—107. How do they supply themselves during war? 108. Does each man provide for himself? or is there any general arrangement, and under what management? 109. Is any portable food used, especially for war? 110. Are their proceedings much hampered by the difficulties of supply? 111 How are requisitions made upon the inhabitants in their own or those of an enemy's country? 112. How do they carry their food, water, and baggage, and the forage for their horses?

Causes and Effects of War.—113. What are the chief causes of war? 114. Do feuds last long between tribes? 115. How do they they treat their prisoners and wounded? 116. Have they any special customs with regard to the first prisoner that falls into their hands? 117. Do conquered tribes amalgamate, or do they become servile castes? 118. How are the women of conquered tribes dealt with? 119. How do they divide the spoil? 120. Are their attacks always succeeded by retreat, or do they follow up a victory? 121. Is it likely that a knowledge of the arts, culture, &c., of other tribes has been spread by means of war? 122. To what extent has the population been checked by wars? 123. Has migration been promoted to any great extent by warlike expeditions? 124. Are scalps or heads taken? and how preserved?

A. L. F.

No. XLVIII.—HUNTING.

There has always been a close connection between war and the chase; and many of the questions relating to the former will apply to this section. It is generally admitted that all races have passed through a stage of existence in which they were dependent on hunting almost entirely for their food. The hunting-practices of savages are therefore of great interest in tracing the origin of customs and institutions which may have survived in a more advanced state of culture. Endeavour should be made to trace the process by which tribes, in a hunting phase of existence, may have been led gradually to adopt a pastoral, and ultimately to settle down into an agricultural, life. The various arts and customs necessitated by the life of a hunter should be noticed, especially such as tend to throw light on the relics of prehistoric times. This is, without doubt, one of the most persistent instincts in human nature, and the tendency to relapse in a hunting life is frequently seen in those whose means are such as to free them from the shackles of progressive industry.

1. How are hunting-parties formed in a tribe? 2. Are they identical with war-parties? 3. What honours are awarded to successful hunters? 4. Under whose command are the parties organized and conducted? 5. What hours of the day or night are employed for this purpose? 6. How is the possession of a carcase decided? does it belong to the killer or to the owner of the weapon? what rule is there as to the possession of an arrow or other weapon found in the body of an animal? 7. Are arrow-marks used to decide the title to possession? 8. How are the spoils divided amongst the tribe? and what are the rights of the non-hunting portion of the community? 9. How are disputes respecting the possession of game settled? (*See* also LAWS and CUSTOMS.) 10. What are the seasons for hunting different animals? 11. Any laws or customs for the preservation of game? 12. How are the hunting-grounds arranged between the neighbouring tribes? 13. Are the regulations on this head respected? or are they a constant source of dispute and war? 14. Are the migrations of the tribe influenced by the habits of the animals they hunt? 15. After a successful hunting expedition do they feed until they are gorged? 16. Are any hospitalities given on the occasion? 17. Is there any evidence of feasts having arisen in this way? 18. What are their methods of preserving meat? 19. To whom do the skins and horns belong? 20. Is any tribute paid in game? 21. What ceremonies or dances are practised on setting out or returning from a hunting expedition? 21*a*. Do individuals voluntarily suffer pain to ensure success? 22. What omens or superstitions have they in connection with hunting? 23. To what deity do they attribute success in hunting? 24. How do they approach and capture the different animals? 25. What precautions are taken against being scented by them? 26. Do they evince an accurate knowledge of the habits of animals? 27. What means do they employ for deceiving game?—*a*, by dressing up in the skins of animals? *b*, by imitating calls and other noises? *c*, by smell? *d*, by colours? *e*, by decoys? *f*, by cunning appeals to any other of their senses or instincts? 28. Do they drive game? 29. Do they

use nets in driving or capturing game? how are they constructed, and of what materials? 30. Any use of palings or trenches in driving or capturing game? 31. Give drawings of any pitfalls used? 32. Snares. 33. Any use of a spring-trap, consisting of a lance attached to an elastic stem, by which the animal is transfixed? if so, give sketches of all the varieties employed, and of any other traps, with the baits used. 34. Describe accurately the weapons employed in the chase? 35. Are they the same employed for war? 36. Are any of them also used as tools for different purposes? 37 At what distances do they use their weapons with effect against different animals? 38. Can they hit a bird on the wing? 39. Any use of bird-bolts or blunt-headed arrows for stunning animals without damaging their skins? 40. Any use of arrows with two or more points? 41. Are arrows with different-shaped heads carried in the same quiver, and used for different animals? describe the uses of the different forms. 42. Is any record kept of game killed? 43. Are fires employed to drive game? 44. Are dogs or other animals employed in hunting? what birds are used in hawking, fishing, &c.? 45. Are they trained to any special functions? 46. By whom are they kept and controlled? 47. Are horses used in hunting? 48. How is the game carried on an expedition? 49. Is there much waste? 50. Is it a reproach to wound without capturing an animal? 51. Describe the different modes of fishing? 52. Describe all the varieties of fish-spears used. 53. Fish-forks. 54. Dams. 55. Weirs. 56. Are arrows used for fishing, and with or without detached heads? 57. Is any connexion of form observable between the harpoon-head and the fish-hook? 57*a*. Is either barbed? 58. Describe the varieties of fish-hooks used. 58*a*. Is any material used in place of a hook to become entangled in the teeth of the fish? 59. Harpoons. 60. Fish-nets; describe the different kinds, and note what is used for floats, sinkers, &c., and their forms. 61. Fish-traps. 61*a*. Is any edible bait used, or is the bait intended to deceive the fish by its appearance only? 62. How are fish preserved and cured? 63. Are they preserved alive in ponds? 63*a*. Are large fish ever attacked at close quarters, *e.g.* by diving? 64. Are captured animals ever preserved alive? and if so, under what arrangements? 65. Any use of the lasso, or other similar contrivance? 66. Is the milk of any wild animal used? and if so, how obtained? 67. If the tribe has no knowledge of agriculture, state what wild fruit, roots, or grasses are eaten, and how prepared? 68. Are the children instructed in hunting? and at what age do they commence? 69. Are the women employed in hunting or fishing? 70. To what extent are firearms employed in hunting? and how long have they been in use? 71. Are they expert in the use of them? 72. Are poisoned weapons used in hunting? and what are the ingredients of the poison? 73. If so, do they cut out the wound before eating the animal? 74. Are any records of hunting-feats preserved? and how? 75. Are any poisons used for killing or stupefying fish?

A. L. F

No. XLIX.—NOMADIC LIFE. No. L.—PASTORAL LIFE.

1. Is the tribe settled or nomadic? 2. If the latter, what induces its migrations? to find fresh pastures for cattle, to escape the severity of summer or winter climate, for purposes of fishing or hunting, for purposes of trade and barter, or for what purpose? 3. Are its movements continuous all the year round, or does it encamp at certain seasons? if so, what is the character of its summer, autumn, winter, and spring camping-country? 4. Is it purely pastoral, or does it grow some produce in the spring and summer? 5. Is any hay or other fodder stored for winter use; if so, how is it prepared, how and where stored? 6. Give a list of the domestic animals kept by the tribe, with their native names (*see* No. LII.). 7. If oxen are kept, what colour and shape are they? are they horned or polled? are they used for draught purposes? is their flesh eaten, or are they kept only for dairy purposes? are any

malformations practised on their horns? 8. Of what size and colour are their horses? are they used for food? Is mare's milk employed? What breed do they most resemble? 9. Describe the sheep and goats: are they horned or hornless? is their milk used for food? what use is made of their wool and hair? if felted, describe the process of felting. 10. If camels or reindeer are used, state for what purposes, and what use is made of their wool or hair. 11. What breed of dogs is kept? and what are they used for? 12. Are cats or poultry kept? if so, describe them. 13. Are there any traditions about the place where the domestic animals were derived from? 14. Are they traded in? if so, to whom are they sold? and at what markets, and what is the relative value of each? 15. How are the horses or cattle broken-in and trained? 16. Is gelding practised; if so, what is the process? 17. What diseases prevail among the domestic animals? and what remedies are employed to cure them? 18. Describe the harness, bits, saddles, stirrups, carts or other vehicles in use, and the manner in which the horses are picketed. 19. If milk is fermented, describe how the spirit is made; also describe the manufacture of butter and cheese. 20. What are the relative duties of men and women in regard to the domestic arrangements, the camping or moving, &c.? who are the neat-herds? who do the milking, brewing, churning, &c.? 21. Describe the tents or yurts in use: are they floored or carpeted? are they covered with felts, with thatch, wattles, or how built? Are the tent-coverings ever fastened down with large stones? and is it probable the use of stone circles might have originated in this way, as has been suggested? If there are special yurts used for summer and winter, describe their differences and idiosyncracies. 22. How are they moved from place to place? and what is the distance generally moved in a day? 23. What furniture do they contain? 24. Of the articles in use among them, which are home-made and which obtained by purchase or barter, and from whom? 25. Do articles reach them from a considerable distance? if so, by what way (*ex. gr.*, Russian knives are found among the Esquimaux, close to the Great Fish River, Japanese things among the Kamskatki, &c.)?

26. Have they domestic gods? if so, how are they arranged in the yurt or tent, and how carried about? 27. What fuel is used? 28. How are the animals killed? are there any superstitions in regard to the method of killing them? 29. Are there any superstitions about using water for washing and other purposes, such as exist among the Mongols, who hold it sacred, and will not pollute it? 30. Note especially any particulars in which the tribe resembles some other tribe known to the inquirer, however distant. 31. How are the dead buried during the period of migration? and what burial-customs are induced by the nomadic habits of the people? 32. What arts are promoted, and what discouraged by nomadic life? 33. What are the particular institutions and customs which owe their origin to the necessities of nomads? 34. To what extent do cattle-lifting and the other concomitants of pastoral life promote war? 35. What particular weapons, tools, or other implements or contrivances may be regarded as characteristic of nomads? 36. What sanitary arrangements are in force in their camps? how are the latrines managed? 37. What precautions are taken to protect the animals from wild beasts? 38. What is the nature of their dealings with the tribes met with on their journeys? 39. What is the military organization induced by nomadic life? and what is the nature of their temporary defences? (*See* XLVII.) 40. Do they work in metals? if so, describe the apparatus employed and the objects fabricated, and state whence the ores are procured. 41. Is the use of stone or bone implements in any case necessitated by nomadic life? 42. Describe the mode of catching the animals, and driving and herding the flocks. Is the lasso used? 43. How is wheat ground upon the line of march? 44. Describe any temporary ovens and cooking-places employed. (*See* XXV.)

H. H. H.

No. LI.—AGRICULTURE.

1. Do the people cultivate the soil, or do they only gat*t* its spontaneous produce? 2. Are the cultivators the whole body of the people, or are they a separate class? 3. Are both sexes employed in agriculture, or is its practice restricted to men or to women? or what parts do the sexes respectively take? 4. What implements are employed—plough, hoe, spade, sickle, mattock? 5. What forms of these, and of what material made, and whether of home manufacture or imported (as are the hoes in some parts of Africa)? 6. Are any of them employed also as tools or weapons? 7. Are any of them, or objects of larger or smaller dimensions, but similar form, used as money? 8. Figure any strange or unknown form. 9. Is any domestic animal employed in ploughing or harvesting? 10. What plants are cultivated, whether for food, stimulation, or ornament? 11. Describe any that are exotic, and ascertain when and whence they were derived. 12. At what seasons and in what manner are they sown and reaped or dug up? 13. Is any attention paid to the growing crops? 14. Is irrigation practised? and what means are used to apply it? 15. How is the harvest gathered and carried home, and how stored—whether in stacks, caves, pits, or granaries especially constructed? 16. What means are adopted for cleaning, thresbing, or winnowing grain, or for the preparation of food from roots? 17. Are any of the roots, or other alimentary substances used, poisonous or unwholesome before preparation and cooking? (No. XXV., FOOD.) 17*a*. Are the poisonous or other peculiar qualities of plants well known? 18. Are there any legends respecting the introduction of any of the food-plants, or their creation by deities? 19. How are the lands to be cultivated, selected, or divided? describe land-marks. 20. Any hedge-rows or plantations to protect crops in exposed situations? 21. Has

any one a permanent right of property in any portion of the soil? or has the tribe in general, or the chief a superior right? 22. Is the same land tilled again and again till it becomes barren, or is fresh ground cleared and tilled yearly? 23. Is the advantage of fallowing understood? or is there any idea of a rotation of crops, or of the use of manure of any kind? 24. How are the crops protected from depredation? 25. What are the relative values of the different cereal or other grains or roots? 26. Do the people possess any domestic animals? if so, what kinds? and what are the apparent peculiarities of breed found in these? 27. Were any of them introduced by civilized men or others from abroad? 28. Are they kept for their flesh, milk, or eggs, or for use in cultivation? 29. How is the milk treated, and in what state is it used? (See No. XXV., FOOD.) 30. Is any kind of sanctity attached to the domestic animals, or to the cow-houses, dairies, or implements used in connection with them! 31. Are any wild or uncultivated plants commonly used as food, or resorted to only in time of scarcity? if so, what are they? and do they appear to yield wholesome nutriment, or are any diseases attributable to their use? 32. Are any of the cultivated plants apparently derived from indigenous wild ones? 33. What produce is imported and exported? and whence? 34. Is the tribulum employed for threshing? (a large plank or board stuck with flint or stone flakes on the underside, which is drawn over the wheat on the threshing-floor.) 35. Are scarecrows or other means of frightening birds or animals used? 36. Does the whole of a crop belong to the individual or family; or are tithes payable? 37. Is any charm or fetish placed in the field to make the crop good? 38. Does the same piece of land continue in the possession of one man, or are there periodical redistributions?

J. B.

No. LII.—TRAINING AND DOMESTICATION OF ANIMALS, AND RELATIONS OF ANIMALS TO MAN.

1. What animals are domesticated or kept in subjection? (See XLVIII., XLIX.) 2. What animals are hunted or fished? (See XLVIII.) 3. What animals are sacred and what worshipped? 4. What animals give names to men? 5. What cries are used to call animals? 6. What animals are gregarious in the neighbourhood, as dogs, horses, &c.? 7. Of what kind are the tame dogs and the wild dogs? and how many different breeds are known? have they the same intelligence and attachment to their masters as the dogs of civilized races? 8. How are the habits of wild animals influenced by contact with man? 9. What hybrid or mule animals are there? 10. Are any animals castrated? 11. Are tame animals branded or marked? (Give drawings of the marks.) 12. Are the souls of animals and men supposed to be interchangeable? and what animals are supposed to represent men? (See XXVII.) 13. What knowledge is there of mythical animals, as dragons, &c.? 14. Have any tombs or remains of supposed dragons, &c., been found? and are these the remains of extinct animals, or purely mythical? 15. What animals are forbidden to be killed and what eaten? 16. What animals are lucky, or the reverse? 17. What monsters exist in the sea or elsewhere? 18. What strange animals are supposed to live in rivers, wells, &c.? 19. How far do wild animals hinder or otherwise affect the movements of men? 20. What animals are migratory? 21. Whence are they supposed to come? 22. What traditions are connected with them? 23. Are the people expert in training animals? 24. What animals are trained? and for what purposes? 25. What are the means employed in breaking them in? 26. Any customs or peculiarities in relation to the breeding of animals. What measures are taken to preserve

the purity of breeds? 27. What animals are used for milk and what for food? 28. Any omens or superstitions in regard to animals. 29. Are they well treated? 30. What vermin is bred upon the person? what is done to destroy vermin? 31. What marks on horses, &c., are considered lucky or unlucky?

H. C.

No. LIII.—SLAVERY.

1. Are slaves kept? 2. How does an individual become a slave? by birth, capture, through debt, crime, &c.? 3. Has the owner absolute power of life and death? 4. Have the slaves particular tasks, and are these of a menial or dangerous kind? 5. Are slaves permitted, or forced, to marry? and with what class? 6. What is the position of the children? are they slaves in the same degree as their parents? 7. Are members of a slave family sold away from the rest? and is this considered a hardship? 8. Can a slave redeem himself or any member of his family? 9. What is his social position afterwards? 10. What is the position of the child of a freeman by a female slave? 11. Is it usual for freemen to take captured slaves as wives? 12. Does this give them the social rank of their husbands? 13. Is the buying and selling of slaves a recognised business? are there markets for the purpose? 14. Are slaves branded or marked, or do they differ in dress from the rest of the community? 15. Are they warriors? or what is done with them in time of war? 16. Are they allowed to carry arms in time of peace? 17. Are there any public brothels in which slaves are kept? 18. Is it considered a disgrace for a free women to have an intrigue with a slave? 19. What is the proportion of slaves to the rest of the population? 20. Is slavery an ancient institution?

C. H. R.

No. LIV.—RELATIONSHIPS.

1. Are relationships traced in the male or female line? 2. How are they estimated? 3. How does property descend? 4. In what position does the family stand with reference to the tribe? 5. Are uncles and aunts on the father's side distinguished from those on the mother's? 6. Is a great uncle distinguished from a grandfather? 7. Is the system of relationship with reference to males the same as that with reference to females? 8. Is a friend generally addressed by his name, or by the title of his relationship? 9. Are the genealogies carefully preserved? if so, for how many genera tions is there any trustworthy record? 10. In what way are genealogies kept? by pictures, symbols, &c., or by oral tradition?

J. L.

Great discrimination is necessary between generic terms and those referring to individuals, such as *parent*, and *father* or *mother*, *grandfather* and *ancestor*. Test how far upwards distinctive terms extend (grandfather, grandmother, great-grandfather, great uncle, great aunt, &c.), and note at what degree it merges into a generic term; repeat the process with the present generation (brother, sister, cousin, male and female, &c.), and then with the next generations (son, daughter, nephew, niece, grandson, nephew's son, daughter, &c.). Ascertain whether these terms are the same when used by men and women

No. LV.—TREATMENT OF WIDOWS.

1. How are widows treated? 2. Are they, or any of them, sacrificed at the husband's grave? or is this custom known to have existed in times past? 3. If not, do they pass to the husband's brother, or to any one else? 4. Are they allowed to marry again? 5. Do they retain any portion of the husband's property? 6. Is any special dress worn by widows? and for how long? 7. Do they observe any time of mourning? 8. Do they carry any memento of the deceased? 9. How are posthumous children regarded?

J. L.

No. LVI.—INFANTICIDE.

1. Does infanticide prevail to any extent? or is it known to have been practised in times past? 2. If so, is it clandestine, or is it recognized by the law? 3. Is any difference made between male and female children? 4. Are any, and if so, what reasons given for it? 5. Are there any special peculiarities which lead to the destruction of the infant? 6. Are there any special customs with reference to twins? 7. Is the father consulted as to the fate of the infant?

J. L.

No. LVII.—CAUSES THAT LIMIT POPULATION.

If men or any other kind of animals were invariably mated early, and if their issue were always reared with care, the produce would increase geometrically, and in no large number of generations would occupy every habitable space. But, as a fact, the number of inhabitants of most countries is very stationary; what, then, are the causes which so exactly neutralize the tendency to increase?

These are best learnt by exhaustively working out the history of 20 or 30 families, finding out how many of their members married, and at what ages, what was their issue, how many of the children died, owing to what causes, and so forth, as stated more fully below. Such an inquiry will necessarily lead to a far more accurate knowledge of the social condition of the people than could otherwise be obtained, and is sure to yield indirectly, as well as directly, a valuable harvest of results.

1. *Conditions of Marriage.*—At what ages do they marry? how many do not marry at all? What are the restrictions which hinder persons from marrying as soon as they are inclined? how as regards the frequency of polygamy or polyandry and the number of wives, &c.? What is the proportion of male and female adults?

2.—*Separation of husband and wife.*—Customs dependent on the institution of polygamy; other circumstances which separate them periodically, or for long periods.

3. *Influences restrictive of fertility.*—How long does the mother suckle her child? At what ages does she begin and end child-bearing? Is any diet adopted by women or other practice followed, as a check on fertility? What is the proportion of children to a marriage? What is the frequency of sterile women? Are drugs, or physical means, used to induce abortion? Is any operation performed on either men or women to induce sterility?

4. *Loss of infant life.*—Still-births, infanticide, and of what sex? Death of child due to severe exertion of mother too soon after childbirth? Do more children die at one time of the year than another? and of what do they die—epidemics, other diseases, want, accidents, war? What is the mortality at different ages, as shown by the sizes of families whose parents are of different ages? What is the proportion of aged men to aged women?

It is not sufficient to collect disjointed facts here and there; the information ought to be full on every point, the materials well put together, and the conclusions fairly worked out.

F. G.

No. LVIII.—BURIALS.

(See also XLVI. § *Tumuli.*)

1. Is the cause of death recognized (wounds, disease, &c.), or is it assigned to some act of commission or of omission of the defunct? 2. Do the friends or relations attend upon the sick man until his death? or is it considered unlucky to be present at the supreme moment? 3. What is done with the body immediately after death? are the limbs straightened or bent up? 4. Is the ordinary clothing left upon the body? or is any special dress used? 5. Is the body left in the house, or removed to any other locality, before burial? 6. Is embalming practised, and what preservatives are used? or portions of the body treated in any way? 7. Is there any funeral procession, and who composes it? 8. Are hired mourners known? 9. Are signs of mourning worn, such as shaving the head, wearing clothes of unusual colours, &c.? 10. Is self-mutilation practised by the mourners? 11. Are speeches (eulogies of the deceased, &c.) made at the grave? and are these pronounced by public orators, or by friends of the defunct? 12. What is the mode of burial? in trees, on platforms, in the earth? 13. Is any coffin used? 14. Are the remains left undisturbed or are the bones removed when decay is complete? 15. What is buried with the body? any implements, weapons, food, or eating utensils, and why? 16. Are wives, servants, slaves, or favourite animals buried with the body, and what reason is assigned for this practice? 17. Are any images of wood or pottery buried with the body? 18. What is the posture of the body in the grave? 18*a*. Is it regarded as of importance whether the head is

directed to any point of the compass? Are there any ceremonies at the digging of the grave? 19. Is a grave or coffin ever re-opened for the interment of a near relation? 20. Is an interment ever made in a canoe, and is the latter provided with all necessary apparatus? 21. Are heads of friends preserved by smoking or otherwise? 22. How are these regarded, as a protection or as mere souvenirs? will the owners readily part with them? 23. In burials by inhumation, is any mound or prominent memorial raised above the grave? 24. Are fetishes placed on the graves? 25. Are these for the good of the deceased or as a protection against him (to keep his spirit quiet)? 26. Are there any superstitious ideas about graveyards? will the natives visit them at all times? 27. Are objects of value buried in the grave, and are they considered safe from theft? 28. What is the difference between the burial of a chief and of a common man or woman? Does it differ only in degree of cost? 29. Are individuals buried in their houses? and are these houses then deserted? 30. Are the persons who have handled a corpse regarded as unclean? for how long? and how do they purify themselves? 30*a*. In what posture is the body carried to the grave?

Cremation.—31. Is cremation practised as well as inhumation, tree burial, &c., and why? How is the body burnt, on a specially prepared pyre or in the house of deceased? 33. Are there any ceremonies observed, or special instruments used, at the lighting of the funeral fire? 34. Are any living creatures, inanimate objects, incense, &c., burnt in it? 35 Is a mound erected over the pyre, or are the bones collected and preserved or buried? 36. If buried, describe the method, *i.e.*, form of grave, of the cinerary urn, accompanying objects, and attendant ceremonies. 37. If the calcined bones are kept above ground, who keeps them, and how are they regarded; is the fate of surviving relations bound up in their preservation? 38. Is desiccation of the dead body practised? 39. Are mummies made? Describe the process and the nature of preservatives used.

C. H. R.

No. LIX.—ASTRONOMY.

Divisions of the Year.—There are two celestial phenomena by which they may be affected :—(1) The solar method, by noting the group of stars which rise just before the sun, or set just after him and in his immediate neighbourhood ; this suffices to fix the time within 10 days ; (2) the lunar method, by counting the number of new moons and reckoning the odd parts of the first and last lunation ; this may suffice to fix the time even to a day ; but a lunar year of 13 complete months is not of the same length as the solar year, to which the seasons conform ; and therefore each method has an advantage and a disadvantage, and the two cannot be used together except by some clumsy compromise. 1. Inquire into the plan used for dividing the year as regards (*a*) seasons and crops, (*b*) sun, (*c*) moon. 2. Is the difficulty of combining solar and lunar years recognized ? 3. If so, is it met or avoided, and how ? 4. Are there names for the phases of each lunation ? and for how many phases ?

Division of the Day.—There is a difficulty in using the height of the sun as a means to divide the day, because at the same hour it stands at different heights at different periods of the year, whether the hour be reckoned from midday or from sunrise or sunset. The difference of its bearing at sunset and sunrise is always considerable, but greatest within the polar circles, where it varies the whole way from N. to S. Near midsummer it momentarily dips below the horizon toward the pole, and near midwinter it momentarily emerges above the horizon, opposite to the pole. 5. Is the fact of the variation of the sun's position at the same hour known and regarded when using it to divide time or to steer courses ? 6. Is the property of the sundial known ? viz., that the shadow of a fixed rod sloping towards the pole, always falls in the same direction at the same hour all the year through ? 7. How is the day divided, by the position of sun or the length or direction of its shadow ? 8. How as regards other means of division of the day? 9. Of short periods of time, as a walk two "pipes" (tobacco-smoking) long? 10. Are there names for any of the points of the compass? are these derived from prevalent winds, or from what?

Steering Courses by Sun and Stars.—For sun *see* last Par. The same star (not planet) has always the same bearing at the same altitude; but the bearing of the star, unless it be near one of the poles of the sky, changes considerably during the night, and its position in the sky differs at the same hour on different nights. To a traveller in equatorial regions, the equatorial stars, as Orion, are always either E. or W. of him unless exactly over his head. 11. When courses are steered by the stars, are these facts recognized? and how are they met? (*See* also No. V, NAVIGATION.)

F. G.

No. LX.—ARITHMETIC.

(*See* also No. LXIV, MEASURES, ETC.)

The use of fingers and toes in counting, as well as of pebbles, sticks, &c., should be carefully noticed; also cases in which the numerals of the language only extend to a very low limit —for instance, not beyond 3 or 5. All examples which illustrate the formation of numerals by words describing the act of counting fingers and toes should be carefully sought; for example, the appearance of words meaning "hand" for 5, "man" for 20. Compound numerals capable of being analyzed into the constituent numbers should be sought for, such as a word for 7, meaning five-two. The numeration should be examined to show how it turns on reckoning by fives, tens, and twenties, which are the almost universal systems of the world, derived from the primitive practice of counting on the fingers. It should be ascertained how far the numeral words now used are borrowed from other people. In the further development of arithmetic, it should be noticed how far the four simplest rules are understood, and by what mental or written processes they are actually worked out. The system of figures or cipher used by a nation, and the rules of their higher arithmetic, often show from what people they must have been obtained, thus throwing light on the later history of their civilization.

1. Do people generally count on fingers and toes, and in a particular order, beginning with one particular finger? 2. Do they use pebbles, heaps of grains, &c., as aids to counting? 3. What names have they for numbers? up to how many? 4. Does any particular number stand as an indefinite expression for "many"? 5. Do any of the numerals show that they originally referred to counting by fingers and toes, such words as "hand" for 5, "hands and feet," or "man," for 20, "two on the feet" for 12? 6. Have any of the lower numerals a meaning besides that of the numbers they signify? 7. Does numeration go by fives, tens, or twenties (quinary, decimal, vigesimal)? or, for instance, does such a numeral as fourteen signify $10+4$? or is there a term for 65 like threescore-and-five, *i.e.*, $3\times20+5$? 8. Are any numerals, especially high ones, borrowed from a foreign language? 9. How far are addition, subtraction, multiplication, and division understood? 10. Are they done mentally, or with the aid of counter or abacus? 11. What is the exact process carried on by the reckoner's mind? 12. Does trade, barter, taxation, &c., involve any complex calculation? 13. Are any figures or ciphers in use? and how used? 14. Any higher arithmetic?

E. B. T.

No. LXI.—PROPERTY.

To what extent private property is recognized; personal and landed property. Tenures of land, customs concerning, &c. Individual, family, and common property. Heirship, succession to. Rights over property of another (*e.g.*, right to trees on land of another, or to game or fish caught by another). Guardianship. Mortgage. Right of resumption at "year of jubilee." (*See* under LAWS, CUSTOMS, NOMADIC LIFE, SLAVERY, ETC.)

No. LXII.—TRADE.

Trade is one of those developments of culture which, when carried to its height, promotes the greatest prosperity of nations, and which is rarely found wanting, in some form, even among the rudest tribes; but the mode in which it is to be recognized, and the degree to which its progress is arrested, have seldom received attention; and it will repay observation to trace, in an obscure form, the real institutions from which, in earliest times, the commerce of the world had its beginning.

Produce.—The exchange of commodities is one step towards augmenting the individual enjoyment of each individual, by enabling him to profit from the labour of many, instead of being solely dependent on his own exertions. 1. What articles of home production are there? 2. Of what raw materials are they made? 3. What articles of foreign manufacture are used? 4. What raw materials are introduced? 5. What articles are sent abroad? 6. What raw materials are sent abroad? 7. Is any article prohibited?

Home Production.—8. Does each household supply itself? 9. Do the people interchange any articles of produce or manufacture? 10. What are the trades carried on by the men? 11. What are the trades carried on by the women? 12. Do the people merely work as slaves for the chiefs, or do they supply the produce of their labour for a consideration?

Division of Labour.—13. Do particular individuals carry on particular trades or occupations, as husbandry, fishing, &c.? 14. Is the occupation hereditary or that of a caste? 15. Is there any superintendence of labour? 16. Are trades restricted to any nationality? Is any trade prohibited?

Labour.—17. Do all classes labour? 18. Do men labour as well as women? 19. Do warriors labour, or labourers take part in war? 20. Is there any pre-eminence assigned to skill in handicraft, or any degradation attached to labour. 21. At what age do boys begin to labour? ditto, as to girls? 22. Is there any mode of apprenticeship, or of training to any occupation? 23. Is there any trace of masters and journeymen?

Trades.—24. What are the general occupations of the people? 25. What are the separate occupations of individuals? 26. Are there workshops (*e.g.*, for boat-building)? 27. Are there quarries for stone? 28. What are the tools employed in husbandry, and in the several trades?

Foreign Trade.—29. Recapitulate what articles are brought in from abroad. 30. Also what are exported. 31. By whom is the exchange effected? and what are the names of the races traded with? 32. How is it effected? 33. What article is brought from the greatest distance? and how? 33*a*. Are there middlemen between producer and consumer?

Barter.—34. Is there any interchange of commodities freely between man and man—food, clothing, cattle, slaves, tools, arms, ornaments? Are presents to strangers binding? and how is the value of such presents regulated?

Relative Value.—35. What is the relative value of a man slave? 36. Woman slave? 37. Wife or wedding dowry? 38. Cattle? 39. Weapons? 40. Tools?

Measures of Value.—41. (*See* also under LXIII, LXIV.)

Markets, Fairs.—42. Is there any common place of trade? 43. Is there a periodical market in the village? 44. Is there a periodical fair? 45. Are these markets or fairs frequented by various tribes or foreigners? 46. Are there market- or fair-tolls or dues paid to chiefs or others? 47. Who collects the tolls?

Right of Way.—48. Is there any right of way for strangers to a market or fair?

Credit.—49. In the case of produce brought from abroad, is the article of exchange given at once or at a future season or crop? that is, is credit given? 50. In case of non-delivery of exchangeable goods, what remedy is there? 51. Is war made on the tribe? are goods of other traders of the same nationality seized? are the people of the nationality of the debtor excluded from trade?

Traders.—52. Do any of the people engage in trade? 53. Is there a distinct class of persons engaged in trade? 54. Are there pedlars? 55. Are there brokers? 56. Are there marriage-brokers?

Association.—57. Are associations formed for fishing, for a canoe, for a trade-expedition by sea or land? 58. What is the principle of sharing? 59. What is the share of the head man? 60. What the share of the absent owner of a canoe, or person sending goods?

Trade-marks.—61. Are there any distinctive or trade-marks on goods, weapons, tools, &c.? 62. Is any trade mark recognized on articles of importation from abroad?

Transport.—63. How is the transport of commodities effected? 64. If by sea or river, is there any consideration for freight? 65. If by land, can porters be hired or beasts of burthen? 65*a*. Are trading voyages undertaken at stated times? are these regulated by winds prevailing at the time, or how? (*See* also LXVIII. COMMUNICATIONS.)

Stock.—66. Is there any accumulation of the labour of former generations in houses, walls, plantations, tools, weapons, ornaments, &c.? 67. Are the people careful in consumption, improvident or thrifty? 68. Is there any accumulation of objects by individuals? 69. Are the crops or fishing-produce cured or stored? 70. What store of food is kept on hand? 71. Has the community any claims, by way of credit or otherwise, on other communities? 72. Are the people, relatively to neighbours, rich or poor? 73. Do they or their neighbours assign any cause for the difference?

H. C.

No. LXIII.—MONEY.—EXCHANGEABLE VALUES.

Consequent on the development of trade, articles assume a relative value, and measures of value are established, which ultimately take the shape of money.

Exchangeable Value.—1. As the existence of such an idea is sometimes obscure and does not present itself on the surface, it is useful to apply the questions under LXII. What is the relative value of a man slave? woman slave? wife or wedding dowry? cattle? weapons? tools?

Measures of Value.—2. What measures of value result from the relative values between various articles of property as above? 3. Is there any common representative of these recognized or which may be used within the tribe? 4. Is there any common representative understood among various tribes? 5. How is compensation attested for the murder of an individual, ransom, or the expenses of a war between tribes?

Money.—6. Does any article esteemed to be of value pass from tribe to tribe, as beads, shells, &c.? 7. Are there small and large measures of value, as beads (single or worked in belts), &c.? 8. What is there in the shape of coins, metal, glass, leather, &c.? 9. Are tools or weapons recognized as mediums of exchange? are they so employed before or after they are finished and hafted, or after they have been in use? 10. Can the forms of any objects used as money be traced to those of tools, weapons, or other articles previously employed as mediums of exchange (as in China)? 11. Are pigs or bars of metal employed as money? and if so, what are their forms and value? 11*a*. Are there any imported imitations of these? and what is the difference of value between them and the originals? 12. Are cakes of salt or hides used as money? 13. Are personal ornaments of gold, silver, copper, iron, or other materials recognized as money? 14. Any marks or stamps upon objects used for this purpose? if so, give drawings of them. 15. Are any such marks copied from European or Asiatic coins? 16. Any penalties for forging stamps, &c.? 17. Give both the local and foreign names for all objects used as money. 18. Does the money actually pass into the possession of the person entitled to it, or is it stored in a common bank and the owner credited with its possession? 19. Is money hoarded, for dowries, &c.?

H. C.

No. LXIV.—MEASURES AND WEIGHTS.

Measures are universally based on the parts of the human body, natural objects, or on units determined by natural conditions. Weights are similarly based upon natural objects, which are of a generally uniform specific gravity, such as seeds of plants. Standards of weight are fixed in certain cases by taking the amount of gold which is equivalent in value to the chief unit of barter, *e.g.*, ox or slave. The multiples and mutual relations are partly conditioned by the system of numeration derived from the fingers and other parts of the body, and the system of weights is closely connected with the practice of employing seeds or pebbles as counters.

Measures of Length.—Is there any measure corresponding: 1. To the breadth of finger or thumb? 2. To the length of finger or thumb? 3. To the distance between finger joints? 4. To the nail? 5. To the hand breadth? 6. To the length of hand? 7. The palm? 8. The greater span (from tip of thumb to tip of little finger)? 9. To the lesser span (from tip of thumb to tip of forefinger)? 10. The cubit (from elbow-point to tip of middle finger)? to the smaller cubit (from elbow-tip to the knuckles?) 11. To the length of the arm? 12. To the fathom (from finger-tips to finger-tips when the arms are stretched out)? 13. To foot? 14. To pace? 15. To stride? 16. To a leap? 17. To the height of a man? 18. To the length of a spear? 19. To the length of ox-goad? 20. To a pole or rod? 21. To ox-yoke? 22. To yoke-strap? 23. To a cord, rope, or chain? 23*a*. To the distance which a man can stretch with a spear? 24. To a spear-cast? 25. To the throw of stone or quoit? 26. To a bow-shot, day's journey (or portion of day) of man, horse, or canoe? 28. What particular articles (if any) are measured exclusively by any of the foregoing? *e.g.*, cloth, timber, land, &c.

Measures of Surface.—Is there any unit based upon the size of the hide of an ox, or of any other animal? 30. Is there any uniform size of manufactured articles, such as mats, cloaks, &c., which is used as a measure? 31. How is arable land measured? 32. Is there a definite unit based on the day's ploughing of a yoke of oxen, &c.? 32*a*. Or is the unit of land measure based on the amount which can be sown with a given measure of seed, such as a peck or a gallon? 33. What is the shape of the land unit? oblong or square? 34. If oblong, what is the proportion between the length and breadth? 35. Is there any higher land unit containing a given number of some smaller unit, such as the day's ploughing? 36. How is the measuring carried out? with rod, goad, rope, or any portion of the plough or harness of the cattle? 37. Is square measure in use?

Measures of Capacity.—37*a*. Is there any measure equivalent to the hollow of the hand? 38. To the handful? 39. To the armful? 39. To the load of a man, of a horse, ox, waggon, or boat? 40. To a hen's egg, gourd, shell, joint of bamboo? To a calabash or jar of uniform size? 41. To a basket? Are there distinct measures for different products? 42. How is corn measured? 43. Wine, &c.?

Weight.—44. Is there a system of weight? 45. Do they employ balance or steelyard? 46. Are the weight units formed by seeds of plants? 47. Have they a recognised system of multiples of weight, the seed of one plant being the multiple of another? 48. Have they any higher units of weight, such as the load of a man, beast, or waggon? 49.

Is there more than one system of weight in use? 50. What articles are weighed by each? How are the precious metals weighed? 51. Is there any special unit for weighing gold? 52. If so, on what is that unit based?

Multiples.—53. How are multiples formed? 54. By fives, tens, twelves, twenties, or hundreds? 55. Are the multiples by doubling, by the hand of 4 fingers, by the hand of 5 fingers, by the foot of 4 hands of 4 inches each, by 4 hands of 5 inches, by 4 scores of 16, by 4 scores of 20, by hundreds of 5 twenties, or by hundreds of 6 twenties?

Standards. 56. Are standards of measure and weight in use? 57. Are these standards sub-divided? How?

Tallies. 58. Are tallies kept of number of articles? 59. How are they notched?

Counters. 60. Are counters used in numbering, such as seeds, shells, pebbles? 61. Is the *abacus* in use?

W. R.

No. LXV.—MARITAL RELATIONS.

1. Ascertain the marriage ceremonies? 2. Is there more than one mode of marriage? 3. How are wives obtained? by purchase? 4. Is there any pretence at capture of a wife? 5. Are there any ceremonies or vigils, previous to the marriage, performed by either husband or wife? 6. Does the wife enter into the family or into the tribe of the husband? 7. What are the respective rights and duties of the husband and wife? 8. Is there more than one description of marriage? 9. Is polygamy permitted? if so, is there any head wife? and what are her privileges? 10. Do the wives live together? or do they have separate dwellings? 11. Is concubinage permitted? 12. Is polyandry permitted? if so, how are the husbands selected? 13. What are the restrictions on marriage? 14. What are the prohibited degrees of relationship? 15. May a man marry a woman of the same family? of the same name? of the same tribe? of another tribe? (*see* also

TOTEMISM, No. XL.) 16. In what estimation are courtesans held? 17. Does a man cohabit with his wife immediately after marriage? 18. Does he visit her by stealth for some time after marriage? 19. Is the bride deflowered by any other than her husband? 20. What are the occasions when men refrain from cohabitation with their wives? 21. Is the marriage ceremony regarded as possessing any religious character? 22. Is there any symbol of a previous marriage to any deity? 23. Are the women allowed much freedom before marriage? 24. When married are they good wives? 25. Under what circumstances, if any, is divorce permitted? 26. May wives who have been divorced marry again? 27. Do a man's relations with other individuals undergo any change on his marriage? (*e.g.*, with his wife's father or mother).

J. L

No. LXVI.—EDUCATION.

Education in its widest sense means training, and there are few peoples which have not some form or other of training the young. Physical training begins in early childhood, and those children's games which mimic the employments of their elders form a kind ef education, later, when the youths associate with the men more serious instruction commences. Ordeals which lads, and sometimes girls, have to undergo at puberty, or before receiving full standing as adults or as warriors, though employed as tests of bravery and endurance, constitute a short but sharp training. During initiation into manhood there is often a prolonged isolation, usually accompanied by various hardships which altogether is an education of no mean rigour, lasting, in some cases, from a few weeks to many months or even years. Discipline is then rigorously maintained, and all kinds of food and other restrictions are enforced, the breaking of which is severely punished—the death penalty may even be inflicted. At this time information is usually imparted to the lads concerning tribal usages and beliefs, taboo restrictions, practical ethics and their code of morals; even a new language may be taught (Lower Congo). The training of sorcerers or medicine-men is usually still more severe, and it is important to learn every detail of the education the novitiates have to undergo. The step is not great from this to the training for a priesthood.

(*a.*) *Physical training.*—1. Is there any recognised system of physical training? 2. Do the children's games afford exercises in strength, agility, or in sharpening the senses? 3. Is there any test of physical endurance or of bravery, either as a distinct custom or during initiation? 4. Are the young men directly instructed when out fishing, hunting, or fighting, or do they learn solely by imitation?

(*b.*) *Mental training.*—5. Is there any mental training apart from periods of initiation? In either case describe what takes place. 6. Is a sacred language ever taught? 7. Under what circumstances are legends or poems taught and recited? 8. Is there a special class of men whose duty it is to learn, repeat, and teach these? 9. Are there any schools, and, if so, what is the system of education? 10. Is there any course of instruction for doctors, musicians, dancers, or any other class of specialists?

(*c.*) *Moral training.*—11. Is there any special occasion on which the customs of the tribe or moral code are taught? It is very important to get the latter and at the same time to make sure that it has been unaffected by Christianity or Mohammedanism. 12. What kind of education have the sorcerers or priests?

A. C. H.

No. LXVII.—GAMES AND AMUSEMENTS.

Describe the games played by men, women, boys, girls. [It is useful to play European games with children to see if they are recognized.]

1 What games are international? 2. What games are noticed among animals? and are any imitated from animalss. 3. Describe the toys used by men, women, boys, girls? 4. Describe any games of ball played, and give drawings of the implements employed. 4*a*. Is "cat's cradle" known? 5. Describe any gambling games, and give drawings of any marks, holes, notches, figures, or numbers upon dice, sticks, bones or cards?

6. Are high stakes played for? 7. Are wives, children, or slaves staked? 8. Does suicide often result from gambling? 9. Are games of chance or physical exercise preferred? 10. Are any games considered manly or the reverse? 11. What animals are used in game fighting? 12. Are they preserved and trained for the purpose? 13. Describe any spurs, defences, or other objects that are attached to them. 14. Are any omens relied upon for success in gambling? or any superstitions connected with the games?

15. Describe any theatricals in force amongst the people, with the masks, dresses, scenes, &c. employed. 16. What is the character of the performances? are they comic, tragic, elevated, or obscene? Have any of them a religious character? 17. Are there special actors? or do all take part in them? 18. Are the orations prepared or impromptu? 19. Are they historical, or relating to passing events? 19*a*. Are the characters well-known to all? 20. Do men, women, boys, and girls act? 21. Do boys dress and act the part of women? 22. Describe any dances performed for amusement? 23. Describe any juggling tricks; and ascertain, if possible, how they are performed. 24. Are animals employed in any of these performances?

25. Describe any foot-races that are run, horse-races, boat races, &c., with the distances and prizes. 26. Feats of agility, climbing, boxing, and wrestling. 27. Describe any games of stone-throwing, weapon-throwing, and arrow-shooting, with the distances and the size of the mark aimed at. 28. Describe any weapons used on these occasions, and state whether they are used for amusement only, or for war as well. 29. Are rats, birds, or other animals shot for amusement? 30. Aquatic sports, such as swimming-matches, shooting rapids, jumping from heights, diving, &c. 31. Equestrian feats, jumping on and off, standing up, shooting, jumping through hoops, &c.

32. Note any of the foregoing sports that are unknown amongst the people. 33. What sites are selected for the sports—natural rocks, hollows, hill-tops, &c.?

A. L. F.

No. LXVIII.—COMMUNICATIONS.

The actual weights transported and the greatest work to be got out of man and beast week after week deserve accurate measurement, also the food they do it on (*see* XXV.). Marks like those made by gipsies or by scoring trees to show the road or to give hints to followers are worth inquiring into. Savages are accredited with an almost instinctive power of finding their way; but many of the cases quoted are found to be less extraordinary than stated. It would be a matter of extreme interest to rigidly test the power of several renowned path-finders, by leading them in a circular path in a new forest and seeing how directly they are able to find their ways back in a straight line.

1. Are there roads of any kind? how made and preserved? 2. Does the roadway through bush and forest consist of a network of paths running in and out of each other.

3. *Swamps.*—How are they passed? Is anything sunk to preserve the roadway?

4. *Fords.*—Are any measures taken to preserve or improve them? Do the natives understand the natural line of fords from salient to salient banks?

5. *Ferries.*—Are any boats kept for the purpose? how maintained? what payment is made? any understanding with neighbouring tribes respecting them?

6. *Bridges.*—Are any of the following kinds used?—*a*, bridges of single trees, or trees from opposite sides crossed and fastened in the middle; *b*, bridges of piles and beams; *c*, trestle bridges; *d*, lattice bridges; *e*, bridges of upright jambs and lintels of large stones; *f*, sloping jambs united at top; *g*, arches of horizontal slabs overlapping and converging, and closed by a large slab at the apex; *h*, bridges of radiating arches; *i*, boat bridges; *k*, raft bridges; *l*, flying boat bridges; *m*, swing bridges; *n*, rope bridges; *o*, suspension bridges.

7. Are corduroy roads known? 8. What points are attended to in selecting the halting-places? 9. Any kind of inn or public house? and how maintained? 10. How are travellers accommodated in villages? 11. Are wheeled vehicles used? if so, describe them? 12. Poles fastened to horses and trailed behind. 13. Are palanquins known, and carried by men or horses? 14. Describe pack-saddles, and all modes of carrying burdens on animals' backs. 15. Are cradles or knapsacks used on the backs of the men? 16. Any public conveyances or horses? 17. What ceremonies or salutes are made by passers on a journey, or on entering houses or villages? 18. What permissions have to be obtained by travellers? 19. Any passes or complimentary introductions to neighbouring tribes? 20. In transporting great weights by large numbers of men is the principle of pulling simultaneously by sound of music or voice practised, as with the ancient Egyptians and Assyrians? 21. Are great weights suspended by crossed beams on the shoulders of a number of men, as with the Chinese? what is the name for this? 22. Anything of the nature of milestones? 23. Drawings of signposts,

roadway marks? 24. Ditto of telegraphic signals? 25. Are any public wells dug? and any regulations established for the use of them?

F. G.

No. LXIX.—TRIBAL MARKS.

(*See* also III. PAINTING AND TATTOOING; XL. TOTEMISM; XLVII. WAR.)

Many people mark their bodies in various ways, either by painting, tattooing, scarification or deformation, or wear peculiar and distinctive clothes, ornaments, or badges. It is important to discriminate between those body or dress decorations which are purely individual and those which have a social significance. Care must be taken not to mistake mourning scarifications, cuts made for sickness or pain, and marks indicating age or sex for tribal marks. It is possible that the people of a particular district may have a local method, or even a transient fashion, for certain scarifications, mode of dressing the hair, or other form of marking or decoration which might mislead a visitor into describing it as a tribal custom. Neither must the different styles of the art of neighbouring districts be mistaken for different tribal marks. Difference in technique or artistic feeling may characterise different tribes without their being in the least intentional. The same remarks apply to clothes and ornaments.

Very little is known about tribal marks in the true sense of the term. It is probable that such marks occur in countries like Australia, where there are clan restrictions as to marriage, the marks in these cases being to warn from incest. It would be interesting to see whether these marks can in any way be associated with the clan totem. In Torres Straits, for example, some women, at least, had their animal totem cut on the small of the back. The animals were in pairs: similar paired totem animals are found in the same district on various objects, curiously recalling the "supporters" in armorial bearings. It is easy to conceive that if the totem animal was frequently cut on objects belonging to the members of a clan, it might in time come to be the symbol of that clan and later of a tribe.

1. Are painted, tattooed, or scarified designs upon the body or particular deformations used and recognised as marks of a clan, caste, or tribe? 2. If so, state on what part of the body the designs are placed, and give careful drawings or tracings, and find out if they have any special names for individual marks. 3. Collect all the variations you can, and endeavour, with native aid, to trace out the sequence (if any) of them. 4. Distinguish between clan, caste, and tribal marks. 5. Warriors on the war-path are usually distinctively coloured, or have weapons, head-dresses, and other ornaments, which differ from those in use on other occasions; are these for the purpose of distinguishing the opposite sides or merely casual? 6. If the former, are there individual variations which nevertheless keep to one common type? 7. If trees or other natural objects are marked, do those marks indicate personal or collective property? Endeavour to trace the signification of such marks, and in all cases fortify your own conclusions by native evidence.

A. C. H.

No. LXX.—MEMORIAL STRUCTURES.

(See also XLVI. § *Megalithic Monuments.*)

1. Are there other memorial structures apart from those erected over the dead? if so, what is their character? 2. Are stones erected in honour of the dead, apart from those over their graves? 3. Are such monuments ever erected to the

living ? 4. Are they put up to commemorate battles, murders, accidents, or other historical events ? 5. To record journeys, discoveries, or conquests ? 6. In honour of, or to propitiate, deities ? or to commemorate religious festivals, miracles, or other events connected with religion ? 7. Are large conical mounds or cairns ever erected for these or similar purposes? 8. Are any objects buried in such mounds, apart from human remains ? 9. Any figures cut in the turf, upon the sides of hills, such as figures of men and animals ? 10. Any mounds in the form of saurians, snakes, or other animals ? and what do they signify ? 11. Are any objects buried in the foundations of buildings or beneath landmarks ?

No. LXXI.—TOPOGRAPHY.

(*See* also LXVIII. Communications.)

1. What boundaries are there ? how are they marked ? 2. What are the names of places or routes followed by the natives ? 3. What foreign slaves or traders are there ? and what routes can they describe ? 4. What geographical beacons or landmarks are there ? 5. What seas are known ? and what is said of the land beyond them ? 6. How do the natives account for the sources of rivers and the formation of hills, valleys, rocks, &c. ? 7. What generic names have they for the natural forms of land and water ? 8. What is their idea of the form of the universe ? 9. What account do they give of the history of creation ? 10. Give drawings of any native maps, and state whether they are done by the eye or by measurement.

H. C.

No. LXXII.—STATISTICS.

The topics suitable to statistics are too numerous to specify, they include every thing to which such phrases as "usually," "seldom," "very often," and the like are applicable, which vex the intelligent reader by their vagueness and make him impatient at the absence of more precise data.

The principal things to be borne in mind in making statistical enquiries are :—

1. That the groups with which they deal should be homogeneous. *Ex.* It would be correct to inquire into the average height, and the frequency of different degrees of deviation from it, of greyhounds, and similarly as regards the speed of racehorses ; but it would be absurd to talk of these averages as regards dogs or horses generally, because there are many varieties of them differing greatly and irregularly in height and speed (see further remarks in par. 5).

2. When the homogeneous groups are largely governed by the variation of a dominant influence, it is necessary to split them up into subdivisions, each referring to a short phase of the variation. *Ex.* It is correct to seek the average height of boys between 11 and 12, 12 and 13, and so on, but it would be absurd to seek that of boys generally.

3. To select cases on a system wholly independent of the quality about which the inquiry is made. *Ex.* It would be correct to estimate the stature of the male adults of a nation by measuring individuals selected by lot ; but it would be incorrect to take townsmen alone, and still worse those who lived in an unhealthy suburb of a town. It requires keen observation and much wariness to avoid errors due to a neglect of this caution, because phenomena that appear independent are often linked together in indirect and subtle ways. *Ex.* If we were to select the upper classes of Londoners according to the initial letter of their names, as printed in the Court Guide and were to choose the letter Z for the purpose,

we should be led utterly astray, as nearly all those names are foreign.

4. As regards the requisite number of cases, a few that are wisely selected and accurately reported are better than very many that are not. Each error sacrifices several good observations before it is diluted until it disappears; but if a faulty bias (as in par. 3) runs through all the observations no increase in their number will eliminate it. Otherwise, the rule is that the precision varies as the square root of the number of observations; thus, twice the precision necessitates four times the labour. It is the best plan to proceed tentatively; if the results fall into more harmonious sequence as you proceed, it is worth proceeding; and if after dividing your statistics into 2, 3, or 4 groups you find the groups agree pretty well, and that their sums form a yet more regular curve than that obtained from any of the subdivisions, you may safely trust it.

5. Variability.—Mention is above made of "homogeneous" groups: this epithet is applicable when individual differences are entirely due to the *aggregate* effect of a great many small and independent variable influences. *Ex.* The stature of an English male adult is due to his being a man of English race, reared under the range of those conditions of food, temperature, clothing, disease, and the like which prevail in England. The large causes common to all are the English breed and the range of English conditions; the small causes are differences of varieties and families, and of food, temperature, clothing, and the rest, within the range. Variability depends wholly on the fact of *multifariousness of causation*, and is subject to the well-known law of deviation, which has no more to do with the particular items of multifariousness than the rules of arithmetic have to do with the quality of the things to be added or multiplied. Two and three make five, whether the objects be pence, or peas, or bills before Parliament; so the law of deviation holds for the stature of men and animals, and apparently, in a useful degree, for every homogeneous group of qualities or compound qualities, mental or bodily, that can be named. It is a very general

statistical law. The obvious effect of multifariousness is to make it an extremely rare event that all or nearly all the influences should be exerted in the same direction. *Ex.* It is a very rare event that all the cards in a hand at whist are found to be of the same colour. This is a simple result of the law of permutation: there are a vast and calculable number of different events each of which is equally likely to occur, and only one of these is the event in question. Proceeding on this principle and making certain rather forced suppositions to render calculation feasible, the law of deviation is mathematically deduced; and comparing fact with theory, wherever comparison is possible, it is found that they agree very fairly and in many cases surprisingly well. Reasoning backwards, we may suspect that a group is not homogeneous, or that the large influences are not sufficiently subdivided into phases (refer back to 3), when it does not conform to this law. The law shows that the frequency of small deviations must be very much greater than that of large ones, and that the larger the deviation is, whether above or below the average, so the frequency of the occurrence diminishes in an accelerating degree. It also shows, owing to the suppositions introduced, that the deviations on either side of the average are symmetrical; this is rarely strictly the case in nature.

Useful Data.—When collecting data of strength, stature, keenness of eye-sight, or of hearing, accuracy of aim in shooting, or any other variable performance, a ready and efficacious process is to use two fixed tests in each particular, and to note the number of those who fail and of those who succeed in either test. We are able to make use of the law of deviation described in the last paragraph, and thereby to calculate with fair precision from these two data, the proportion of those who would fail at any other test of the kind. Similarly, we can calculate the value of the test that would be beyond the powers of just one half of those submitted to it; in other words, we know what would be the average performance. *Example*—Suppose strength is to be tested. Select two stones and weigh them. Then offer small prizes to those who can lift both of them in succession, beginning with the lightest. Note the number who fail and the number who succeed in each test, and that is all. But it is safer to use three test-stones as a check upon the calculation. Also, before finally selecting the stones, make a few preliminary trials and fix upon such as it is likely that, roughly, about a quarter of the whole number would fail with the first, half with the second, and three-quarters with the third. It is impossible, briefly, to explain how the calculations have to be made. The method is fully described in my work on "Natural Inheritance," p. 62 (Macmillan & Co., 1889).

F. G.

No. LXXIII.—POPULATION.

Count wherever you can. The contingents of fighting-men afforded by a district, as compared with that procurable from other districts, gives some idea of their relative population, and it is not difficult to make out the particulars of a small district in detail. In some countries the numbers attending a religious festival may give a clue, so may the number of marriage-feasts and burials.

F. G.

No. LXXIV.—CONTACT WITH CIVILIZED RACES.

1. Were the first civilized strangers who visited the races reported on, sailors, traders, refugees, convicts, deserters, settlers, or missionaries?

2. Did they communicate the vices rather than the virtues of civilized life?

3. What was the influence of the missionaries? Did they impart religious instruction only? Was the conversion of the

tribe reported on real, or did they only add a belief in a new sort of magic to their old superstition?

4. Are the Aborigines apt at, and did they make rapid progress in, learning the elements of knowledge?

5. Is there any physical bar which prevents the race from elevating itself in the social scale?

6. Has any existing civilized race acquired knowledge of the arts of civilization in less than several generations? And if civilization be not gradually and spontaneously developed is it possible to force it rapidly on any particular race without causing its destruction or decay?

7. On first contact with a civilized race aboriginal races usually retire or give way, but no decrease in numbers is at first perceptible. At what period did the decrease in number of the race reported on become perceptible?

8. Was any taint in the blood or other cause of decay known to exist in the aboriginal race before they came in contact with civilized men?

9. Were the women in the habit of using any particular food affecting their reproductive powers? (The Maoris do.)

10. Can the decay of the race be partially attributable to sudden change in the habits of life, want of the excitements proper to savage life, and listlessness resulting from passions subdued (but not eradicated), in obedience to the commands of the Christian religion and enlightened laws? such change having been enforced before "culture" and a knowledge of the arts of civilization has provided other pursuits and enjoyments.

11. What effect, in causing disease, has a partial change of diet and dress? *i.e.*, is disease produced by the occasional use of European clothing and a sudden return to the nakedness of savage life? by temporary residence in towns and a return to the smoky, unventilated cabins used by savages?

12. What have been the effects of scrofula, smallpox, typhus, and other diseases unknown before the arrival of white men?

13. What remedies were used by the Aborigines? or did they refuse all remedies?

14. To what extent have diseases affecting the sexual organs been introduced by white men?

15. Can any system (which the superior race would submit to) be suggested by which the fatality attendant on the contact of white and aboriginal races would be avoided or mitigated?

16. Would it be desirable, and if desirable, would it be possible, to forbid the settlement of whites in isolated positions surrounded by Aborigines, and to require them to settle in specified localities, from which they should only extend by the acquisition of contiguous blocks of land?

17. Are the laws of England suited to the abnormal state of society necessarily existing when white men first intrude on an aboriginal race? and is it capable of adequately protecting the rights and interests of the latter?

18. What effect has the custom of holding lands in common upon aboriginal races?

19. If the communal tenure is a bar to progress in civilization, would it be possible to induce the race reported on to divide their lands and cultivate them for the benefit of families or individuals?

20. In cases where land has been so cultivated, what has been the result?

21. What is the condition of any individuals among the Aborigines who have been educated from childhood by Europeans, and have consequently adopted European habits and customs? and are their families as numerous on an average as those of Europeans?

22. What effect has the partial contact of European with black races, *e.g.*, the Zulus? Has the race reported on welcomed or resisted the approach of civilization?

23. Compare the condition of the aboriginal race in districts where they mix with Europeans with that where there are few or no Europeans.

T. G. B.

No. LXXV.—ETHNOLOGICAL COLLECTIONS.

It is of importance to obtain from natives any portable specimens of their handiwork, tools, weapons, dress, ornaments, fetishes, &c., and, where possible, the native descriptions of the objects, whether the tools, for instance, are for any special work, &c.

Models should be secured when the originals cannot be obtained or are too large for transport, *e.g.*, canoes, houses, &c.

Not only are the finished objects worth collecting, but also the raw material used in their manufacture, where this has any special character, as grasses for plaiting, dyes, or paints used in staining, gums for fixing arrow or spear-points. The commonest things in use are generally the most valuable from an ethnological point of view, though masterpieces of native art are of artistic value, and therefore should not be despised.

At the first moment of leisure the objects should be labelled with the locality where they were obtained, and their use, and any other particulars. Never trust to memory alone. The best means of doing this will differ with the climate. For stone implements, shell, or any similar surface, write in lead pencil upon the object; pencil is far better than ink, as it is but little affected by damp, and is practically indelible, unless the specimen is much handled. Gummed labels will serve for dry climates, but they should be avoided if possible. It is better to use labels of parchment or tough paper, tied on like a luggage-label, where the shape of the object permits. A list of the objects should be made, with a slight sketch of each beside the description.

Comparatively few ethnological specimens are liable to deterioration. Corrosive sublimate, or, failing that, arsenical soap, will serve to prevent the destruction of feather ornaments, skin dresses, &c., by insects. Pure napthaline is pleasant to work with, and if placed in cases with feathers or skins, will prevent moth from entering, though it is scarcely powerful enough to destroy them once their operations have begun, unless in very tight-fitting boxes. Carbolic paper is also a preventive, and can be obtained in rolls.

Articles of pottery will require special precautions in packing. If paper be obtainable, each piece should be enveloped, so that, in case of breakage, all the fragments will be found together. Hay, dry grass, crumpled paper, or raw cotton, will serve for packing, and provided that there is some of the material between the pots, the more tightly they are packed, the greater is their security.

C. H. R.

No. LXXVI.—PAPER SQUEEZES.

THE requisites for taking squeezes are (1) Tough paper, unsized. Special paper is made for this, and can be obtained at David Nutt's, Strand; but any tough, thick wrapping paper will do; and newspaper may be used. (2) Bristle brush; the best form is the long narrow one made for washing carriage wheels. (3) a basin or bucket of water. Wash the surface of the stone, or other sculptured material, removing every trace of sticky clay, &c., and leave enough water on it to hold the paper by capillary attraction; dip the paper in water and lay it on the stone (having first torn it to the right size), leaving a full amount to go into any deep hollows; then press the paper in by the hands if the sculpture is deep. Begin to beat it with the brush in the middle, and proceed outwards; as the paper expands in beating, it is well not to get it fixed at the edges first. It should be beaten over only a few square inches at one stroke, and the beating must be continued, in spite of the paper breaking on the prominent points, until it is completely bedded into every grain and crack of the stone. If there are deep parts, strips of paper must be torn and soaked, and beaten on to cover the rents where the first paper is split in yielding inwards. If desired, the strips may be pulped in the fingers and pressed into the hollows by the back edge of the brush (squeezing out the water thus as far as possible) so as to fill up the sculpture level on the face. This produces a solid *papier-maché* cast. In any case add an outside sheet to hold together the first sheet, or pulp, only beating it enough to make it stick tight. As a rule, let the paper remain on till quite dry.

Difficulties.—Limestone is often too absorbent, and will not leave water on the surface to hold the paper. If the face is upright the paper must be held up along the top edge, beaten on quickly, and then lifted off the stone and laid to dry on a flat surface, such as smooth sand. The sculpture is often too polished and smooth for the paper to get any hold, so that when it begins to contract in drying it draws out of the hollows, and may retain no impression from a low relief. If so, as soon as it begins to dry lift it off by peeling it up from one edge (holding the corners), and lay it flat to finish drying. Wind is the greatest trouble. On this account paper should never be larger than necessary; sometimes temporarily beat it on at the edge while doing the rest, and lift and rebeat the edge finally when the rest is done, or plaster the edges down with mud. It is always well to beat the edges on very thoroughly in finishing to prevent the paper being blown up while drying. Strings across the face of the stone are useful, especially if the face overhangs.

When dry the papers may be packed tight together in a box without any injury, or rolled up if necessary. If the stone yielded salt to the squeeze, the paper may be soaked in a tray of water to extract it. When casts are required, heat the paper on a stove, and brush over with beeswax enough to choke the grain, but not to face it. Then plaster may be cast on it, taking care that it does not run round the edges. Tissue paper beaten on with a tooth brush may be used for gems or coins, adding several thicknesses. But for such small objects tinfoil is the best, either beaten by a tooth brush or squeezed by the fingers.

A photograph, tracing, or drawing usefully supplements a squeeze, and if the surface of the stone be smooth enough, a rubbing with heel-ball may be made. Another method of making the squeeze more distinct is to dab it with colour mixed with water containing a little gum or size. This process is of course subsequent to all the operations of squeezing, and while the squeeze is drying upon the stone.

The simplest and quickest method of all is to make a rubbing, using grass or leaves in place of heel-ball. Common Japanese paper is the best for rubbings; it is very strong, and not being sized, it is little affected by damp..

W. M. F. P.

No. LXXVII.—PHOTOGRAPHY.

In addition to the ordinary information of photographic hand-books, a few special details for travellers may be noted. A tin-plate camera is desirable, as it cannot be broken or cracked by heat, but it must be specially ordered. The light tight slide of the body is best fitted by a pad of black linen folded over 8 or 10 times, as this gives great elasticity, and can be refolded with extra turns in it if it should not be tight enough. If plates of small size are used, it is best to have a plate box, holding 20 or 30, made in one with the camera, the plates standing beneath parallel with their place in the camera; changing is then done by the fingers in a dark bag, permanently fastened on to the side of the camera and plate box, furnished with a short sleeve to admit the hand. No plate holders are thus required, the ground glass is withdrawn from the camera, and the dry plate inserted in its place. The shutter of the camera back slides into the bag when focussing. The dark bag should be of two thicknesses of black linen, with strips of tin foil coating the inner linen, stuck on with touches of varnish; and inside the linen a similar black silk bag. Each of the three bags should be made separately, so that the stitch holes will not coincide when put together. Washing negatives is often difficult in travelling, but by having six soup-plates that will hold a ¼-plate without touching the bottom, and placing these in a row, filled with water, each negative may be passed through six waters, remaining in each during the time of one developing; and this washing is almost always quite sufficient, while it requires but half-an-hour extra time to shift those in the plates successively after the developing is all done.

It is very useful to take some paper upon which prints can be made on the spot for presentation to the natives (*e.g.*, bromide or platinotype). In photographing groups, always focus *before* the natives are placed in position; this can readily be done by placing an object on the spot where they will afterwards be made to stand.

Other hints might perhaps be given, *e.g.*, the obvious advantage in many ways of paper negatives over glass; but on these points it will be better to consult the trade journals or apply to one of the leading firms, who will advise the amateur as to the materials best suited to the climate where they are to be used.

W. M. F. P.

INDEX.